Routedge Revivals

Cooperation in the Multi-Ethnic Classroom

First published in 1994, this book describes how cooperative group work can enhance relationships in the classroom, reduce prejudice and alleviate problems of victimisation and peer rejection. It combines quantitative experimental analysis with detailed case studies; considers the impact of the family on pupil behaviour; and concludes with practical recommendations to foster social acceptance in the classroom.

There is a strong emphasis on helping teachers to develop group work in their classrooms as an effective means of *averting* trouble and inducing a genuinely better attitude to collaboration with their fellow pupils. The difficulties in implementation which can arise if teachers are not motivated, or if pupils are disruptive, are honestly confronted.

The book will also help educational and developmental psychologists involved in resolving behavioural difficulties resulting from social tensions in multi-ethnic classrooms.

Cooperation in the Multi-Ethnic Classroom

The Impact of Cooperative Group Work on Social Relationships in Middle Schools

Helen Cowie, Peter Smith, Michael Boulton and Rema Laver

First published in 1994
by David Fulton Publishers Ltd

This edition first published in 2018 by Routledge
2 Park Square, Milton Park, Abingdon, Oxon, OX14 4RN
and by Routledge
711 Third Avenue, New York, NY 10017

Routledge is an imprint of the Taylor & Francis Group, an informa business

© 1994 David Fulton Publishers Ltd

All rights reserved. No part of this book may be reprinted or reproduced or utilised in any form or by any electronic, mechanical, or other means, now known or hereafter invented, including photocopying and recording, or in any information storage or retrieval system, without permission in writing from the publishers.

Publisher's Note
The publisher has gone to great lengths to ensure the quality of this reprint but points out that some imperfections in the original copies may be apparent.

Disclaimer
The publisher has made every effort to trace copyright holders and welcomes correspondence from those they have been unable to contact.

A Library of Congress record exists under LCCN: 94231225

ISBN 13: 978-1-138-57110-5 (hbk)
ISBN 13: 978-0-203-70302-1 (ebk)
ISBN 13: 978-1-138-57114-3 (pbk)

David Fulton Publishers Ltd
2 Barbon Close, London WC1N 3JX

First published in Great Britain by
David Fulton Publishers 1994

Note: The right of the authors to be identified as the authors of this work has been asserted by them in accordance with the Copyright, Designs and Patents Act 1988.

Copyright © David Fulton (Publishers) Limited

British Library Cataloguing in Publication Data

A catalogue record for this book is available from the British Library

ISBN 1-85346-284-5

All rights reserved. No part of this publication may be reproduced, stored in a retrieval system or transmitted, in any form, or by any means, electronic, mechanical, photocopying, recording or otherwise, without the permission of the publishers.

CONTENTS

NOTES ON CONTRIBUTORS v

PREFACE vii

CHAPTER ONE: Peer acceptance, friendships and bully–victim problems in junior-school classrooms: an overview of research findings and theory 1

CHAPTER TWO: Ethnicity, relationships and attitudes in children 28

CHAPTER THREE: Cooperative group work in primary schools 43

CHAPTER FOUR: The background to the project 66

CHAPTER FIVE: In-service training and support 79

CHAPTER SIX: The effects of cooperative group work on social relationships 115

CHAPTER SEVEN: Individual differences and case studies of children 154

CHAPTER EIGHT: Conclusions and recommendations 188

BIBLIOGRAPHY 203

INDEX 211

NOTES ON CONTRIBUTORS

Helen Cowie was Director of counselling courses at Bretton Hall College of the University of Leeds and is currently Professor of psychology and counselling at the Roehampton Institute. She has completed research on children's writing and cooperative group work. Her published works include *Understanding Children's Development* (with Peter K. Smith) and *Learning Together – Working Together* (with Jean Rudduck).

Peter K. Smith is Professor of psychology at the Department of Psychology of the University of Sheffield. He has researched in to children's play and social development, and has recently directed the DfE-funded Sheffield Anti-Bullying Project. He is co-editor of *Practical Approaches to Bullying* with David Thompson.

Michael Boulton is a lecturer in the Department of Psychology at the University of Keele. He has researched and published widely on children's social development, especially rough-and-tumble play and bully–victim problems in schools.

Rema Laver is a research associate at the University of Sheffield. Her work experience has encompassed a range of research and clinical posts within the University of Sheffield, Sheffield Health Authority and Sheffield City Council. She has a special interest in psychotherapy.

PREFACE

Many children have problems in social relationships at school, or experience barriers to integration and friendship by reason of factors such as race, sex or disability. The project described in this book aimed to use cooperative group work as a curriculum approach which might help to reduce the difficulties, and encourage cooperation and friendship across these barriers. Our success was limited, but we feel that we have learnt a great deal about the feasibility of using cooperative group work methods and the difficulties in doing so in classes containing many children who may find such cooperation difficult, even though these children may need it most.

Our initial interest in this approach came from two sources. Helen Cowie had been working with Jean Rudduck, on a project funded by B.P. Education, to document uses of cooperative group work methods in primary and secondary schools. The rationale was that working together in groups, solving a common problem, was a very useful skill in many industrial work contexts. At the same time, Peter Smith and Michael Boulton had been studying children's social relationships in schools and playgrounds. The two approaches came together in an initial study funded by the E.S.R.C., under its initiative 'education for a multi-cultural society'.

In this study we used CGW methods in two primary schools to examine the impact on ethnic relationships and attitudes. The results were quite promising, but came from a small and selected sample. This book describes the follow-up study, in which we used a larger sample of schools and teachers, and extended our range of outcome measures to look at social relationships generally, and bully–victim problems, as well as ethnic relationships.

Peter Smith was the grant holder and Helen Cowie provided the training and in-service work on CGW methods throughout the project. Michael Boulton was the main research worker in the first year, Louise Bowers in the second year and Rema Laver in the final six months. The book is a collaborative effort amongst us, although, unfortunately, Louise Bowers was not able to take part. Michael Boulton is primarily responsible for the first two chapters; Peter Smith and Rema Laver for chapters four and six; Helen Cowie for chapters three, five and seven; and Peter Smith and Helen Cowie for chapter eight.

Besides Louise Bowers who worked on the project in the second year, we are most grateful to Lucia Berdondini, who helped in some of the analyses contributing to chapter seven and in much of the data organisation. We would also like to thank Sally Clarke, Nicky Copping, Kate Folkard, Adam Murphy, Bente Olson, Jane Ross, Claire Tydeman and Rachel Wills, who helped in data collection at various times.

Jim Lewis and John Allen offered invaluable support and advice in the initial planning of the in-service programme. Jim continued to be involved during the second year of the project and has published, with Helen Cowie, a number of articles on the subject of CGW methods. The study could not have been carried out without the collaboration of the schools, teachers and pupils (all names of teachers and pupils are pseudonyms). Our activities were sometimes an intrusion, but we know that, for at least some, the CGW approach continues to influence their professional development.

Helen Cowie
Peter K. Smith
Michael Boulton
Rema Laver

Sheffield, December 1993

CHAPTER ONE: Peer acceptance, friendships and bully–victim problems in junior-school classrooms: an overview of research findings and theory

Introduction

Forming good relationships with peers is an extremely important aspect of a child's world. Children who have difficulties in this domain are much more likely to suffer from problems in other areas of their lives, for example they may have a low sense of self-esteem and underachieve in academic work. Having the capacity to relate well to others is like a passport to positive feelings about self and others.

Some children show remarkable stability in their friendships, staying with the same friend throughout the school years and even, in some cases, into adulthood. Others have a wider network of relationships with peers which changes over time, with circumstances and according to the particular interests of the moment.

Ben, aged 10, has been friends with Alex since they met at first school. He explains it in this way:

> Alex shows his friendship back to me. He likes me. He plays with me, shares his toys with me. Alex agrees with me and shares my feelings about things we like. He enjoys my company.
>
> He stands up for me when someone is being unfriendly. I stood up for him when he was being bullied and he stands up for me.
>
> We do quarrel but we usually make it up. Sometimes we have an argument and then next time we meet we forget about it. It's in the past and it doesn't matter any more. I don't have too many friends. If I had millions of friends and I had an argument with him, I could walk off. But instead I try to make it up with him.

Shaista and Nazia have been firm friends since Shaista joined the class at the beginning of the year. They share everything at school and often play together at weekends. Nazia says of Shaista:

> I like her because she keeps secrets and she makes me laugh. She's very helpful and friendly – and she's thoughtful. She knows the answers to things and helps me if I can't do something.

Shaista says:

> When I first came to this school I didn't know anybody but Nazia – and that's because she lives next door and she called round for me when we first moved. At school she sat beside me and was friendly. She's my best friend now and I can tell her things. I share my secrets.
>
> At my last school I had a best friend. She were different from me because she were Indian. And then everyone in my school – all the muslim children – said, 'Why do you be best friend with an Indian?' I didn't know what to say. I just ignored them.

Children's close friendships are typically characterised by openness, good humour and honesty. Older children in the primary school are also likely to report that they share intimate thoughts with their close friends, and that they value qualities of loyalty and trustworthiness. They demonstrate through their friendships that they are sensitive to one another's feelings. Popular children are acknowledged by their peers for being friendly, sociable, kind, competent, willing to help and supportive. For children who do not have this kind of interpersonal experience from peers school can be a very unpleasant place.

The past decade has seen a rapid growth of interest in children's social relationships with peers. These relationships can be extremely complex. In many cases, peer relationships can be a source of great support during the childhood years and provide valuable experiences for growth in cognitive, social and emotional domains. However, it is now equally clear that social relationships can be a source of great anguish for some children and problems with peer relationships can lead to experiences that may be damaging both in the short term as well as over a period of many years that extends well into adulthood.

It would be impossible to review all of the theoretical and empirical work on children's social relations in one chapter, even if the review was limited to the most recent advances in our knowledge. Instead, in this chapter and the following one, we will focus on three aspects of the social worlds of junior school children that may be especially important for their well-being. These are peer acceptance and friendships, bully–victim relationships, and relationships with children from different ethnic groups. Of course it would be wrong to give the impression that these three facets of children's social relationships are completely independent. They are not separate and the mechanisms by which they mutually influence one another are beginning to be understood. Nevertheless, it is convenient to begin by considering these three topics separately, not least because our current knowledge of them has come from almost independent research traditions. In later sections of this chapter and the ensuing one, some of the ways in which these three aspects of peer relationships may interrelate will be discussed.

Peer acceptance and friendship

The distinction between peer acceptance and friendship

Acceptance by one's peers and friendship are not synonymous terms (Berndt, 1984; Bukowski and Hoza, 1989; Mannarino, 1976). Children themselves typically make a distinction between peers that they like and those that are 'true friends', although of course there may be some overlap. This may lead to a situation in which a child is generally liked and/or accepted by most of her or his classmates, but who nevertheless has no close friends. Similarly, a child who is poorly accepted and/or disliked by most classmates may still have satisfying mutually close friendships with one or a few classmates.

The ways in which one is accepted by peers and the ways in which one makes friendships, may differ in important ways. This also appears to hold true for the maintenance of peer acceptance and friendships, and for the benefits that accrue from them. Furman and Buhrmester (1985), for example, suggest that such things as intimacy, affection, loyalty and availability can be obtained in the context of friendship whereas a sense of inclusion is more likely to develop in the context of general peer relationships (for further discussion see below). For these reasons we will begin by looking at what we know about peer acceptance, prior to focussing on friendships *per se*.

Peer acceptance

Peer acceptance generally refers to how much an individual is liked or disliked by her or his peers. While such a construct can be (and has been) studied in a number of different ways, categorisation of children in these terms has usually been based on sociometric techniques. Perhaps the most influential study in this area was that by Coie, Dodge and Coppotelli (1982). Certainly it has stimulated many other researchers to investigate and report on children's peer acceptance. Typically, individual children are asked to nominate 'some' (often three) classmates that they 'like the most' (or 'like to play with' or other similar positive nominations) and 'some' that they 'like the least' (or other corresponding negative nominations). In most cases, the 'social unit' from which data are generated has been the class a child is in. In some studies, children are asked to consider just same-sex classmates, whereas in others they can select from both boys and girls.

Based on the pattern of nominations received by every child in the class, each individual is classified as belonging to one of five or six sociometric status types. In general, *popular* children are those that receive many 'like the most' nominations and few if any 'like the least' nominations. *Rejected* children receive many 'like the least' nominations and few if any 'like the most' nominations. *Neglected* children receive few if any of both 'like the most' and 'like the least' nominations. *Controversial* children are those that receive many 'like the most' and many 'like the least' nominations. Finally, *average* children are those

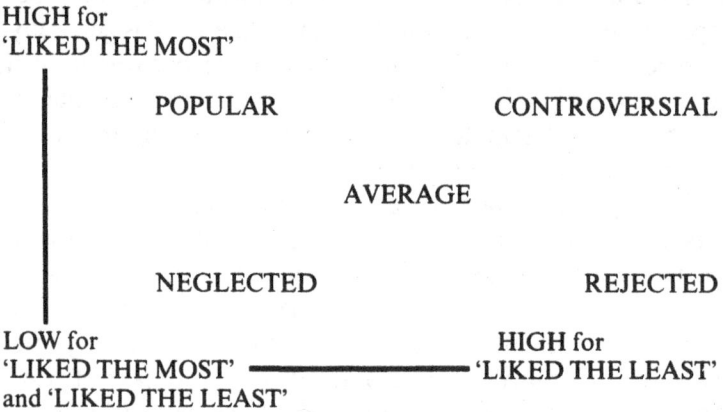

Table 1.1 Different types of sociometric status

that receive an average number of both 'like the most' and 'like the least' nominations; and *other* children (usually near the average) are those that fit none of these five categories exactly. Table 1.1 shows a schematic representation that may help to conceptualise these different sociometric groups.

The distinctions between these different groups of children are thought to be important and researchers have identified distinct sets of causes, correlates and consequences for each. Here we shall focus on what have been considered 'problematic' groups – the rejected and neglected groups – since, as we shall see, research has shown that the low levels of peer acceptance associated with them may carry increased risks of various negative outcomes.

The distinction between rejected and neglected pupils has proven to be especially useful for understanding low levels of peer acceptance. Rejected children, in general, seem to be more salient members of the peer group than neglected children, and this probably stems from their inappropriate behaviour with peers. Neglected children on the other hand appear to go largely unnoticed by the majority of their peers, at least to the extent that they are not actively disliked.

In trying to understand the antecedents, correlates and consequences of each type of sociometric status, researchers have to consider an array of different variables for all three. For example, aggression, cooperation, playgroup entry tactics and play styles are just four of the categories of *behavioural* measures that have been studied. Some of these are shown in Table 1.2. These have been augmented by measures of children's *social cognition*, including the social goals they pursue during peer interactions and their ability to detect the intentions of peers, as well as measures of children's affect, particularly their loneliness, and *non-behavioural characteristics* such as physical attractiveness and even birth order.

Sociometric status and behaviour

In this review, we will try to capture some of the more important differences that have been found to characterise the six sociometric status groups. In this respect, perhaps aggression has received most attention. It appears to be an especially salient variable distinguishing rejected children from all others. Coie, Christopoulos, Terry, Dodge

Table 1.2 Some behavioural characteristics of the five main sociometric status types

	leads peers	cooperates	acts shy	seeks help	fights	disrupts group
POPULAR	HIGH	HIGH		Low	Low	Low
CONTROVERSIAL	HIGH		Low	HIGH	HIGH	HIGH
REJECTED	Low	Low		HIGH	HIGH	HIGH
NEGLECTED	Low	Low		Low	Low	Low
AVERAGE						

and Lochman (1989) stated that 'It is true that when peers and trained unfamiliar observers provide information about rejected children's behavior, the most compelling reason for peer rejection appears to be aggressive behavior' (p. 224).

This conclusion needs to be qualified in an important way. Dodge and Coie (1987) have emphasised the distinction between reactive and proactive aggression. The former is considered to involve a hostile reaction and/or retaliation to some external event (such as frustration or provocation), whereas the latter is thought to occur in the absence of any immediate aversive stimulus, without anger, and may include such behaviour as coercion and bullying. The available evidence suggests that proactive aggression is most likely to be associated with rejected status (Coie and Kupersmidt, 1983). On the other hand, reactive aggression does not appear to be closely related to it. Indeed, some results suggest that aggression in response to provocations and/or prior aggression by other children appears to be positively correlated with acceptance by one's peers. Thus, standing up for oneself by not being pushed around unfairly appears to be a useful strategy children may use to gain acceptance by their peers.

Several studies, then, have shown that unprovoked aggression is a correlate of rejected status – children who are classified as being rejected on the basis of sociometric techniques tend to show significantly higher levels of this type of aggression with peers than any of the other status groups. These results, while interesting in their own right, are limited in that they do not tell us whether the elevated levels of aggression typically preceded and/or caused a child's rejected status, or instead whether most individuals concerned were initially rejected for some other reason and only once they were rejected did they begin to show higher than average levels of proactive aggression.

To help overcome this type of limitation, researchers such as Kenneth Dodge and John Coie in the U.S.A. developed methods whereby initially unfamiliar children were brought together in special play sessions over a period of weeks or months. They were then able to study the way the behaviour of the children influenced the development of their sociometric status. Results clearly showed that elevated levels of proactive aggression preceded the acquisition of rejected status, suggesting that the former caused the latter in the majority of cases (Coie and Kupersmidt, 1983; Dodge, 1983).

Despite this pattern of results, it would be wrong to give the impression that there is a strong one-to-one relationship between rejected sociometric status and high levels of proactive aggression. While this does appear to hold in a general sense, two variables that mediate the relationship are age and sex. Rejected status is more strongly related to aggression in children above seven or eight years of age than below. One explanation for this age effect is in terms of social norms (Coie, Christopoulos, Terry, Dodge and Lochman, 1989). Aggression is more prevalent in children prior to their reaching junior school age and so it may not be seen as unusual or deviant, at least to the extent that it is seen in this way by slightly older children who engage in fewer instances of aggression. In a similar sort of way, the relationship between rejection and aggression appears to be stronger for boys than for girls, perhaps because girls show less aggression than boys.

Another reason why we should be cautious about accepting that rejection and unprovoked aggression are always strongly related is that not all rejected children show higher than average levels of proactive aggression. Recent work using cluster analytical techniques suggests that rejected children do not form a homogenous group. In one study, Coie, Christopoulos, Terry, Dodge and Lochman (1989) reported that four sub-groups of rejected children could be identified. The first group consisted of rejected-aggressive children, the second group contained rejected children who were physically unattractive but not aggressive, the third group consisted of the rejected children who engaged in strange behaviour (such as making strange noises and acting silly) but not aggression, and the fourth cluster contained those rejected children who were average on all of the above traits.

Some other researchers have also distinguished between rejected-aggressive children and rejected-withdrawn children. The former tend to be seen by peers and/or by teachers as being immature, easily angered, bossy and difficult to understand (Crick, 1991). They also tend to be non-cooperative and highly aggressive (Cillessen, van IJzendoorn, van Lieshout and Hartup, 1992). In contrast, rejected-withdrawn children tend to be perceived by teachers and/or peers as being highly submissive and withdrawn but only moderately aggressive (Crick, 1991).

Not all highly aggressive children are classified as rejected. For example, some studies have found that controversial children, who receive many 'like the least' nominations *and* 'like the most' nominations from their classmates, typically engage in both high levels of aggression as well as high levels of prosocial behaviour (Newcomb and Bukowski, 1983; Coie and Dodge, 1988).

Neglected status children have been the focus of fewer studies than have rejected children. Some early studies found that they tended to be characterised by social withdrawal, that is low levels of social participation with peers. However, more recent studies have (as with rejected status children) found that different sub-groups of neglected children may be identified (Rubin, Hymel, LeMare and Rowden, 1989; Crick, 1991). For example, using measures of peer and teacher perceptions, Crick (1991) found two sub-groups of neglected children. The neglected-withdrawn children tended to be seen as submissive and quiet and hence they probably received relatively little attention from teachers and peers. In contrast, the neglected-non-withdrawn children were viewed as being less submissive and withdrawn, but more mature and better liked by peers.

The above discussion of recent research leaves little room for doubt that the behaviour children display in their interactions with peers is important when it comes to how much they are accepted and liked by those peers. In the next section we focus on friendship *per se*. We examine how friends and non-friends differ in terms of the behaviour they typically engage in with one another. We also consider the benefits children derive from having close friends, and discuss the short and long term consequences of low peer acceptance – be it rejection or neglect – and of having few or no close friends.

Children's friendships

Childhood is a time when friendships are formed. Some may be transitory, lasting only a few weeks, whereas others are enduring and may last a lifetime. What benefits do children get from having friends, and how important are they to them, both in the short and long term? Asher and Parker (1989), reviewing the studies on this topic, concluded that 'On the whole, seven friendship functions appear with some regularity across various formulations: (a) fostering the growth of social competence (b) serving as sources of ego support and self-validation (c) providing emotional security in novel or potentially threatening situations (d) serving as sources of intimacy and affection (e) providing guidance and assistance (f) providing a sense of reliable alliance, and (g) providing companionship and stimulation' (p. 6).

Parker and Gottman (1989) looked at the importance of children's friendships from a developmental point of view. They observed children as they were in the process of becoming friends. It appeared that friends try to achieve lots of excitement and stimulation in their play, and they very often create and re-create exciting themes that enable them to develop in important ways. It was suggested that children learn how to manage their emotions, deal with conflicts and take on the perspectives of others through their play with friends.

Given that such a diverse range of positive outcomes resulting from having friends has been suggested, the question of how children actually select their friends has received considerable attention from researchers. Epstein (1989) suggested that three factors are important in this respect – proximity, age and similarity. Proximity exerts a very obvious influence over children's choice of friends. Several studies with children of school age have found that children tend to live closer to friends than to non-friends (Fine, 1980; Coates, 1985). Epstein also argues that many children form friendships with mixed-age mates, and that similarity of character and personal characteristics influence which individuals are selected as friends. Not surprisingly, once children have established a friendship with a peer, they are more likely to spend time with them than with non-friends (Hartup, 1989).

Cooperation, friendships and peer acceptance

As we have seen, a child's level of (unprovoked) aggression goes a long way to determine her or his level of popularity within the peer group. This also appears to be the case for more prosocial categories of behaviour as well and cooperation is particularly important in this respect. Coie, Dodge and Coppotelli (1982) found that popular children were perceived by classmates to be more cooperative than both rejected and neglected children (see table 1.2).

Levels of cooperation are also relatively high among children who are friends. Newcomb, Brady and Hartup (1979), for example, compared the behaviour of friends and non-friends in a block-building task: friends showed more evidence that, by smiling and laughing with each other, they enjoyed working together on this task. Moreover, friends also talked more about completing the task and were more interactive generally than non-friends.

In another study, by Charlesworth and LaFreniere (1983), children were given the opportunity to cooperate spontaneously with others. The children were provided with a film viewer that had a small eyepiece. Only when the apparatus's lighting arm was cranked by another child could anything be seen in the eye piece. Friends were found to cooperate more than non-friends – the sessions were generally more harmonious and there was much more turn-taking. This higher level of cooperation between the children who were friends resulted in them having greater average viewing times than the non-friends.

Clearly, cooperation is a feature of existing friendships. But is it a condition for the emergence of friendships in the first place? This is an important question because if the answer is 'yes', then encouraging cooperation between children may help overcome some of the problems they can experience in their peer relationships.

Asher and Williams (1987) suggested that children consider a number of questions as they choose their friends and associates. These are (a) Is this child fun to be with? (b) Is this child trustworthy? (c) Do we influence each other in ways that I like? (d) Does this child facilitate and not undermine my goals? (e) Is this child similar to me? and (f) Does this child make me feel good about myself? Children are thought to evaluate one another in these ways as they form and maintain their friendships or associations with peers. It is clear that several of these concerns are related to cooperation, especially (b), (c) and (d).

Smoller and Youniss (1982) interviewed 6- to 13-year-old children about friendships. One question posed was 'What do you think might happen to make X and Y become friends?' The younger children thought that doing things together or doing something special for the other person was the best way for strangers to make friends. Among the 9 and 10 year olds, sharing and helping one another were mentioned most often.

A study by Furman and Childs (1981) illustrated how quickly children attend to the cooperative qualities of others they have only just met. On the first day of a week-long summer camp children indicated that they liked some, rather than others, because they perceived them to be generally cooperative. These impressions were then found to influence the course of friendship development and consolidation throughout the rest of the week.

Behaving cooperatively towards peers in the classroom can also influence liking and friendships. Johnson, Johnson and Scott (1978) compared social outcomes in groups of children either working cooperatively on mathematics assignments or working on their own. The children working cooperatively expressed a more positive view of the personal worth of their peers and were more attracted to them, than did the children working individually. In a similar study (Johnson, Johnson, Johnson and Anderson, 1976), children in cooperative classrooms also believed that other pupils liked them more than did children working in traditional classrooms.

Epstein (1983) found that in 'open' classrooms that were characterised by cooperation between pupils, fewer students were neglected by their peers compared to traditional classrooms. Specifically, fewer children were overlooked as 'best friends'.

This sort of research suggests that cooperation is a trait that can both precipitate friendships and help to maintain them during the childhood years. In chapter three we discuss ways in which cooperative qualities can be enhanced in the classroom as a key part of the rationale for our study.

Implications of low peer acceptance and having no close friends

We have seen how some children may be poorly accepted in their peer group and have discussed some of the possible functions of friendships during childhood. In this section we will consider some of the consequences of poor peer relationships, be it in terms of a lack of close friends or low peer acceptance.

One short-term consequence that has been the focus of recent research is subjective levels of loneliness. Studies have shown that loneliness can be reliably measured during the childhood years (Asher, Hymel and Renshaw, 1984), and that it can be fairly stable even over a one-year period (Hymel, Franke and Freigang, 1985). Children appear to understand the concept to mean more or less the same thing as adults (Cassidy and Asher, 1992). The words of an eleven-year-old boy we interviewed serve as a poignant illustration of the hurt children can feel at being left out by their peers:

> What don't I like about school? Well the worst thing is when my friends won't play with me. They say, 'we're already playing a game so you can't play'. I just sit there on my own but no one comes to talk to me. That's when I wish I didn't have to go to school. They make you feel like you aren't important. It happens a lot, but I don't know why.

Asher, Parkhurst, Hymel and Williams (1990) reviewed the results of five studies with large samples that each examined levels of self-reported loneliness in the different sociometric status groups. In all five studies, the rejected group emerged with the highest levels. Somewhat surprisingly, the neglected group did not differ in their reported levels of loneliness from the average status children. This pattern of results led Asher and Parker (1989) to state that 'Apparently, it is not simply lacking friends in a class that leads to strong feelings of social isolation or alienation, but rather, it is being actively disliked by many of one's peers' (p. 15). Once again, this result suggests that the distinction between rejected and neglected status is a meaningful one. It may even be the case that neglected status children *choose* to remain isolated from many of their peers.

Parker and Asher (1988) investigated the relationship between peer acceptance and friendships. Specifically, they wanted to learn how many low-accepted children had close friends and, moreover, how satisfying those friendships were. They identified low-accepted children who had at least one mutual best friend, and compared the quality of those friendships to those of average and high-accepted children. As

Parker and Asher expected, fewer low-accepted children (54 per cent) had best friends than average-accepted (79 per cent) and high-accepted (91 per cent) children. In terms of relationship quality, there were some similarities but also some important differences between the friendships of the low-accepted, and the average and high-accepted children. They were similar with respect to the reported levels of companionship and conflict within the friendships, as well as the extent to which the friends were seen as a 'special' person in their lives. However, the low-accepted children reported that their friends were less supportive, trustworthy and loyal, and that they had more problems resolving conflicts with friends than both of the other two groups. Thus, overall, while more than half of the low-accepted children had one or more mutual best friend(s), they did not seem as satisfied with their friends than the better accepted children seemed to be with theirs. Many of the benefits that children may derive from having friends were not evident in the close relationships with peers experienced by low-accepted children.

In a school environment, another consequence of low peer acceptance or having no close friends would be a lack of play partners or at least having fewer peers to play with. Although children's conceptions of friendship appear to change with age, actually playing together seems to be important for children of diverse ages. Davies (1982) stated that children 'see proximity, or being with someone, as the first and basic element of friendships' (p. 68).

Surprisingly few studies have actually examined the relationship between children's sociometric status and/or their reports of who their friends are and who they actually play with on the playground. One researcher who did do so was Ladd (1983). Several of his results support the notion that being of low popularity with peers exerts a negative influence on the pattern of peer interactions on the playground. Rejected children were found to spend more time alone and to be unoccupied on the playground (e.g. wandering aimlessly), than popular children. They also spent more of their time in smaller groups and with younger school-mates. Ladd suggested that because of this pattern of peer interaction on the playground, rejected children 'have fewer opportunities to develop the knowledge and skills needed to operate effectively in larger social contexts' (p. 305).

Boulton and Smith (unpublished) have also looked at how often children of different sociometric status groups were alone on the playground, the age of their companions and the type of interactions they engaged in with them. It was found that neglected children at eight years of age spent significantly more time alone than any of the other status groups. However, this was not the case among the eleven year olds in the sample. The data suggested that neglected children at eleven years of age might compensate for their social isolation from age-mates by playing with younger children – neglected children at eleven years of age directed far more of their rough-and-tumble play initiations at younger children than did the other status groups. This would serve a useful purpose by enabling the neglected children to play with some pupils on the playground. However, such a tactic may also have some costs associated with it. By interacting with younger children in an activity such as rough-and-tumble play, which is generally favoured by younger children anyway, the impetus towards engaging in more age-appropriate play with same-age peers may be lost. If so, and it must be said that this idea needs further testing, neglected children could continue to be at a disadvantage because they may be less likely to acquire the skills possessed by many of their contemporaries. Consequently, they would continue to be less attractive companions to them.

What about the longer-term implications of being neglected/rejected by one's peers? In a comprehensive and widely-cited review, Parker and Asher (1987) examined the evidence linking low levels of acceptance by peers during childhood and later personal adjustment problems. They considered many important conceptual and methodological issues in this field of research. For example, they noted that two types of research designs have been employed in these studies – follow-back designs and follow-up designs, and that data have come from both peer nominations and teacher nominations. In each case, there are advantages and disadvantages associated with the different methodological options, and Parker and Asher argue that we need to be aware of them all if we are to fully appreciate the complexities involved.

In their review, Parker and Asher considered research that looked at several different outcome measures (dropping out of school, juvenile and adult crime, and adult psychopathology) that could possibly result from low levels of peer acceptance during the school years.

Most of the evidence suggests that, for many individuals, the decision to drop out of school is preceded by an earlier period of low peer acceptance. Parker and Asher stated that,

> What makes dropping out of school particularly interesting when compared with other indexes of later academic maladjustment is that dropping out, to the extent that it is undertaken voluntarily and represents a flight from something unpleasant, is an unambiguous rebuke of the school's . . . social setting. (p. 363)

Parker and Asher also found that there is much evidence, especially from follow-back studies, that criminality is often preceded by periods of low peer acceptance.

The suggestion that adult psychopathology is preceded by low peer acceptance during the school years is less than clear cut, and Parker and Asher explain this in terms of the literature being 'largely incomplete and conflicting' (p. 374). Nevertheless, some studies have found that negative adult adjustment is preceded by periods of low peer acceptance. Whether the problem with peers is the actual cause of the later psychopathology, or merely an incidental occurrence, is yet to be determined.

Conclusions

In concluding this section, it is clear that we should be concerned with peer acceptance and friendship in childhood. Johnson (1980) states that 'Experiences with peers are not superficial luxuries to be enjoyed by some students and not by others. Student–student relationships are an absolute necessity for healthy cognitive and social development and socialization' (p. 125). However, as we have seen, there is huge diversity in the extent to which individual children are accepted and liked by their peers, and in the extent to which they are deliberately left out. It is for these reasons that we set out to investigate how children who may be having difficulties establishing or maintaining a healthy level of integration within their peer-group setting in school may be helped (see chapter four). Before we do so, however, we will consider another aspect of children's social relationships which has the potential to cause distress and suffering – bullying.

Bully–victim problems in childhood

What is bullying?

Bullying has been defined and conceptualised in many different ways, and we shall look at some of these in more detail below. Nevertheless, Farrington (1994) noted that there is widespread agreement, among researchers at least, that bullying involves five basic elements:

(i) it may take several different forms, including, but not limited to, the physical, verbal, and psychological;
(ii) it is intended to and does cause fear, harm and/or distress to the victim;
(iii) it involves an actual or perceived imbalance of power;
(iv) it is unprovoked by the victim;
(v) it occurs repeatedly over time.

Researchers differ in the extent to which they accept some or all of these elements as being necessary in order to classify an act as constituting bullying. For example, in terms of the latter criterion, Roland (1987) defined bullying as, 'a *longstanding* violence, physical or psychological, conducted by an individual or a group directed against an individual who is not able to defend himself in the actual situation' (emphasis added). Similarly, Olweus (1993) stated that 'I define bullying in the following general way: A person is being bullied when he or she is exposed, *repeatedly and over time*, to negative actions on the part of one or more other persons (p. 87, emphasis added). Olweus justified the inclusion of the longevity clause in his definition by stating that 'Even if a single instance of more serious harassment can be regarded as bullying under certain circumstances, the definition ... emphasizes negative actions that are carried out "repeatedly and over time". The intent is to exclude occasionally non-serious negative actions that are directed against one person at one time and against another on a different occasion' (p. 87). In support of this line of reasoning, Arora and Thompson (1987) asked secondary school pupils about their own views of the nature of bullying. Most pupils thought that bullying involved repeated incidents over a period of time with the same individuals.

However, an analysis of children's telephone calls to the Bullying Line in the U.K. suggests that this may not correspond with all children's conception of bullying (LaFontaine, 1991). LaFontaine noted that 'the evidence from the Bullying Line is that bullying need not last long to cause pain and distress in the victim' (p. 17). Given that those children who ring up the Bullying Line are likely to be those most disturbed by being bullied, this cannot be regarded as a representative sample. Nevertheless, these results do suggest that some children may not regard very persistent acts of harassment to be necessary in order to feel they are victims of bullying.

Just as researchers differ in the precise way that they define bullying, so too do children's conceptions of this type of aggression. One child that we interviewed, an eleven-year-old boy, was adamant that bullying was, 'only hitting and kicking'. Another boy of the same age took a much broader view. When asked what bullying was he said 'It's when somebody does something nasty to somebody else. Like beating them up, or teasing them, or sticking a [drawing] pin on their chair, or messing up their work, or moving their chair, or saying they said something when they didn't say it, or calling them names, or spoiling their game and things like that. I think it's anything that you can do to upset somebody. Kids are good at that sort of thing you know.'

Our interviews with children also led to many comments that

challenged stereotypical perceptions that the bully is always much bigger or stronger than the victim. For example, over and over again, eleven-year-old children in one class nominated the smallest boy as a bully. It appeared that this boy was able to get away with bullying, at least as far as the children themselves were concerned, because he threatened to call in his elder brother should anybody stand up to him. One boy complained that 'we can't stop him spoiling our game because if we touch him he'll get his big brother to beat us up after school. I think that's why everyone is scared of him. But he's a weed really.'

It is important to be aware that different people view bullying in different ways. We also believe that it is equally important that such disagreements do not stop our attempts to understand 'bullying', however it is defined, nor hinder us in our endeavours to eradicate the suffering that it can sometimes bring.

Prevalence of bully–victim problems

Particularly over the past five years several researchers have provided data on the prevalence of bully–victim problems among school-age children. The actual figures vary, sometimes quite considerably. To some extent these differences can be attributed to inconsistent definitions of bullying, the means by which the data were generated (the three most common methods being self-report, peer nomination and teacher nomination) and sample characteristics. Table 1.3 summarises the results of several studies that have used self-report questionnaires, in most cases based on the pioneering work of Olweus in Scandinavia. From these data it is evident that bully–victim problems are a feature of life in schools for many children from various countries.

A separate approach to assessing levels of bully–victim problems in school pupils is by means of peer nominations. Typically, children are interviewed individually and are asked to name those children in their class who are bullies, and those children who are victims. In almost all cases, a definition of bullying is provided to ensure that the pupils are nominating in the way required by the investigators. Table 1.4 shows the results of one such study (Boulton and Smith, 1994). It represents the percentage of children that were nominated as bullies by 25 per cent of their classmates, by 33 per cent of their classmates, by 40 per cent of their classmates and finally by 50 per cent of their classmates. It also shows the corresponding figures for those children who were nominated as victims. The actual level of bullying regarded to be present in the sample obviously depends on the cut-off point taken, in other words the number of classmate nominations required to classify an individual

Table 1.3 Levels of bully–victim problems reported in the literature using self-report questionnaire techniques

Researcher(s)	Method	Sample	Location	Main findings
Olweus (1987)	Self-report (original questionnaire)	130,000 children in grades 2 to 9	Norway (nationwide)	9% bullied 'now and then' or more frequently. 7% bullied others 'now and then' or more frequently.
O'Moore and Hillery (1989)	Self-report (devised by Roland and Munthe)	285 boys and 498 girls (total = 783) aged 7 to 13 years	Ireland (Dublin)	54.9% bullied 'occasionally' (i.e., 'once or twice' or 'sometimes'). 8% bullied 'frequently' (i.e., 'once a week' or more often). 43.3% bullied others 'occasionally' (i.e., 'once or twice' or 'sometimes'). 2.5% bullied others 'seriously' (i.e., 'once a week' or more often).
Hirano (1991)	Self-report (based on Olweus)	10 to 11 years (number not specified) 12 to 14 years (number not specified)	Japan	15% bullied 'sometimes' or more often. 12% bullied others 'sometimes' or more often. 10% bullied 'sometimes' or more often. 14% bullied others 'sometimes' or more often.
Boulton and Underwood (1992)	Self-report (based on Olweus)	154 boys and 142 girls (total = 296) aged 8, 9 and 11 years	U.K. (Sheffield)	28% bullied 'once or twice'. 14.5% bullied 'sometimes'. 6.1% bullied 'several times a week'. 25.2% bullied others 'once or twice'. 13.3% bullied others 'sometimes'. 3.8% bullied others 'several times a week'.

Table 1.3 (continued)

Researcher(s)	Method	Sample	Location	Main findings
Ruiz (1992)	Self-report (based on Olweus)	163 boys and 121 girls (total = 284) aged 11 to 14 years)	Spain (Seville)	26% bullied 'several times a week'. 22% bullied others (frequency not specified).
		309 boys and 266 girls (total = 575) aged 14 to 16 years		5% bullied 'several times a week'. 10% bullied others (frequency not specified).
Whitney and Smith (1993)	Self-report (based on Olweus)	1,271 boys and 1,352 girls (total = 2,623) aged 8 to 11 years	U.K. (Sheffield)	27% bullied 'sometimes' or more often. 10% bullied 'once a week' or more often. 12% bullied others 'sometimes' or more often. 4% bullied others 'once a week' or more often.
		2,152 boys and 1,983 girls (total = 4,135) aged 11 to 16 years		10% bullied 'sometimes' or more often. 4% bullied 'once a week' or more often. 6% bullied others 'sometimes' or more often. 1% bullied others 'once a week' or more often.

as a bully, or, separately, as a victim. Even taking a fairly conservative cut-off of 40 per cent, table 1.4 shows that about 23 per cent of children in this sample were perceived to be bullies by their classmates and 10 per cent were perceived to be victims. These results are not atypical.

In interpreting these figures it is important to realise that there may be some overlap between the children classified as bullies and those classified as victims. Olweus (1987) found that 6 per cent of the children that were bullied frequently and 18 per cent of those that were bullied occasionally, bullied others themselves. Olweus suggested that since the characteristics of bullies and victims were unlikely to correspond, the numbers of bully-victims would be small. In the sample of 158 junior school children described in table 1.4, about 5 per cent of them were classified as bully-victims.

A third approach to assessing levels of bully–victim problems in school pupils is based on teacher nominations. Stephenson and Smith (1989) developed a questionnaire for teachers that elicited information on the extent and nature of bullying. It was administered to 49 teachers of 1,078 final-year primary-school children at 26 schools. Overall, about 23 per cent of the children were reported to be involved either as bullies or as victims.

The figures we have presented give a general indication of levels of bullying in schools. Nevertheless, some marked age and sex differences have been reported in some studies. Because of their great importance for understanding bullying, and for any attempt to take action to stop it occurring in schools, these two factors will be considered in separate sections. In both cases, the discussion will be extended to consider the nature of the problem, as well as its extent.

Table 1.4 Percentage of boys and girls nominated as bullies, and as victims, by 25%, 33%, 40% and 50% of classmates

Nominations from classmates	25%	33%	40%	50%
Bully				
Boys (n=83)	57.8	53.0	43.4	30.1
Girls (n=75)	10.7	5.3	1.3	1.3
Both (n=158)	35.4	30.4	23.4	16.5
Victim				
Boys (n=83)	30.1	20.5	8.4	4.8
Girls (n=75)	37.3	22.7	12.0	2.7
Both (n=158)	33.5	21.5	10.1	3.8

Sex differences in bullying

Some studies have found that boys are more likely than girls to be involved in bully–victim problems. In a study in Dublin schools, O'Moore and Hillery (1989) reported that significantly more boys than girls stated that they had been bullied once a week or more often, and the same pattern was evident in terms of reported levels of bullying others. In a study in Sheffield schools, Boulton and Underwood (1992) also found similar sex differences, with boys more than girls reporting both being bullied and bullying others.

Our largest scale survey (Whitney and Smith, 1993) was carried out with over 6,000 pupils in 24 Sheffield schools. These confirm that sex differences can be evident across a broad range of ages, as shown in table 1.5. Overall, boys were more involved in bully–victim problems; these sex differences were substantial for 'bullying others', but rather small for 'being bullied'. Similarly, Perry, Kusel and Perry (1988), using a peer-nomination technique, found that while boys were named as victims more often than girls, 'the difference is not large' (p. 810).

The results on sex differences in levels of bullying others are in accord with one of the most robust sex differences reported in the child development literature, namely that boys tend to be more aggressive than girls. But to understand differences in the levels of bullying experienced by girls and boys more fully it is necessary to

Table 1.5 Percentage of boys and girls who report being bullied, or bullying others, 'sometimes' or more during the last term, at various year groups in primary and secondary schools. Based on data from Whitney and Smith (1993).

	Primary school pupils					Secondary school pupils					
	Y3	Y4	Y5	Y6	Y7	Y7	Y8	Y9	Y10	Y11	Y12
Been bullied BOYS	38	32	28	11	22	17	14	13	10	9	0
Been bullied GIRLS	31	27	28	23	14	9	9	8	9	9	0
Bullied others BOYS	11	17	16	10	9	8	5	9	8	11	3
Bullied others GIRLS	2	5	6	8	10	2	4	4	7	3	3

consider the actual form that bullying takes. Work in Scandinavia by Olweus (1991), and by Bjorkqvist, Lagerspetz and Kaukainen (1992) shows that boys are more likely to experience direct forms of bullying, such as being hit or kicked, than indirect forms, such as being excluded or having nasty stories told about them behind their backs. The opposite was the case for girls. Several studies have supported this dichotomy. Whitney and Smith (1993) found that among junior/middle-school pupils, more boys (40 per cent) than girls (33 per cent) reported that they had been physically hurt, whereas more girls (25 per cent) than boys (12 per cent) reported that no one would talk to them. These differences were even more marked among the secondary-school pupils. More than twice as many boys than girls (34 per cent versus 16 per cent) reported that they had been physically hurt, and three times as many girls than boys (12 per cent versus 4 per cent) indicated that no one would talk to them.

Sex is also an important variable influencing who bullies whom. Numerous studies have found that boys tend to be bullied almost exclusively by other boys, whereas girls are more likely to be bullied by children of either sex (Olweus, 1987; Boulton and Underwood, 1992; Whitney and Smith, 1993). Of course, there are exceptions to these general trends. The comments of one eleven-year-old boy indicate that being bullied by girls may have an even more detrimental effect on self-esteem than being bullied by other boys. He told us that 'when I was teased by Tracy and the other girls, it was terrible. The other boys, like Tom and Paul called me a wimp and stuff like that. They said, "you can't even fight girls". They kept going on and on and on. I hated that.'

Age differences in bullying

Almost all studies also feature age differences in being bullied. Generally the youngest pupils in schools appear to be most at risk of being bullied by other children (Boulton and Underwood, 1992; Olweus, 1991; O'Moore and Hillery, 1989; Whitney and Smith, 1993). In a large-scale survey Whitney and Smith (1993) found that there was a steady decrease in the extent to which pupils, aged eight through to sixteen, were being bullied (see table 1.5).

This clear age trend is not evident in terms of bullying other pupils and sometimes there is a rise from one age level to the next (see table 1.5). Whitney and Smith (1993) found levels to be fairly stable through the junior-/middle-school years, but Olweus found an increase over this period among boys but not girls. In another study, Boulton and

Underwood (1992) found that more eleven- and twelve-year-olds reported bullying other pupils 'once or twice', 'sometimes' and 'several times a week' than was the case with eight- and nine-year-olds.

Among secondary-school pupils, there is often an increase in the numbers of individuals who bully other children, especially over the first three or four grades (Olweus, 1991; Whitney and Smith, 1993).

The most likely explanation of these age trends is relative strength and opportunity. Quite simply, the older a child is in school, the greater the numbers of younger pupils are available to be bullied, should the child be inclined to engage in this type of aggressive behaviour pattern.

Friendship/peer acceptance and bully–victim problems

What is the relationship between children's participation in bully–victim problems and their levels of peer acceptance and rejection? In some studies, children not involved in bully–victim problems have been found to be more popular than bullies who, in turn, have been found to be more popular than victims (Olweus, 1978; Lagerspetz, Bjorkqvist, Berts and King, 1982; Stephenson and Smith, 1989).

The finding that victims tend to be low in popularity has been replicated in several studies. Perry, Kusel and Perry (1988) looked at the associations between peer nominations of victimisation on the one hand, and levels of acceptance or rejection on the other. They found that 'extremely victimized' children were significantly more likely than other children to be classified as rejected, a finding that was substantiated by the fact that the correlation between victimisation and peer rejection was significant.

Boulton and Smith (1994) also assessed the relationship between bullying/victimisation and peer acceptance/rejection. Among boys, rejected children received significantly more bullying nominations than popular, average, neglected and other status children, and rejected children of either sex received significantly more victimisation nominations than (male and female) popular, average and other status children. A similar pattern emerged in a series of analyses based on tests of association: both bullies and victims tended to be overrepresented in the rejected group, and to be under-represented in the popular group, relative to not-involved children.

We also demonstrated a tendency for bullies to be overrepresented in the controversial group and so, by definition, they were liked and disliked by above average numbers of classmates. Such a finding could help account for Stephenson and Smith's (1989) finding that teachers rated bullies as having average popularity with other children. Moreover, we might speculate that being well-liked by some classmates could help explain why bullies continue in their negative behaviour: it may not matter to the bullies that they are (probably) disliked by their victims and the friends of their victims, since they have their own friends who are not put off by their engaging in bullying behaviour.

A related suggestion is that bullies may form cliques within the peer group, whose members provide mutual social support and/or friendship. Such a phenomenon was reported for highly aggressive cohorts of 10- and 13-year-old children (Cairns, Cairns, Neckerman, Gest and Gariepy, 1988). Cairns *et al.* found that 'Even though highly aggressive children and adolescents were less popular than control subjects in the social network at large, they were equally often identified as being nuclear members of social clusters' (p. 815).

Somewhat unexpectedly, the results for the popularity of bullies are more mixed than for those from studies of the popularity of victims. Olweus (1978), and Stephenson and Smith (1989) found that bullies were of average popularity, whereas Roland (1989) found evidence to suggest that bullies were essentially as lonely and rejected as victims. All these studies have involved sociometric techniques – based on asking children who are their friends, who they play with, and so on – for assessing popularity. An alternative approach to addressing the issue of peer popularity in relation to bully–victim problems would be to actually *observe* the interaction of children in free-play situations. In one study (Boulton, unpublished), children classified as bullies, victims, or not involved, were observed on the school playground. There were no significant differences between the social network sizes of bullies, victims and not-involved children. This social network variable was an index of how many different children a target child interacted with in a non-aggressive way in the playground during the observation period. However, at any one time, victims tended to be in smaller groups than bullies and not-involved pupils. Victims were also found to spend more of their time alone than the other two groups. These results were an important additional source of support for the notion that victims tend to be lower in popularity than other pupils. Based on this convergent evidence, victims, at least relative to other children, appear to lack an important protective factor against their being bullied in the playground, namely being embedded in a 'large' network of close friends/associates. Having 'many' close friends/associates could serve either to discourage potential bullies from picking on the child in the first place or alternatively the close friends/associates might help to drive a bully off.

In contrast to victims, bullies had the largest social network of all the three groups and tended to be in larger groups at any given moment in time. They also spent the least amount of time in the playground on their own. This evidence challenges Roland's (1989) finding that bullies tend to be as lonely and unpopular as victims. There was also some, although not overwhelming, evidence to suggest that the children regarded by their peers as bullies tended to spend a lot of their time in the same groups.

Stability of bully–victim problems

The evidence collected from recent surveys should be a cause for concern simply because of the proportions of pupils reported to be involved. The fact that it tends to be a stable phenomenon further strengthens the need for action. Olweus (1979) reviewed 16 studies concerned with the stability of aggressive behaviour and reaction patterns, and concluded that the evidence indicated a considerable degree of stability, and that, to a large extent, personality variables were largely responsible for it. Olweus (1978) has also considered the issue of the stability of bullying *per se*. He reported that, among boys, those who were classified as bullies and those who were classified as victims at 13 years of age were likely to retain similar status some three years later, even though in many cases they had changed teachers, schools and/or classmates.

With respect to the junior-school period, Perry, Kusel and Perry (1988) studied 9- to 11-year-old victims over a short (3 month) interval, and found that the victimisation dimension was stable. Boulton and Underwood (1992) asked children two questions about how often they had been bullied in school, one relating to the term they were then in, and the other to the previous term. Analysis indicated a significant degree of stability in reported levels of being bullied across these two time points.

Boulton and Smith (1994) then carried out a more detailed assessment of the stability of bullying, and being bullied, during the junior-school period. Children who were perceived by their peers to be bullies/victims at the beginning of a school year remained so throughout that school year and also remained so during the next academic year. The pattern of bully and victim nominations received by both boys and girls over four assessment periods, extending across one school year and into the next, tended to be stable. These data support the proposition by Perry, Kusel and Perry (1988) that 'a stable propensity to be victimized is established by the time children reach middle school' (p. 812).

Our data also suggested that a correspondingly stable propensity to bully peers exists at this age. These results are particularly disturbing given that the composition of the classes changed from one school year to the next. It appears that it is not the actual composition of a group of children that is the crucial factor in determining which individuals will engage in bullying behaviour and which will be bullied. Perhaps relatively stable individual characteristics are more important in this respect, but further research is certainly required.

Correlates and consequences of bully and victim status – the need for action

Being a bully or a victim appears to be associated with some negative outcomes for children both in the short term and in the long term. One variable that has been studied in this respect is self-esteem. Several studies have shown that bullies, victims and not-involved children may differ in their levels of self-esteem. Victims usually have lower levels of self-esteem than the other two groups, whereas bullies tend to have comparable levels to not-involved children (Olweus, 1978, 1984; Lagerspetz et al., 1982; Boulton and Underwood, 1992).

Using Harter's Self-Perception Profile for Children (1985), a standardised self-esteem inventory, Boulton and Smith (1994) examined in which specific areas of self-perception, if any, bullies, victims and not-involved children differed. Victims (male) scored lower on self-perceived athletic competence than (male) bullies and (male) not-involved children; (male and female) victims scored lower on global self-worth than (male and female) not-involved children, and (female) victims scored lower on self-perceived social acceptance than (female) not-involved children. The latter result may be because bullying for girls, more than for boys, takes the form of social exclusion.

It would be tempting to conclude from the results presented above that being bullied causes a drop in children's self-esteem. However, few studies have specifically addressed the causal relationship between low self-esteem and victimisation. Studies employing correlational designs produce data that are of limited use since they cannot indicate whether low self-esteem pre-dates victimisation or whether victimisation itself is the cause of low self-esteem. Longitudinal designs are required, but to date none have been reported.

Boulton and Underwood (1992) interviewed children that were perceived by classmates to be bullies, victims or not involved in this type of problem. All of these children were asked how they felt when they themselves were bullied. Not surprisingly, most indicated that they experienced negative emotions. They were also asked if they felt better, or worse, or the same about themselves prior to their being bullied. Most (81 per cent) indicated that they had a more positive image of themselves before they had been bullied. This result suggests that in the majority of cases, it is the bullying that precedes the low self-esteem rather than the low self-esteem being the cause of the bullying. However, about 14 per cent of the children indicated that they had felt worse about themselves prior to the onset of their being bullied and so it seems that for a minority of pupils, low self-esteem might pre-date their being bullied.

The finding that low self-esteem is associated with being bullied in school provides a strong case for taking action to combat it. This point is further strengthened by the documented cases where children's lives have been made so miserable by bullying that they have been forced to change schools against their wishes. In extreme cases, pupils have resorted to suicide. Unfortunately, calls for action to remove bullying from our schools often seem to need the publicity of these tragic cases.

The negative effects of both bullying others and being bullied may extend into adult life. Gilmartin (1987) found that about 80 per cent of men who reported that they had problems in their relationships with women had experienced bullying at school. It would be premature to conclude that the early bullying caused these subsequent difficulties with intimacy, but this possibility cannot be ruled out.

For those children who bully others there may also be some long-term negative outcomes. Olweus (1991), for example, reported that 60 per cent of boys who were classified as bullies in Norwegian secondary schools had at least one court conviction by the time they were 24 years of age. Furthermore, 35 to 40 per cent of them had three or more court convictions compared to only 10 per cent of the control boys in the study. In the U.K., Lane (1989) also reported that bullying others in school was a strong predictor of delinquency.

A long-term study cited by Lewis and colleagues (1989) carried out with 800 children in the U.S.A. suggested that pupils who bullied others at 6 years of age were likely to grow up to become aggressive, anti-social adults who were more likely to be convicted of offences. They were also likely to have problems with their social relationships – they were more likely than others who did not engage in bullying at this early age to physically abuse their own children, to have less satisfactory marriages and to have less satisfactory friendships

In general terms then, pupils who regularly bully other children in school may learn that they can get what they want by using and abusing their power, in one form or another, over weaker children. This interactional style may even be retained as the individual develops into an adult.

Clearly, there are a host of reasons why we should be concerned about pupils' involvement in bully–victim problems. Olweus (1993) states that

> bully/victim problems... confront our fundamental democratic principles: Every individual should have the right to be spared oppression and repeated, intentional humiliation, in school as in society at large. No student should be afraid of going to school for fear of being harassed or degraded, and no parent should need to worry about such things happening to his or her child. (p. 107-8)

It is for these various reasons that we decided to target this type of problem in our research project.

We were also concerned about another aspect of children's social relationships that has the potential to lead to damaging experiences: namely prejudice, exclusion or harassment on grounds of race or ethnic group. In the next chapter we examine what has been discovered about children's ethnic relationships and attitudes.

CHAPTER TWO: Ethnicity, relationships and attitudes in children

Introduction

There have been many studies, conducted over several decades, of attitudes and relationships among children of different ethnic groups. Some of the earliest studies, mainly carried out in the U.S.A., focussed on which race or ethnic group children 'identified' with. In general, although with a few exceptions, these early findings showed that most ethnic majority children selected an own-race character on tests using drawings, photographs or dolls as stimulus materials from which children were asked to indicate the one that looked like, or was most like, them. A substantial proportion of young ethnic minority American children selected an other-race rather than an own-race character on tests of this type (Clark and Clark, 1939; Stevenson and Stewart, 1958; Asher and Allen, 1969). Similar findings were reported in minority children in various cultural/national contexts, including the Maoris in New Zealand (Vaughan, 1964), the Bantu in South Africa (Gregor and McPherson, 1966), as well as in the U.K. (Jahoda, Thompson and Bhatt, 1972; Milner, 1973).

Some more recent studies carried out in the U.K. have suggested that ethnic minority children may not be as likely to choose an other-race character to be most like them as the earlier studies had found (Boulton and Smith, 1992; Davey and Mullin, 1980). In a study with 8- to 10-year-olds, for example, Boulton and Smith (1992) found that 76 per cent of Asian pupils and 72 per cent of White pupils, selected the own-race photograph as the one that was 'Most Like Me', a non-significant difference.

Another focus of research in this area concerns children's choices for friends and/or partners to share activities with, that is their ethnic preferences. Some studies have used sociometric methods to generate data, but a minority have used observational techniques of one sort or another. Some early studies found a clear own-race preference among

White children, even at the pre-school level (Renninger and Williams, 1966) and some evidence that Black children preferred partners who were White (Stevenson and Stewart, 1958). However, more recent work in the U.S.A. (Finkelstein and Haskins, 1983; Howes and Wu, 1990) and the U.K. (Davey, 1983; Jelinek and Brittan, 1975; Boulton and Smith, 1992) suggests that an own-race preference may be a feature of many ethnic majority *and* minority children.

Jelinek and Brittan investigated patterns of friendship in a large sample of 1,288 primary- and 3,012 secondary-school children. Friends tended to come from the same ethnic group at eight years of age, but the preference was significantly greater in the older children, with the most marked increase for peers of the same ethnic group occurring between ten and twelve years of age. Similarly, Davey concluded that his results, 'leave little doubt that own-group friendship is strongly established at an early age in multi-ethnic primary schools' (p. 140).

Boulton and Smith (1992) examined the extent to which children exhibited an own-race preference in a sample of eight- to ten-year-old Asian and White pupils. We used a technique devised by Wilson (1987). The children were interviewed individually and asked if they would play a game that involved looking at and sorting into groups, some photographs of children they did not know. The participants in the study were shown six head and shoulders photographs – a girl and a boy from three ethnic groups – African-Caribbean, Asian and White. The participating children were asked about their preferences for partners in various activities – 'sit next to in class', 'have in your team for a game', 'help you with your school work', 'invite home' and 'play with in the playground'. They were asked to indicate their first and second choices for each of these activities. In general, Asian and White boys and girls showed a strong preference for the own-race own-sex photograph. Beyond this, gender appeared to be a much more important selection criterion than race – in almost every case, the three same-sex photographs were preferred significantly more than the three other-sex photographs.

It might be tempting to conclude from these results that race is a less salient factor in determining children's preferences for partners than gender. Moreover, expressing a preference for one or other group in this test, be it on the basis of race or sex, does not necessarily imply that one is negatively disposed to the least preferred group. The methodology of limiting the number of children's choices in this way could mask the possibility that there is actually little if any real difference in the level of preference for one's own race versus another race, and for children of one's own sex versus the other sex.

However, there is some evidence to suggest that a noteworthy proportion of children *do* hold negative attitudes about other ethnic groups and that race *is* an important factor that influences which partners children select in real-life contexts. The results of the studies to be reported below might be construed as indicating the existence of actual prejudice, as opposed to a marginal preference for one's own racial group, something that can not be inferred from the forced choice preference techniques described above.

In an early study carried out in the U.S.A., Radke, Sutherland and Rosenberg (1950) asked seven- to thirteen-year-old children to assign positive and negative traits to pictures of Black and White children. Altogether 80 per cent of the White children made pro-White and anti-Black assignments, suggesting that ethnic majority children have a much more favourable view of their own racial group than of ethnic minority groups.

In contrast, ethnic minority children have been shown in some of the earlier research to perceive their own race in a less favourable way than they perceive the White majority. Among his sample of eight-year-olds, Milner (1975) reported that when presented with a Black doll and a White doll, 58 per cent of the African-Caribbean children indicated that the Black doll was the 'bad doll', and 82 per cent that it was the ugly doll. A large proportion of these same children (78 per cent) stated that the White doll was 'the nicest'. Similar figures were obtained for the Asian children that were interviewed – 45 per cent, 77 per cent, and 84 per cent respectively. Corresponding results were obtained by Davey (1983). He found that White children were significantly more likely to assign positive traits (such as 'works hard' and 'friendly') and significantly less likely to assign negative traits (such as 'stupid' and 'lazy') to members of their own race than to those of the African-Caribbean or Asian groups. The African-Caribbean and Asian children in this sample gave about the same proportion of both positive and negative traits to their own racial group as to the White group and, in addition, each of these ethnic groups gave significantly fewer positive, and more negative traits to the other ethnic minority group.

Two recent British studies have also shed light on the issue of preferences being made on the basis of race. Bennett, Dewberry and Yeeles (1991) showed eight- and eleven-year-old White children who attended a largely White junior school a selection of photographs of unknown children. They were asked, 'Can you tell me if there are any children whom you think are nice?' and a similar question relating to children they thought were not nice. In each case they were asked to say why they did or did not like the children they had selected. The results supported the in-group preference found in previous studies – a third of the children selected as 'nice' photographs of White children only and only 12 per cent selected Black children only. However, there was little evidence for other-group rejection – only 12 per cent selected Black children only as those who were 'not nice'. This pattern of results was replicated with children from an ethnically-mixed school.

Boulton and Smith (1992) replicated the investigation of Davey (1983) discussed above, with a number of slight changes to the methodology. Asian and White children were interviewed, and asked to assign a number of positive and negative traits (see above for examples) to one, some or all of three ethnic groups – African-Caribbean, Asian and White. There was also the option of assigning traits to a 'nobody' option. The latter point was deemed important because it would enable children to indicate positive attitudes to one, some or all three of the target ethnic groups, but at the same time enable them to indicate that they did not have a negative attitude to any of them. Once again, there was strong evidence for an own-group preferences and other-group rejection by both the Asian and the White children. Asian children tended to give most positive traits and least negative traits to the Asian group, with little difference so far as the allocation of both positive and negative traits to the White and African-Caribbean groups was concerned. The White children also gave significantly more positive and significantly less negative traits to their own ethnic group. The White children assigned more positive and less negative traits to the African-Caribbean group than to the Asian group. The 'nobody' option was found to be little used in terms of the allocation of positive traits by both Asian and White children, but about 20 per cent of Asian children's allocations of negative traits and 32 per cent of White children's allocations were directed at the 'nobody' option.

In comparing these results with those obtained by Davey ten years before, it appeared that Asian children in the sample were less positive and more negative in their attitudes towards White children. Similarly, the White participants were distinctly less positive and more negative in their attitudes towards Asian children. In so far as we can take this comparison to give an indication of change over the last decade, it would seem that children's racial attitudes should be an area for increased concern.

Results from projective tests, such as those reported above (see also Aboud, 1988, for a review of other research), have come almost exclusively from studies that have used unknown children to generate ethnic attitudes. The processes involved in the development and maintenance of attitudes and preferences towards members of particular racial groups may vary as a function of familiarity with the target that is being asked about. For example, while a child may hold generally negative stereotypical views of another racial group, they may actually be good friends with individuals that belong to that racial group. In order to investigate this possibility, Boulton and Smith (1993) looked at the extent to which Asian and White children reported that they liked own-race and other-race members of *their own class,* as well as the correlations between this and the children's preferences for sharing activities with others from their own race and the other race that they did not know.

Both Asian and White children rated own-race classmates higher for liking than they rated other-race classmates. This supports the idea of a strong own-race preference that originally came from studies using projective tests. Most of the correlational data did not support the view that the preferences obtained in the projective test were systematically related to liking of known peers. Thus, for example, a child that showed a strong preference for unknown members of her/his own race on the preference test, was just as likely to report a high degree of liking of other-race classmates as to report a low degree of liking of them. Our findings, therefore, suggest that children's racial attitudes/preferences may vary as a function of familiarity with the target.

Most of the available data from other studies suggest only minimal correspondence between preferences based on projective tests and those actually observed in children's peer groups. For this reason, it is important to use *direct observations,* as well as projective tests, to study the relationship between liking of peers and race, and some researchers have done so. Most of this work has been carried out in the U.S.A.

Finkelstein and Haskins (1983) observed 38 Black and 25 White American kindergarten children during classroom instruction and during recess on the school playground. Observations were made during the autumn and then during the following spring. The results indicated that these five-year-olds entered kindergarten with a clear own-race preference and that this *increased* as the school year progressed.

Schofield and Sagar (1977) observed spontaneous seating patterns within a mixed-race middle-school cafeteria, again in America. Two indices of seating aggregation were computed – one concerned with sitting next to a schoolmate, and the other concerned with sitting face-to-face with a schoolmate. Sex was found to be the strongest factor affecting grouping, with children clearly favouring same-sex companions. Nevertheless, race was also very important in this respect for both boys and girls aged thirteen and fourteen. There was a marked preference for same-race companions.

In another American study, Schofield and Francis (1982) investigated the quantity and the quality of cross-race and within-race interactions in four racially mixed classrooms. The children were aged 14 years. The researchers coded the race and the sex of partners, the affective tone (positive, neutral, negative) and the orientation (task, social, ambiguous) of the interactions. Overall, the children were found to interact significantly more with own-race peers than with other-race peers, and the patterns of behaviour shown by the four sub-groups of race/sex participants indicated that cross-race interactions tended to be more task-related than within-race interactions, whereas within-race interactions had a more social orientation than cross-race interactions.

The two studies by Schofield and her colleagues also found that preferences for other-race peers may be different in boys and girls. In the earlier study, boys were found to have significantly more cross-race interactions than girls and, similarly, in the latter study planned comparisons revealed that the strong own-race preference of the girls was responsible for the overall significant own-race preference in the total sample of girls and boys. The boys interacted cross-racially at approximately the rate that would be expected if race was not a factor in interaction choice.

Boulton and Smith (1993) observed a sample of Asian and White junior-school children on the playground in the U.K. The race of the partners that each participant selected to be with/play with on the playground was recorded. The results are summarised in table 2.1. They clearly show a strong racial cleavage among both girls and boys. They are also in accord with the results obtained by Schofield in her research in the U.S.A., namely that this effect is more marked in girls than boys.

In summary, the results from studies of children's racial attitudes and preferences for partners suggest that, in many cases, relationships between children of different ethnic backgrounds continue to pose a

Table 2.1. Percentage of playground companions that were Asian and White observed among Asian and White girls and boys

	Proportion of companions that were Asian	Proportion of companions that were White
Asian girls	89.6	9.4
Asian boys	79.9	16.2
White girls	7.0	84.4
White boys	19.9	62.7

Please note: row totals do not add up to 100% because some of the playground companions were from other ethnic groups, mainly African-Caribbean.

challenge to school systems which aim for understanding and cooperation between pupils from different backgrounds. In study after study, children have been shown to exhibit a strong preference for members of their own racial group over members of other racial groups. This appears to hold true for both ethnic minority as well as ethnic majority groups.

Aboud (1988) has carried out research which linked children's ethnic preferences/attitudes on the one hand, and their cognitive development on the other hand. Based on her work, it seems that the middle school years may be a good time for intervention programmes directed at enhancing children's inter-ethnic relationships and friendships. Aboud stated that:

> although beginning at 7 years children are cognitively capable of being less prejudiced, they may choose to be influenced by prejudiced parents and peers, or they may not have the exposure to information which allows them to use their newly developed cognitive capabilities. A golden opportunity might be lost if children were not given the chance to exercise these new capabilities with the appropriate kind of information about ethnic groups. (p. 128-9)

We decided to investigate how children's relationships with other-race pupils could be improved. The details of our first study, with the main findings, and the rationale leading to our main study, are described in chapter four.

The interaction of friendship/peer acceptance, bully–victim problems, and ethnic attitudes and preferences

We have seen how the different aspects of children's social relationships may, on occasions, either put children under stress or be incompatible with the positive social values of caring and tolerance that many teachers and parents strive to encourage in children. We are also beginning to understand how the different types of relationships children have with their peers might interact with one another in ways that can either ameliorate the potential stress or even magnify its negative effects. For example, a child who is victimised, but at the same time enjoys a number of good friends, may be better able to cope compared with another child that is also victimised but lacks supportive friends. This example illustrates how children's potential to adapt to stresses that stem from their peer relationships may depend on the many different types of social relationships that they experience. In the following section of this chapter, we examine some of the other ways that the three aspects of children's social relationships that we have focussed on may be interrelated.

Race and bullying

Researchers are beginning to address the issue of the relationships between race and racial attitudes on the one hand, and bullying on the other. One finding that has been replicated many times is that in multi-ethnic schools, racial harassment may be extensive.

In a survey in secondary schools, Malik (1990) found that one in three pupils reported that they had been bullied and about a third of these, and more Asian than White pupils, indicated that on some occasions the perpetrator was someone from another ethnic background. Similarly, Kelly and Cohn (1988) found that while about two-thirds of secondary-school students reported that they had been bullied, often in the form of name-calling, it was highest among the Asian pupils. Whitney and Smith (1993) found that 15 per cent of junior/middle-school pupils, and 9 per cent of secondary-school pupils, reported that they had been called nasty names about their colour or race.

The figures are even higher in some other schools. Tizard, Blatchford, Burke, Farquhar, and Plewis (1988) reported that about a third of their sample of junior-school pupils in London indicated that they had been teased about their colour and that more Black children did so than White children. Mooney, Creeser and Blatchford (1991) asked 11-year-old pupils to say how children in general, and themselves in particular, are teased. About 17 per cent of these pupils indicated that children in general are teased because of their race and about 8 per cent indicated that they themselves had been teased in this way in that particular school year. This study also found that 58 per cent of pupils reported that racial teasing occurred at their school. Bullying on racial grounds is not limited to the U.K. – Russell (1986) found that racist name-calling was not uncommon in multi-ethnic junior schools in Australia.

Boulton (unpublished) set out to examine the proportion of ethnic minority and ethnic majority girls and boys in multi-ethnic middle schools that were perceived to be bullies and/or victims by their classmates. There was not a significant difference in the extent to which Asian pupils and White pupils were nominated as bullies by their classmates and, separately, in the extent to which they were nominated as victims.

We also examined the patterns of association between children's ethnic perceptions and ethnic preferences on the one hand, and the degree to which they bullied own-race peers and other-race peers on the other hand. As was noted above, Boulton and Smith (1992) found little correspondence between Asian and White eight- to ten-year-old children's stated racial preferences for unknown other-race individuals and the extent to which they actually played with other-race schoolmates on the playground. This finding suggested that the *general* racial preferences (which may or may not reflect actual prejudice) of children of this age do not usually influence the degree to which they select known other-race peers as playmates, although it may do so in some cases. In this other study, the aim was to see if children's attitudes to other racial groups in general terms would influence which children, if any, they chose to bully in school. This issue had not previously been examined to our knowledge. The results showed that there were no significant correlations between preferences for sharing activities with other race children that were unknown to the participating Asian and White boys, and the extent to which these two groups were perceived by classmates to bully other-race schoolmates that they did know. This was also the case for these two groups of children for the correlations between ethnic stereotypes on the one hand and bullying of known other-race classmates on the other hand. Thus, while a boy might or might not have a generally negative view of other-race children, as determined by their pattern of responses in the tests based on photographs of unknown children, this did not appear to influence whom he actually chose to bully in school. In one sense, this result is encouraging since it suggests that bullying is not always racially motivated even in multi-ethnic schools. The same sort of comparisons could not be carried out for the Asian and White girls in the study because too few of them were named as bullies by a sufficient proportion of their classmates to enable meaningful comparisons.

In this study, we also documented the types of bullying that children reported they had experienced. Particular attention was paid to a comparison between the types of bullying directed at own-race peers and other-race peers. As was noted above, racist name-calling can be common in some multi-ethnic schools but the extent to which other forms of bullying are directed at own-race and other-race pupils was not known prior to the study.

The results showed that proportionally more Asian children than White children reported that they had been teased about their colour/race, and that when it did happen both Asian and White children reported that it was carried out by other-race pupils. In contrast to the findings for racial teasing, proportionally more White children than Asian children reported that they had been teased in some other way and this was mostly carried out by other-race pupils. The association between race of the bully and race of the victim for this type of bullying was not significant.

In a separate study, Moran, Smith, Thompson and Whitney (1993) examined ethnic differences in experiences of bullying. This time a modified version of Olweus's bullying questionnaire was used rather than peer nominations as previously. Despite this difference in methodology, the results were strikingly similar, suggesting that they are robust. Once again, there was no significant difference in the extent to which Asian and White children reported that they had been bullied. Similarly, one half of the bullied Asian pupils report that they had been called racist names but none of the bullied White children reported that they had been called names about their colour or race.

Based on these data it appears that overall, while there is very little difference in the levels of teasing carried out by Asian and White children, the nature of the teasing is different. White pupils are more likely to base their teasing of Asian pupils on matters of race/colour whereas Asian pupils are more likely to base their teasing of White children on something else.

All instances of bullying have the potential to cause pain and distress to the victims, but racial bullying may have even more deleterious effects. The Swann Report (1985) and Mooney *et al.* (1991) highlighted the distinction that can be made between racial name-calling and other forms of name-calling. Whereas racial teasing is a reference not only to the child but also to their family and their ethnic community as a whole, other forms of teasing relate only to the individual child and her/his own particular characteristics.

Moran, Smith, Thompson and Whitney (1993) asked children if they did not like any of the children in their class and if so, to say why. Of the seventeen Asian pupils that reported not liking someone, twelve gave bullying as the major reason and half of these explicitly mentioned racist name-calling.

Cohn (1988) investigated pupils' reactions to racist name-calling in six secondary schools in London. She found that 'the most prevalent, powerful and abhorent names are those to do with race and colour' (p. 36). The pupils were also asked to state the specific names that children use. More than sixty different racially abusive names were mentioned by the over 13-year-olds and over forty by the under 13-year-olds.

While all teasing that causes distress should be a target for elimination by teachers and parents, there is clearly a need for White pupils to be the targets of attempts to reduce instances of racial teasing. Again, it is possible that if these patterns of interaction between Asian and White pupils, especially racial teasing by the latter, are not challenged at middle school, if not earlier, then they may be even harder to change in the future.

Troyna and Hatcher (1992) give disturbing insights into the experiences of Black children in predominantly White primary schools. Racist incidents are, in their words, 'a way of life'. The Black children interviewed by Troyna and Hatcher said that they found racist name-calling more hurtful than any other kind of name-calling. Typical responses included:

> 'I don't like people calling me things about my colour, I don't like it. I feel strong about my colour.' (p. 57)
> 'Nearly every day I get called Blackie.' (p. 58)
> 'Like this boy called Robert, he keeps calling me a "Baboon", and Simon calls me the same and Aaron he calls me the same as well.' (p. 60)

For many of the Black children in this study, being called racist names was only part of an on-going experience of discrimination in the community, as Troyna and Hatcher show in their commentary on an account by Zabeel, an Asian boy:

> Some of the white children were aware of this, but others had little understanding of racism in society. Zabeel's experience of racism outside school provides him with some important lessons which he makes use of in dealing with racism from white children: the value of support networks among black people, the effectiveness of force in deterring racist harassment, the lack of confidence in the ability of authority to provide a solution, the belief that if you appeal to them then you may very well end up getting the blame. (p. 65)

At the same time, Troyna and Hatcher point out that there is wide variation in the reports which Black children give of racism. This they attribute to differences in the patterns of children's social interactions and – significantly – to the policies which individual schools have on the issue of anti-racism.

Race and friendship/peer acceptance

We noted earlier how many children were found to express a clear preference for members of their own racial group in projective tests that involved photographs of other children that they did not know, and how many pupils were found to spend more time with own-race schoolmates than with other-race schoolmates in the classroom and playground. Some studies have also examined the way that race may mediate children's liking of classmates and their selection of friends.

Boulton and Smith (1992) asked a sample of Asian and White middle-school pupils to indicate how much they liked each one of their classmates. They were asked to respond on a 3-point scale that included 'not at all', 'a little' and 'a lot'. Both groups expressed a significantly higher degree of liking of own-race classmates, an effect that was evident in both boys and girls separately.

Kelly (1988) investigated the relationship between race and friendship among pupils in three secondary schools in Manchester. In two of these schools, 24 per cent of boys and 21 per cent of girls indicated that they had never been friends with someone from a different racial group, and the value for the boys in the other school was even higher at 35 per cent.

Some of our playground observations also suggest that race influences not only which peers children chose to play with but also who they deliberately exclude from their games. We found that the extent to which Asian and White children reported that they had been deliberately excluded from games and other activities did not differ significantly. However, for both groups it was other-race pupils who were said to be responsible.

Some researchers claim that schools may influence the extent to which pupils exhibit an own-race preference. In the study of 5-year-old Black and White children in America by Finkelstein and Haskins (1983) referred to above, the extent to which children chose to interact with same-race schoolmates and other-race schoolmates was observed both in the classroom and on the playground. In both contexts there was a strong tendency for children to select same-race as opposed to other-race children. Nevertheless, this tendency was strongest during classroom instruction than during playtime. Finkelstein and Haskins state that,

> when teachers do influence the context of peer relations by assigning children to seats or work groups in the classroom, children exhibit a somewhat increased frequency of cross-color interactions. (p. 507)

In many schools, there are few systematic attempts to enhance children's cross-ethnic friendships and this may work to consolidate the evident own-race preference of a large proportion of pupils. Finkelstein and Haskins found that the tendency of children to select play partners from their own racial group increased during the kindergarten year. They stated that, this finding, especially when combined with results of other studies showing strong same-color preferences in older students, implies that school experiences reinforce and strengthen the predisposition of both black and white children to interact with children of their own color – and this despite the fact that children apparently have ample opportunity to interact with other-color peers in the classroom. (p. 507)

Teacher/pupil relationships in multi-ethnic classrooms

Wright (1992), on the basis of classroom observations in four innercity primary schools, suggested that teachers' attitudes towards Black children have a strong influence on peer relationships. She reported that in classrooms where the teachers treated the Asian children negatively – by, for example, losing patience with them, failing to involve them in group discussions, ignoring their attempts to contribute, assuming that they did not speak English – White children would echo these 'perceived personal deficiencies to tease and taunt their Asian classmates' (p. 19). In her view, African-Caribbean children in her study were 'always the most criticised and reprimanded children in the group' (p. 19). As a Black childcare assistant observed:

> Marcus (an African-Caribbean boy) really likes answering questions about things. I can imagine he's quite good at that because he's always got plenty to say ... but they (white teachers) see the black children as a problem here. (p. 21)

From the White teachers' perspective, the accusations of racism could seem unfair:

> I am not saying I am pristine and my halo is glowing, but at least I am aware of my own shortcomings and I do make positive steps to overcome what has been instilled in me for years. Whether or not things come out sort of unconsciously without me knowing. I am sure that if I knew things were coming out then I would take positive steps. (p. 26)

Although Wright (1992) appreciates the stress which teachers face in an extremely demanding job, like Troyna and Hatcher, she argues strongly that schools can counteract the effect of racism through active commitment to a policy which is endorsed by all members of staff and involves all groups of children who experience hostility. Furthermore, she is of the view that:

those who still advocate colour-blind approaches in schools are avoiding the reality that staff, like most other people, do treat people differently on the bases of perceived 'racial' characteristics. Further, many nursery and primary staff are still reluctant to accept that younger children can hold incipient racist attitudes and exhibit hostility towards members of other groups. (p. 103)

Gillborn (1990) explored teacher/pupil relationships in his ethnographic study of life in a multi-ethnic, innercity comprehensive school. He, too, found that ethnicity was an important part of the social relationship networks among Black pupils. Shared ethnicity could unite, for example, Asian boys in defending a fellow pupil from racist attacks. Gillborn observed frequent instances of racist name-calling and physical attacks on Black pupils. This kind of victimisation was a common, almost daily, experience for Asian pupils which, in his view, was often underestimated by the staff. Ethnicity, he concludes, has a strong impact on the way in which Black pupils, in particular South Asian males, experience school, especially with regard to friendship choices and the experience of racial harassment. He, like Wright, is critical of a colour-blind approach which ignores the reality of everyday life for Black children in our schools.

Besag (1989) considers that schools have an important role to play in combatting racial bullying but recognises that the problem is a recalcitrant one. She writes:

Schools alone cannot combat racism... Schools can, however, escalate or de-escalate the situation by the attitudes and practices at work within the school. One tutorial lesson a week will change little; it is the quality of all daily interactions throughout the school day which will be influential in bringing about a more positive situation. Social attitudes are man-made, they are the result of schooling in prejudice; therefore if a positive attitude is presented throughout all aspects of the school day, then some inroads can be made to counteract the current situation which appears to be characterized by an uncomplaining acceptance that prejudice is a widespread and commonplace feature of contemporary life in Britain. (p. 49)

Conclusions

Our discussion clearly suggests that peer acceptance/friendship, bully-victim relationships and ethnic relationships may be linked in a variety of ways. All of the research we have considered leads inextricably to two firm conclusions. One is that the social worlds of children are complex, probably to the same extent as those of adults. The other is that social relationships can be problematic for a disconcerting proportion of children and for a whole host of different reasons. These two points repeatedly emerged as we planned and carried out this research project. It was clear to us that intervention strategies need to be tested for their efficacy, but at the same time we did not expect to find any easy solutions to the complex problems associated with children's multi-faceted social relationships. All the evidence seemed to indicate the need for schools to develop an active stance on racism and for the staff to create a climate in which racist behaviour and domineering, aggressive behaviour is challenged. How could this be done?

In the next chapter we outline the reasons why we decided to investigate the potential of cooperative group work techniques to improve aspects of children's social relationships that may harm them in some way, or which run counter to our concern for fostering attitudes of care and tolerance. As we will see, there is strong support for the view that the creation of a cooperative climate in the classroom can markedly improve the quality of interpersonal relationships in the peer group. Cooperative learning methods integrate prosocial values into the curriculum and, as Sharan (1990) points out, the positive effects of these methods on the enhancement of friendship in ethnically heterogeneous classrooms is documented in many classroom studies at all age levels.

CHAPTER THREE: Cooperative group work in primary schools

Introduction

Most educators acknowledge the idea that much of children's learning takes place in a social context. Group work in the classroom, many educators would claim, is an established part of current practice; and they would point to the fact that children in primary schools regularly work round tables in small groups.

A commitment to cooperative methods assumes a readiness to view knowledge not as a commodity owned by the expert teacher but as something which can (at least in part) be constructed, developed and criticised by the group. In fact, committed users of cooperative learning strategies often claim that some topics can only be understood fully through the active interplay of different perspectives from members of an involved group. The justification for group work has a long history. The Plowden Report (1967), advocating progressive, child-centred ideals in education, argued that children benefit from frequent opportunities to experience interactions within a range of different groupings. They suggested that children learn to communicate effectively with one another; gain in self-confidence as they share ideas of mutual concern; and widen their network of friendships. Later, the Bullock Report (1975) stressed the relationship between language and learning right across the curriculum and throughout children's years at school. Each report recommended the greater use in schools of exploratory talk in small interactive groups as a means of enabling pupils to develop in their capacity to relate new knowledge to previous understanding.

Concern to foster meaningful dialogue in small cooperative groups was a distinguishing feature of many curriculum projects taken up by schools in the 1970s. For example, *Man: a Course of Study*, a project used in the U.K. and the U.S.A., was founded in a commitment to the view that group work brings cognitive benefits to children as they challenge one another's beliefs and work together to solve problems collaboratively. Many educators openly acknowledge the value of this approach.

Here is how one teacher expresses his belief that cooperative learning strategies enable students to arrive at a deeper understanding of an issue:

> There's the possibility of greater diversity and the ability to . . . develop ideas which are generated by children rather than generated by the teacher. Very often (in instructional teaching) you have to cut off and say, 'We've got to go on to the next point'. But if you've got group work then you've got the facility of developing and moving through and allowing the children to develop ideas rather more extensively. (Cowie and Rudduck, 1988a, p. 58)

This teacher comments on the positive effect which cooperative learning has on his students' academic achievement. In the Vygotskian tradition, it is this social context which is a key ingredient in learning. Although Piaget acknowledged the role of social experience in intellectual growth, Vygotsky is the developmental psychologist who has placed most emphasis on the essentially social nature of individual thinking processes. In his view, children develop as thinkers by internalising processes which were originally experienced in a social context.

Vygotsky (1978) and later Bruner (1986) claimed that there are clear benefits when a more knowledgeable peer or adult interacts with a less expert child. Learning is about 'the negotiation of meaning' rather than its transmission and, for it to be effective, it must be rooted in personally significant issues, human settings and social relationships. Cooperative learning, from this standpoint, creates opportunities for the active construction of meanings to take place through dialogue. The contexts of such dialogue should allow for a range of views and experiences to be taken into account and give the students some say in what is to be learned and how learning goals are to be achieved.

Vygotsky's view is that learning is a cooperative venture. Like Piaget, he argues that action is the way in which the child responds to the world. However, in his view, children also learn by turning round and reflecting on their thoughts using language and so come to see things in a new way. Furthermore, learning is achieved through cooperation with others in a whole variety of social settings – with peers, teachers, parents and other people who are significant to the child. In other words, the child's capacity to learn is embedded in his or her capacity to learn *with the help of others*.

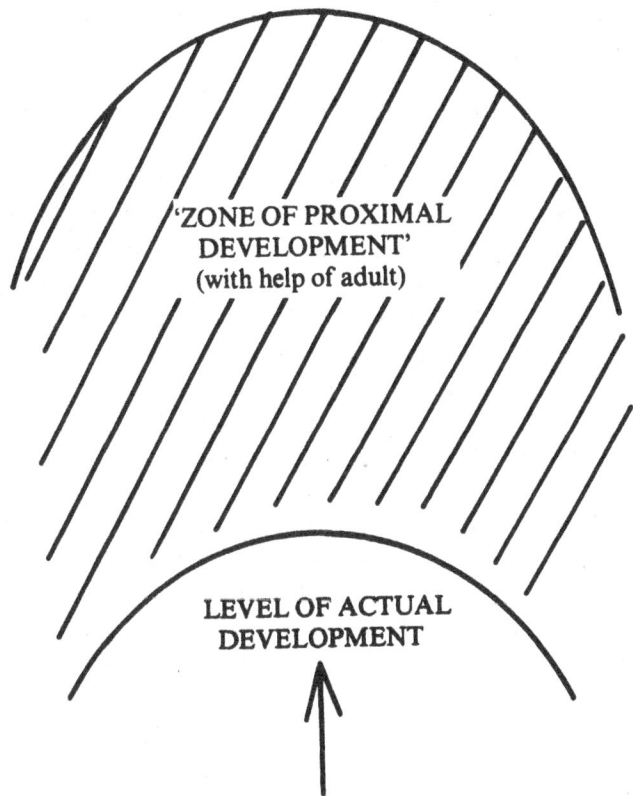

Figure 3.1 Vygotsky's zone of proximal development (Z.P.D.)

A central concept is the zone of proximal development (Z.P.D.) – the distance between the child's actual developmental level and his or her potential level of development under the guidance of more expert adults or in collaboration with more competent peers. The child learns by jointly constructing his or her understanding of issues and events in the world.

Unlike Piaget, Vygotsky did not wait for the child to be 'ready'. Instead, he argued, children learn from other people who are more knowledgeable than themselves. It is the 'loan of consciousness' (to use Bruner's phrase) that gets the child through the Z.P.D. The process of collaborating with other people not only gives the child more information about a topic but also confirms those aspects of the topic which the child does understand. The process of cooperation enables the child to move on. The intervention is most effective when it is contingent upon the child's existing repertoire of skills and knowledge, that is when it is within the child's Z.P.D. So, when the child is challenged – but not too much – then he or she is more likely to learn new things without experiencing failure.

Others highlight the part which cooperative learning methods play in children's social and personal development. Cooperative group work provides a setting where children can explore relationships with one another and can share issues in a trusting setting. When they are experiencing difficulties, this kind of group work can be helpful and supportive. It is a context where children can learn to be confident in themselves. They can also explore conflicts and learn to resolve them. The classroom is seen as a microcosm of society where children can come to learn about roles and relationships and learn about interactions which will stand them in good stead in their future lives as adults (Brandes and Phillips, 1979; Hopson and Scally, 1981; Pike and Selby, 1988).

Educators in this tradition do not downplay the importance of academic attainment but their underlying philosophy is that personal and interpersonal experience forms the basis for both personal and intellectual growth. If the basic needs of the person are neglected then academic work will suffer. A priority would be to establish trust and cooperation in the classroom. Such practitioners claim that cooperative learning methods contribute to a climate of acceptance and tolerance in the classroom. Students who have experience of working cooperatively with one another are likely to have higher self-esteem and to view their peers more positively (Kutnick, 1988).

Here is one head teacher's view on the role of cooperative learning in the innercity junior school where she works:

> I am absolutely committed to the encouragement of cooperation in this school because of our aim of enabling the children to respect themselves, respect others, respect the school and the environment in which they live. At one time we would have respected others first, but you can't do that until you respect yourself. It is about values – values in relation to other people. It is hard in a school like this because before you can get children to work cooperatively together they've got to be able to have a certain amount of self-esteem and a lot of children have not got that. But that doesn't mean you haven't got to keep working at it.

She stresses the importance of a secure emotional base for the children before they can begin to fulfil their potential, claiming that cooperation in the classroom is directly related to the growth of effective communication skills, to a climate of trust, and an environment which is friendly and supportive. Fun and enjoyment form part of this process. Orlick (1978; 1982) expresses his belief that cooperative games can create enjoyable opportunities in which children learn to value themselves and others:

> Through cooperative ventures, children learn to share, to empathise with others, to be concerned with others' feelings, and to work to get along better... The fact that children work together toward a common end, rather than against one another, immediately turns destructive responses into helpful ones. (Orlick, 1978, pp. 6-7)

Over time, in classrooms where these qualities of cooperation are consistently promoted and valued, the children, it is claimed, become more tolerant of one another and more skilled at dealing with interpersonal conflicts and tensions. In addition, teachers who hold these views claim that the cooperative attitudes developed through interaction with peers contribute to a sense of social responsibility in their students, for example, to children who are new to the class or who come from another culture, or who are unsure of themselves. Teachers, they argue, have a key part to play in counteracting the competitiveness which pervades Western culture and which can inhibit the natural development of children's sensitivity towards one another:

> We are exposed to competition in every aspect of our lives; it pervades the home, the classroom and the media alike, and is frequently a source of stress, particularly with children who quickly see themselves as failures. Yet it is cooperation that has always been an intrinsic part of human nature. (Masheder, 1986, p. 5)

> Problems to do with poor communication, lack of trust and mutual respect, an inability to cooperate, are evident at the level of world society and in our national life, as well as in the local community and classroom. The classroom is, in this sense, the world in miniature. (Fisher and Hicks, 1987, p. 67)

Furthermore, as we saw in chapter two, there is a growing concern about the discrimination experienced regularly by children from minority groups. Recent reports have widely documented this racial discrimination in schools (Commission for Racial Equality, 1988; Eggleston, 1985; Rampton, 1981; Swann, 1985), and have recommended in no uncertain terms that it is the responsibility of schools to give their pupils, regardless of gender, social class or ethnic background, the confidence and the ability to make their voices heard within their own community and in society at large. Cooperative learning, it seems, offers a coherent way of putting these principles into practice.

What does cooperative learning look like?

(1) Perspectives from the U.K.

Here are some perspectives from the U.K. Cowie and Rudduck (1988a) contend that the central feature of cooperative learning is the opportunity to learn through the exploration and expression of diverse ideas and experiences in cooperative company. They argue that, in the cooperative classroom, the pupils will be encouraged to work with one another rather than in competition with one another, that they will be predisposed to use the resources of the group in order to share ideas, deepen knowledge and understanding, and that they will come to acknowledge the variety of perspectives which people bring to any issue or situation. They also argue that, in order to create a cooperative working climate in their classroom, teachers need to make a transition to new teaching and learning styles which incorporate democratic and participatory principles. Groups that work well together, they argue, will have the following characteristics:

* group members are, between them, putting forward more than one point of view in relation to the issue or task they face;
* group members are disposed to examine and to be responsive to the different points of view put forward;
* the interaction assists with the development of group members' knowledge, understanding and/or judgement of the matter under scrutiny;
* they are engaged in a task designed in a way which supports the distinctive potential for learning through group work. (p. 13)

In other words, cooperative group work depends on a shared commitment to the task and a negotiated understanding of the rules and procedures appropriate to that particular group. The activity itself should promote certain values, such as sensitivity to others, a willingness to listen, supportiveness, the freedom to take risks, tolerance for all contributions, no matter how tentatively expressed; it should also involve frequent opportunities to reflect on and evaluate shared experiences. Cooperative group work from this perspective can be part of any subject where there is some issue, problem or controversy that can be explored through the careful consideration of different points of view.

The function of talk in enhancing the thinking processes of children was the focus of Barnes and his colleagues (Barnes, Britton and Rosen, 1969). On the basis of their detailed observations of teacher–pupil interactions in the classroom they concluded that teacher-centred talk devalued what pupils had to say, and discouraged them from thinking and talking creatively. Although they acknowledged that primary-school children were encouraged to share personal experiences, they found that in secondary schools there were very few opportunities for the pupils to make links between this personal knowledge and the material which they learned in school. Barnes et al. argued that a crucial aspect of the learning process arises through dialogue which is personally meaningful – the kind of talk which can be facilitated best in the context of the small group. They were impressed by the quality of the talk which emerged in this informal setting. Of course the groups varied widely in their capacity to solve problems effectively, to speculate, to criticise and to consider a range of perspectives. But they were more likely to adopt a tentative, exploratory stance when the teacher was not present, and they frequently drew on their own experience to make a point or to help the group to arrive at a new level of understanding. These ideas seemed controversial at the time and remain so, as we shall see in the following paragraphs, but this work was influential in promoting the idea in some educational circles that pupils could be trusted to relate their own personal knowledge, perceptions and experiences to the processes of learning and understanding.

Galton and Williamson (1992) also value 'non-controlling' classrooms and give clear, practical guidelines on how to achieve a collaborative climate in the classroom. But they recommend a more structured approach to the management of small groups. They indicate that it is essential for the teacher to be quite explicit about the value she places on collaboration and to communicate this to the children. In addition, they recommend, children need to be taught the skills of collaboration and communication through well-designed activities, including those which enable them to cope with conflict. It is important that critical feedback takes place in which teacher and children take the opportunity to comment on and evaluate what took place within the groups. If the teacher does not establish clear criteria against which the pupils can judge their own performance in the group, they may remain confused about what the purpose of the activity was. It is important, argue

Galton and Williamson, that children be given the experience of a range of roles within their groups, including being a leader, clarifying the goals of the group, carrying out maintenance work like tidying up, resolving conflicts and keeping the group on task. The children should also understand the criteria against which they can be evaluated by self, group and teacher.

Dunne and Bennett (1990) have also investigated children's work and talk in groups. They delineate the following three models:

Model 1: working individually on identical tasks for individual products

On the surface this model does not look like a cooperative group work structure since individuals are asked to provide individual products. Yet, when children in a group are working on the same task it is possible for them to share the experience and contribute to one another's interest, motivation and understanding. Their talk may influence one another's actions, ideas and the quality of the end product. But it is unlikely that this will occur unless the teacher specifically demands and encourages this kind of behaviour, and is concerned with issues such as which person talks to whom and in what relation group members are towards one another. An example would be where the teacher introduces the task and emphasises that the children are working as a group, not on their own. She would exhort them to 'join in and help one another. Try to solve any problems within your group. I will be available for any problems which your group cannot solve.' Alternatively, the children could work individually on the tasks and then meet as a group at the end to debrief, either about the task which they have just done or about the way in which they have worked together, or both.

Model 2: Jigsaw

Here children work individually on 'jigsaw' elements for a joint outcome; cooperation is built into the task structure as is individual accountability since if the individual child sits back and lets others do all the work the group will not complete its task. Group members are likely to ensure that each person pulls his or her weight. An example of such a task would be the production of a group story or a newspaper. This can cater for a range of contributions. Non-readers can use drawing; those for whom English is a second language can contribute in their first language and interpreters found from within the group. Another example might be found in topic work. Children might be asked in 'expert' groups to find out about aspects of life in a certain period of history (say, in the time of the Celts) – being a serf, being a woman, being a noble. The experts then return to home groups to instruct one another and then to create a short role-play showing aspects of life of that time.

Model 3: working jointly on one task for a joint outcome
For this kind of task children need to work cooperatively since only one product is required of the group. Activities will therefore have to be coordinated and it is possible that a group leader will emerge or could be selected, in order to create the necessary organisation. Each individual's work will have an impact on the group product but will be worthless until it becomes a part of that product. Brainstorming is an example of this kind of activity. So, too, is whole-group discussion, as when children read a story and then, in groups of four, make a critique of it, or create a poster to illustrate it.

Dunne and Bennett found a dramatic increase in the extent and the involvement of the children when they worked in cooperative groups. Teachers commented on the children's capacity to develop their own ideas, reach informed conclusions and 'use rich mathematical language'. Low attainers benefited; most children became more independent; and there was a higher quality of work all round. For Dunne and Bennett the research demonstrated the great need to promote, as Barnes had attempted to do in the 1970s, the value of talk for thinking in the classroom; and showed that high level talk was encouraged by group work of a cooperative kind. One disturbing aspect of their research is that the same problems which Barnes faced in implementing his ideas widely in schools remain at the present time in the 1990s.

Here are some examples of group work built on these principles, drawn from cooperative learning resource materials in the U.K.

DISCUSSION
Here a larger group of pupils and their teacher, or a smaller group of pupils without the teacher's constant presence, work to share understandings and ideas. An example from a resource book on the teaching of poetry to young children (Balaam and Merrick, 1988) illustrates the role of group work in enhancing children's imaginative responses to literature. After the teacher has read the poem *Alone in the Grange* by Gregory Harrison to the class, children may be asked in small groups to talk about an issue which is highlighted in the poem – living alone. They may be asked to describe with one another someone they know who lives alone, how that person behaves, what that person looks like. Later, the groups move on to explore what the poem tells them about the old man who lives in the Grange. The focus here is on the interpretation of something which is ambiguous as well as the sharing of experiences. Discussions may lead to enhanced individual understanding or they may require negotiation in the interests of arriving at a consensus.

PROBLEM-SOLVING TASKS

Here children meet together to confront a problem and evolve a solution. Often the same task is set simultaneously to a number of small groups of three or four pupils, and there may be a final review of solutions in a plenary with mutual criticism. Group members acquire a range of skills as they work together on their issue. They learn how to generate ideas through brainstorming; they develop in their powers of observation; they may be required to collect data in the course of the investigation; communication is enhanced at the point where they present their solution for evaluation by the teacher and other groups. The problem may be a mathematical one or it could be to do with relationships in the class. The Quality Circle is one kind of problem-solving group in which the children identify a problem issue (for example, children's boredom at breaktime) in the school community and work together over a period of time to suggest a solution (Cowie and Sharp, 1992; Cowie, 1994).

GROUP PROJECTS

These are different from problem-solving tasks since there is usually a concrete outcome. Pupils may be working in a team to write a piece of music or to design a logo collaboratively; they may be working collectively to produce a mural or a flowchart based on technology, language or science work. It may be necessary for the teacher to assign roles to members of the group, such as writer, reader, designer. At the end there is often a communal group review of the process and evaluation of the product.

SIMULATION

Here, pupils take on the situation of a real-life group. In *The Banana Game* simulation (Tigwell, 1990), for example, participants discover how a familiar fruit reaches us and who is involved in its production and journey. Players adopt the roles of six groups: growers/pickers, packers, shippers, importers, wholesalers and retailers. A price is fixed for the banana crop and each group has to agree on how much of that price they deserve. Pupils learn how trade can affect the prosperity of different groups of people and experience how the gap between rich and poor is maintained and even made wider by the trading system. As in all simulations, there must be time at the end for children to share feelings about issues – individual rights, injustices, power, needs – which have arisen for them in the course of the game. Within simulations children are free to contribute their own perspectives and draw on their own experiences; where specific roles have been assigned, the simulation can merge into the next category – role-play.

ROLE-PLAY ACTIVITIES

Here each pupil is given a character or perspective within the framework of an event or situation. The role becomes a mask and the characters interact according to their interpretation of the given role. Roles are usually assigned to reflect different perspectives on an issue or event. If we return to the poem *Alone in the Grange*, the children in groups may be asked to visit the Grange in the roles of reporters, curious townspeople, anxious shopkeepers. Alternatively, within groups of five or six, one child takes the role of the old man while the others take it in turns to interview him about himself and his home (Balaam and Merrick, 1988). Through their engagement in the drama, the children are offered the opportunity to explore the poem's meanings more deeply.

(2) Perspectives from the U.S.A. and Israel

In the U.S.A. and Israel, where work on practical applications of cooperative principles began in the 1970s, a number of distinctive instructional methods have been developed. Those which have been most extensively developed and evaluated are *Student Team Learning, Teams Games Tournament, Jigsaw* and *Group Investigation.*

STUDENT TEAM LEARNING

This method was pioneered by Slavin (1983) and was rooted in a theoretical model which promotes the view that, if social interactions among individuals from different social and ethnic backgrounds are to be made more positive, then mere contact is not enough; rather the interacting group members must be working towards a common goal.

In *Student Teams and Achievement Divisions* (S.T.A.D.), groups were deliberately heterogeneous, mixed by ability, race and gender. The teacher first presents a lesson, after which the students meet in four- to five-member teams to master a set of worksheets on the topic. They are then quizzed individually. Quiz scores are turned into team scores through a weighting system which takes into account previous performance by individuals. The reward is given to the team with the highest score. The highest scores are recognised in a weekly class newsletter.

TEAMS GAMES TOURNAMENT

In *Teams Games Tournament* (T.G.T.) (DeVries and Slavin, 1978), students, in heterogeneous groups of four to five, study worksheets together and question one another to check that the material has been learned. A tournament is then held in which individual representatives of each group compete with one another. Points are awarded on those individuals' performances and the reward is given to the most successful team.

JIGSAW

Jigsaw (Aronson, 1978) was designed to involve participants in direct instruction. It is called 'jigsaw' because information about the topic under investigation is divided into four or five sections so that each student has access to only part of the material to be mastered and must therefore work with others in order to fit together all the pieces of the 'jigsaw'. Children begin in home groups which are accountable to one another for mastering the information to be learned. The material is divided into 'expert' sections. At this point, children move into 'expert' groups in which they study one section; they then return to their home groups and teach the material which they have mastered to other members of their group. Finally, students are individually tested on their knowledge of all aspects of the topic. Here there is interdependence of task but not of reward. Jigsaw is a good method for building a positive sense of interdependence within the group as well as a sense of individual accountability.

GROUP INVESTIGATION

This method, developed by Sharan and Sharan (1976), is the most complex of the American cooperative learning strategies. Here, children select sub-topics within a general area determined by the teacher, often in the field of science or social studies, and then organise themselves into groups of two to six. In cooperation with peers, they identify problems, plan the procedures needed to understand these problems, collect the data relevant to their plan and prepare a report of their work. The social context of the peer group allows them the chance to examine data carefully and analyse findings critically in collaboration with others. Finally, there is a group presentation to the whole class which is evaluated by teacher and peers. The technique is similar to *Jigsaw* in incorporating interdependence of task. Furthermore, the students take substantial responsibility for deciding what they will learn, how they will organise themselves to learn it and how they will communicate it to their peers.

Forming and maintaining the group (U.K. and U.S.A.)

Cooperative games were first developed as a form of cooperative learning in the U.S.A. but have been incorporated into curriculum initiatives in the U.K. (for example, into *World Studies*).

Cooperative games

The distinctive feature of cooperative games is that 'everybody cooperates... everybody wins... and nobody loses' (Orlick, 1978). Orlick views play as the ideal medium for social learning since it is intrinsically motivating for young children and it involves participants in 'the processes of acting, reacting, feeling and experiencing' (Orlick, 1982). Furthermore, cooperative games do not distort this natural activity by rewarding competition, aggression towards others, cheating and leaving people out. Cooperative games are designed in such a way that cooperation among players is necessary in order to achieve the objectives of the game. Children play together for common ends rather than against one another for exclusive ends. In the process, it is hoped, they learn prosocial skills of sharing, being sensitive to others, becoming considerate, working together.

Orlick identifies five essential freedoms which are central to cooperative games – freedom from competition; freedom to create new games; freedom from exclusion of those deemed to be less expert or less experienced; freedom to choose aspects of games which are appropriate and to devise new rules and procedures; freedom from hitting through involvement in physically aggressive games. One example is *Magic Carpet* where children in groups of about seven take turns in giving one another magic-carpet rides on a gym mat. Other examples include the wide variety of parachute games which can only be played by groups of cooperating participants.

There is a time factor involved in group work. Group norms evolve; there are stages in the formation of a group which need to be understood. It is normal, for example, for groups to experience a period of 'storming' before a productive climate can be established. Dealing constructively with interpersonal conflicts within a group can be a healthy experience for group members, but they need to be taught the skills. In the absence of an understanding of group processes, teachers may find the short-term 'deterioration' in pupils' behaviour during group work alarming and cut it short before long-term goals have been achieved. There are some distinctive activities which are essential for group formation and the maintenance of group cohesion.

Trust-building exercises

These take many forms but are essentially about enabling group members to get to know one another and to build up trust within the group. Initial sessions focus on learning names and discovering characteristics of fellow group members. They are often designed to be fun – they break the ice in early stages of the group. Non-verbal birthday line-up is an active game which requires people to line up in order of the month of the year in which they were born. In the process, participants find themselves communicating with people whom they did not already know. At later stages in a group's formation it may become safer for participants to share feelings and experiences within the group. They may, for example, have a round in which members complete the sentence 'My hopes for this group are that . . . ' Again, the process of sharing is held to build trust and goodwill within the group which creates a good climate for productive working together.

At regular points during the life of a group it is necessary to take time to reflect on processes which are taking place within the group. These evaluations continue to build trust but they also have the important function of creating opportunities for group members to bring to the surface any difficulties which are around, for example interpersonal conflicts. They enable groups to build on productive working practices and to challenge practices which impede the progress of the group. This aspect of group work is sometimes called *group processing* and sometimes called *debriefing*.

Group processing/debriefing

Here group members have the opportunity to reflect on an experience. This can take five minutes or a whole lesson; it can happen immediately after the experience or at a later date. The main point of the activity is that it is viewed as an essential part of the cooperative learning experience. Debriefing takes many forms. It can be structured or unstructured, directive or non-directive. A formal debriefing session might, for example, be designed by the teacher to ascertain how much the participants had actually learned about a specific topic: in this case, questionnaires or checklists would be appropriate and the teacher would retain a controlling role. A more informal debriefing session would be used to enable participants to deepen their understanding of the issues which had been explored during the lesson or the events which had occurred: here strong emotions might well emerge and the teacher's role would be facilitative rather than directive. Debriefing typically goes through three stages which can be summarised as a series of questions:

what happened?
how did participants feel?
what does this mean to the group?

Techniques vary. Children can fill in smiley faces; they can write telegrams to one another; they can complete open-ended sentences like 'At the beginning of the activity I felt . . . ' The main aim of debriefing is to help participants move towards a new level of understanding and to be responsive to the themes which emerge as being important.

Cooperative group work in practice

The theory is there to support cooperative learning and, as we have seen, there is no shortage of tried and tested methods for the teacher to adapt in the classroom. There is also a widespread belief that, in primary schools at least, a large part of the day is devoted to group work. Yet a closer look at group work in action by a number of classroom-based researchers reveals a different picture. It seems to be difficult for teachers to sustain group work which is cooperative in nature. HMI (1983), in a survey of middle schools, pointed out that there were few opportunities for children to engage in extended discussion or collaborative work in groups, or to exercise choice, responsibility and initiative within the curriculum. Kerry and Eggleston (1988), investigating topic work in the primary school, observed that teachers were often at a loss when it came to assigning children to groups. The friendship pair was most common, followed by the 'hidden streaming' of grouping children by ability. Although many teachers believe that the children in their classes are working with one another in small groups, the reality is that the practice of group work rarely reflects the values which are central to cooperative learning. Mortimore and his colleagues (1988) and Tizard and her colleagues (1988) confirmed this in their observations that collaborative and cooperative group work appeared far less frequently in primary classrooms than other forms of activity. Galton and Williamson (1992) in their overview of classroom-based studies of group work note that children in groups are often asked to work in silence; the task is usually an individual one; asking for help from a peer is not usually encouraged. As Bennett and Dunne (1992) suggest, group work is often little more than a seating arrangement and the tasks which the children are being asked to complete could just as easily be accomplished alone. Dunne and Bennett (1990) have expressed doubts about the effectiveness of small-group work as currently practised in schools. Their extensive research into the actual talk that goes on when children are doing 'group work' revealed some disturbing findings. It was not that the children were failing to stay 'on task', rather that the quality of their talk was not 'task-enhancing':

Talk tended to be about procedure, discussions of how much work each child had completed, talk of each other's social or intellectual competence and so on. The category of talk most likely to be task-enhancing was one we call 'instructional input', where children shared knowledge and provided, or received, explanations. Only 16 per cent of all talk appeared in this category, although there was a great variation across the groups studied ... The great majority of requests and responses were of low order: a specific question, for example. 'How many twos in 54?', followed by a specific response, and not all responses were correct. (Bennett, 1991, p. 584)

Dunne and Bennett's interpretation of these findings was that the missing ingredient in group work as practised in British classrooms was *cooperation*. The children were seated in groups but they were working as individuals. Again we see an example of apparently innovative practice being undermined by the persistence of traditional values. The British view of school as a place where individuals compete with one another is hard to change. Grouping was little more than an organisational device.

Galton, Simon and Croll (1980) in the ORACLE study found that children, although frequently grouped round small tables, worked for nearly 80 per cent of their time on individual tasks. Only 9 per cent of tasks could be categorised as cooperative and then they tended to be craft or art activities. Often the teacher would spend her time during that lesson helping individual children who had particular difficulties in maths and language, rather than facilitating the group work. The implicit message was that this was not serious work. Thus, in practice, teachers tended not to interact with groups of children but worked either with individual pupils or talked to the whole class; within the groups, children tended to work on their own. It would seem that the primary teachers in this study were largely traditional in teaching style. Knowledge on the part of the teachers about cooperative learning methods was slight.

Similarly, Galton and Patrick (1990) in the PRISMS project in infant and junior classrooms found that although children were seated *in* groups for 56 per cent of the time they were expected to work *as* a group for only 5 per cent of the time. When they were seated in pairs they were only expected to *collaborate* with their partner for 4 per cent of the time. By contrast, although they were seated at individual desks for only 7.5 per cent of the time, they actually worked individually for 81 per cent of the time. This confirmed the findings of the ORACLE study that the amount of collaborative activity was small.

Why, since the emphasis in so many primary schools is on seating in groups, is there so much reluctance on the part of teachers to enable their pupils to work cooperatively? One explanation may be that teachers find this seating arrangement a useful one for dealing with mixed-ability classes (Galton and Williamson, 1992). When children are grouped by ability it seems to be easier to adjust the work to the level of the children. At a deeper level, there seems to be ambivalence among teachers about the actual benefits which group work brings. There seem to be clear barriers, both perceived and real, which make it difficult for children to achieve active participation in cooperative groups and for teachers to create opportunities for the letting go of power which cooperative group work requires of them. Interviews with teachers (Cowie and Rudduck, 1988a; Lewis and Cowie, 1993) indicate that the establishment of truly cooperative educational practices takes time and involves letting go of some firmly-held traditions. A fundamental problem is that many teachers fear what may happen if they lose the control which whole class teaching seems to offer. Children, too, expect their teachers to be in control of what they do and may not immediately respond positively to the opportunity to take responsibility for their own actions. Clearly it takes time and practice to keep a realistic balance between maintaining discipline in the class and fostering a collective sense of social responsibility. Despite recent Government exhortations (DfE, 1992) for schools to educate for citizenship, it is still rare to find situations where pupils are trusted to take collective responsibility for their own learning.

Teachers also worry that without their constant oversight of the groups the pupils will not stay on task. A particular concern is that children will adopt certain roles within the group, some of which are not conducive to learning. These roles could include the dominant member who overrules all the others; the 'hitch-hiker' who sits back while everyone else does the work; the clown who distracts everyone from the task; the isolate who is marginalised by the group. These are very real anxieties which it would be unwise to ignore.

The evaluation of cooperative learning strategies

Experimental investigations into cooperative learning, carried out in the U.S.A. and in Israel, have for the most part focussed on outcomes in two major areas – academic achievement and student social relationships (Hertz-Lazarowitz and Miller, 1992; Johnson and Johnson, 1982; Kagan, 1986; Sharan, 1980; Slavin, 1987).

Slavin (1987) carried out a meta-analysis of 46 empirical studies of cooperative learning and achievement. The 46 investigations looked at group work across the curriculum among students of different ages and from a variety of backgrounds. Statistically, 63 per cent of the studies showed significant gains for experimental as opposed to control groups. In only 2 per cent of the studies did control students achieve more highly than experimental students. The positive effects appeared in secondary and primary schools, in urban and rural areas, and across all areas of the curriculum.

Slavin found that the majority of studies showed cognitive benefits to low, average and high achieving students. He was also able to distinguish different outcomes from different forms of cooperative learning. There was some evidence, for example, that tightly structured methods such as S.T.A.D. and T.G.T. had the greatest effect on basic skills, whereas higher-order skills were developed by more open-ended methods like Group Investigation. Slavin identified two major influences on the academic achievement of students working cooperatively – group rewards and individual accountability.

At the same time, Slavin (1987) also acknowledged the effect of peer interaction itself in providing the kind of 'cognitive conflict' which is necessary for children if they are to be enabled to move through the Z.P.D. He suggests that

> research has established that under certain circumstances the use of cooperative learning methods increases student achievement more than traditional instructional practices. In addition, these methods consistently improve students' self-esteem and social relations among students, in particular, race relations and acceptance of mainstreamed students. (p. 1161)

Hertz-Lazarowitz (1992) presents a multidimensional model of the classroom in which she identifies six distinctive but interrelated mirrors – the physical layout of the classroom, the actual learning task, the teacher's instructional style, the teacher's communicative mode, pupils' social behaviour, pupils' academic behaviour – each of which contains a continuum of learning style, from solitary through interactional to collaborative. In her model she describes conditions which facilitate each type of learning and, through her meticulous observations of real-life classroom interactions, she concludes that, even when tasks are structured to facilitate cooperation, interactive behaviours do not necessarily occur, and neither do helping behaviours. She notes that pupils' level of cooperation can vary from low to high when it is analysed on the basis of the interactions which actually take place. For example, if pupils are invited to write a group story, each child might write his or her own story and then combine them mechanically into the group story. This would be categorised as low cooperation. By contrast, if all the pupils engaged in discussions, clarifications, revisions and editing in order to write the group story, this would be categorised as cooperation at a high level. The pupils in the second group would have used complex social skills such as participation, taking turns, reflecting on one anothers' contributions and evaluating one anothers' responses to constructive criticism. By breaking down classroom interaction processes and behaviours into 'mirrors', Hertz-Lazarowitz offers a model which attempts to conceptualise the various dimensions simultaneously and also provides teachers with a developmental sequence of how to progress from a traditional to a highly interactive classroom.

The specific effect of cooperative learning strategies on relationships between students in multi-ethnic classrooms has also been widely researched in the U.S.A. Numerous studies of friendship between students of different backgrounds have confirmed that students in cooperative classrooms are more likely to make friendship choices outside their own ethnic group than do students who have been taught in the traditional didactic mode. As we have seen, Slavin (1983) found this to be the effect of Student Team Learning where, although the work was carried out cooperatively, final assessment was on the basis of individual performance. Aronson (1978), using *Jigsaw*, found a positive effect on tolerance, acceptance and trust among children from different ethnic backgrounds. Johnson and Johnson (1987) report equally positive outcomes in the promotion of learning and in increased altruism among group members when evaluation is based on group rather than individual performance.

So, despite differences in the models of cooperative learning which underpin the methods, the American research suggests that the effects are lasting; when retested several months after the experience of cooperative learning, the students have significantly more friendships outside their ethnic group than controls. As Kagan (1986) suggests,

> the results of cooperative learning studies indicate that with relatively little time and expense, by reorganising the social structure of the classroom, radical improvements in race relations can be obtained consistently. (p. 235)

The challenge of the multi-ethnic classroom highlights for teachers the value of cooperative learning in developing positive relationships among students. Several of the investigations into cooperative learning have measured self-esteem. Again, there is evidence that there are increases in students' self-esteem (Blaney et al., 1977). Furthermore, students who work together report that they like school more than those who are encouraged to work individually. They also like other students more and they are more likely to say that they want their classmates to do well at school (Sharan, 1985).

In Israel, Eitan, Amir and Rich (1992), concerned about the drop in self-esteem which occurs so often when minority children enter multi-ethnic classrooms, compared the impact on self-esteem of three types of intervention – cooperative learning in small groups, a programme which focussed on social relationships, and an intervention which combined both these programmes. They found that, although all had an impact, those interventions which included cooperative learning had the most positive impact on the self-concept, both academic and social, of these children. They recommended that educators integrate academic with social elements (as cooperative group work does) when designing appropriate teaching methods in multi-ethnic schools.

Sharan (1990) reviews studies which examine the impact of cooperative learning methods on pupils' status in the multi-ethnic classroom and confirms the view that traditional classroom structures impede the social integration and academic attainment of ethnic minority children. By contrast, when conditions are created for greater interaction on an equal basis among children from different ethnic groups, there are positive outcomes in terms of social status and academic attainment. He concludes that there is strong research evidence to support the view that cooperative learning creates opportunities to improve intergroup relations in multi-ethnic classrooms. At the same time, he acknowledges that there is still widespread disagreement in the field about the precise nature of the components of cooperative group work which facilitate this process.

These studies seem to provide strong evidence that intensive, regular cooperative contact among children from different ethnic backgrounds can forge real and lasting friendships and can significantly reduce prejudice among participants. But there is still a concern among the researchers that we do not fully understand how this happens.

How firmly can we accept these results? So far as cognitive/academic gains are concerned, Brown and Palinscar (1989), while convinced of the value of cooperative learning methods, are somewhat sceptical about some of the studies, for example, the types of experimental study which Slavin considers. They criticise the use of multiple-choice tests of content retention rather than tests of improved thinking skills. More importantly, they point out that we are given little information about the mechanisms or processes which take place within the groups. As a result, it is impossible to do more than speculate about which thinking processes are actually being practiced and developed in the groups.

Brown and Palinscar think that we should be cautious and should probe more deeply into the examination of the process itself. We need to 'unpack' what we mean by cooperation. For example, they note that group members spontaneously adopt a variety of roles within a group – the executor or doer; the sceptic or critic; the educator; the record keeper; the peacemaker. These roles are enacted in public so that children can observe the enactment of roles which correspond to thinking strategies that they themselves must subsequently perform independently and silently. The actions of the other members of the group have the potential, therefore, for guiding them through their own Z.P.D. A group member might always adopt one of these roles or the roles might shift among members. Their own research indicates that children can be trained in the skills of being learning leader. This reduces the cognitive load for any one member in two ways. First, they have less of the thinking burden placed on their own shoulders alone. Second, they see others' enactment of the roles and can learn from that.

> Sharing the burden not only permits a collaborative level of functioning far in advance of the individuals' ability to maintain discourse cohesion, but it also provides important modelling of essential argument forms. (Brown and Palinscar, pp. 401-2)

Galton and Williamson (1992) and Bennett (1985) also express reservations about the body of American research reviewed by Slavin. They point out that the tasks given to children in these studies are usually highly structured in comparison to more general tasks given to control groups. Differences could have been due to the nature of the task rather than the cooperation. The interventions were often very short in duration. A major criticism, too, is that the researchers did not observe the groups in action so there was little advice to be given to teachers on how to facilitate the positive effects which were claimed. Nor do these studies give any insight into difficulties which group work engenders. Many of the earlier studies were not carried out in normal classroom conditions and, as artificial experiments, may well not be transferable to ordinary lessons. However, it is clear that more recent research, for example the detailed work of Hertz-Lazarowitz, does focus on real-life observations in classrooms and on-going interactions which teachers as they prepare for, participate in and evaluate their cooperative work.

Studies which focus more directly on the *process* of learning, indicate that academic achievement should be viewed in its social context, and that cognitive and social processes interact in complex ways. Webb

(1985) showed that initial behaviour in groups changes over time and suggested that this is an important factor to be taken into account. Furthermore, she investigated the characteristics of groups and found distinct differences among group members. The experience of working in a group was not the same for each participant. There were gender differences and differences in terms of children's academic ability. The ability of the pupils also interacted with their status within the group: pupils' attributions of their own contributions to group process varied according to their academic ability. Hertz-Lazarowitz (1992) has also noted how groups change over time. Only when group members have internalised skills which both enable participants to move from individualistic to social behaviour in groups, and to maintain the smooth running of the group, are they able to engage in complex cognitive interactions at a higher level. Teachers need to foster different sets of skills at different stages of the process.

Barnes (1976), Cowie and Rudduck (1988a), and Salmon and Claire (1984) have placed emphasis on coming to understand how pupils in cooperative groups begin to explore and negotiate their own meanings through dialogue, active participation and engagement in issues of personal significance. Using interview data and observations of groups in action, these researchers made qualitative analyses of the processes at work when students learn cooperatively from one another. Their findings show that students express a greater understanding of complex issues when they have had the opportunity to explore them with their peers. Cowie and Rudduck, for example, document case studies of students exploring controversial issues such as the siting of a power station (a simulation) or solving a problem in technology (a role-play) (Cowie and Rudduck, 1988b, pp. 99-121).

But these qualitative studies also highlight aspects of cooperative learning which hinder its full acceptance as a legitimate approach to learning. These writers note the strong personal and organisational barriers which operate against the widespread use of cooperative learning in school contexts, and they point to the deeply embedded idea that academic learning is an individual activity. Even teachers who talk about the benefits of group work will often betray their doubts by saying how time consuming it is and how difficult it is to get through a syllabus in any other way than the traditional didactic mode.

Case studies of students working cooperatively confirm that participants in cooperative group work express a range of views on its social benefits. Some students report a sense of well-being and a sense of responsibility for peers when they are given regular opportunities to work cooperatively with one another (Cowie and Rudduck, 1988b, pp.

91-98). Furthermore, they respond positively to invitations to play an active part in resolving interpersonal conflicts in the group (Cowie and Rudduck, 1990). However, a proportion of pupils and teachers remain sceptical about the value of cooperative learning methods. In addition, there are also reservations about the support which is given to teachers who use cooperative methods in their classrooms. Salmon and Claire (1984) found that young people did have the potential to work collectively on issues of common concern in their classrooms but only provided that there was a willingness to establish and maintain these common goals and a sense of mutual understanding between teachers and students. They noted that this process took time to develop and often ran counter to established practice.

Overall research seems to indicate that cooperative learning methods can be used by teachers to achieve academic and social goals at the same time without adversely affecting either, but that teachers experience difficulties in actually implementing these methods. The method is a promising one but we need to know more about the conditions under which it works best.

In the next chapter, we examine the specific context in which the present study took place.

CHAPTER FOUR: The background to the project

In the first two chapters, we have reviewed how many children may experience difficulties in social relationships in school. Some children have difficulty making friendships and are sociometrically 'rejected' or 'neglected'. Others get bullied frequently or take part in bullying classmates. Also, in multi-cultural classrooms there may be infrequent social interactions across ethnic groups and there is evidence that children in junior schools may be quite prejudiced about children from different ethnic backgrounds.

These relationship problems can have quite serious consequences in the long term, both for the happiness, well-being and self-esteem of pupils, and very probably (although here evidence is more indirect) for their academic achievement. It appears important to attempt to intervene in cases where these problems are serious. The junior school seems a very appropriate age at which to intervene. By this age, more than at infant school, problems of sociometric rejection/isolation and of bullying, have become readily identifiable. It is also, according to some authorities (Aboud, 1988) an optimal period at which to intervene to reduce racial or ethnic prejudice. By secondary school age, intervention may become more difficult as behaviour patterns become more entrenched and an 'anti-school' attitude more obvious in many of the children we are concerned with.

Chapter three documented the possibilities of cooperative group work as a way of organising much of the school curriculum, which could also have beneficial outcomes for these aspects of social relationships. Bringing children together from outside friendship groups to work collectively on common tasks might be hoped to increase understanding and cooperation, if not actually bring about friendships, among children who might otherwise interact very little. It should help to include withdrawn children and to encourage interaction between children of different ethnic groups as well as between boys and girls. Given appropriate debriefing work by the teacher, it could also be a useful forum for uncovering problems of domineering or bullying behaviour and working on them.

Our own interest in this started in 1988. The Economic and Social Research Council (E.S.R.C.) had publicised a research initiative called 'Education in a multi-cultural society'. They invited bids for research projects on this theme. We submitted a project 'Ethnic relations and sociometric status in middle school: an intervention study', which was successful in receiving funding. Peter Smith was the grant holder, Michael Boulton the research associate and Helen Cowie provided in-service training on cooperative group work methods for the teachers involved. The experience of this initial project, the main results of which are given in Smith, Boulton and Cowie (1993), was important for our main project described in the remainder of the book. The next section summarises the design and the outcomes of this initial project.

Ethnic relations and sociometric status in middle school: an intervention study (1988/89)

This project was carried out with teachers and 8- to 9-year-old children from three ethnically mixed middle schools in Sheffield. In all three schools, the main ethnic groups were Asian and White. The Asian children were largely from Punjabi, Urdu and Gujerati speaking backgrounds. They were not selected because ethnic relations were considered to be a special problem. Indeed, all three schools adhered to the anti-racist policies expressed by the Local Education Authority.

In each school we worked with two classes. During the year, one of the two classes continued with the normal curriculum which remained unchanged and so was regarded as a control. The other class in each school experienced a curriculum that involved elevated levels of cooperative group work. The three teachers that used these techniques received a total of five days in-service training in how to do so, under the supervision of Helen Cowie. The initial objective for these three teachers was to use cooperative group work in their class for at least one hour each day. The in-service sessions were backed up by intermittent visits by members of the research team.

Diary records were kept by all of the teachers throughout the year to assess the actual extent to which cooperative group work methods were used. In the control classes, the average percentage of time given over to them was 19 per cent, a value significantly lower than that of 34 per cent in the intervention classes.

The teachers that used the cooperative group work methods usually started with a trust-building exercise before going on to use group activities such as problem-solving, role-play activities, cooperative games and discussion groups. The sessions usually ended when the groups reported back to the whole class, along with debriefing, in which the teacher could bring out into the open and discuss the successes as well as any problems such as non-cooperation between the children. The debriefing activities were regarded as an important element in the whole process of cooperative group work as they allowed for the potential gains in understanding on the part of the children to be consolidated and reinforced by the teacher.

The effects of the type of curriculum on the pupil's ethnic attitudes and preferences were determined via a range of quantitative and qualitative assessments. Some of the quantitative data were obtained from tests which used photographs of unknown children as stimulus material. Others were based on sociometric techniques designed to assess relationships with classmates. These were given in individual interviews in three phases during the school year – October 1988, March and June/July 1989.

Open-ended interviews were also carried out to provide qualitative data. Pupils were interviewed during the final term and teachers at the end of the project. They were asked about their feelings towards cooperative group work methods and (for teachers) the impact they perceived them to have had on the children's peer relationships.

The results showed a general trend of improved social relationships in the cooperative group work classes relative to the control classes. While some of these effects were modest and significance levels varied between the different assessment tests, they were consistent across a range of indicators.

One test was designed to measure children's preferences for sharing activities with unknown boys and girls from three different ethnic backgrounds. The base-line data from the first assessment phase (see Boulton and Smith, 1992) showed a strong same-gender followed by same-race order of choice. Our results showed that Asian girls and White boys in the cooperative group work classes changed away from this pattern to a more equal distribution featuring other race and other gender children. However, this effect was not found for Asian boys and was, in the one finding that went against our predictions, reversed in the case of White girls – they showed an even stronger own-gender/own-race preference over the course of the study.

In the other test using unknown children as stimulus material, the aim was to measure positive and negative perceptions of one's own and other ethnic groups. The children were asked to assign a number of positive and negative traits to groups of African-Caribbean children, Asian children and/or White children. They also had the opportunity to assign any or all of these traits to a 'Nobody' option. The changes revealed an increasingly positive view by Asian children of White children in the cooperative group work classes but not in the control classes. Unfortunately, no such effect was found among the White children.

In terms of attitudes towards classmates, some of the results were encouraging. Among the children in the control classes there was a tendency for both Asian and White classmates to be liked slightly less from one assessment phase to the next. However, children in the cooperative group work classes tended, over the school year, to show a slightly greater liking for classmates generally.

Both Asian and White children in the study also perceived more of their classmates to be cooperative with time; this effect was again more evident in the cooperative group work classes relative to the control classes.

The qualitative data also supported the idea that the cooperative group work curriculum had a positive effect on social relationships. The children themselves were generally enthusiastic about engaging in this type of activity. Typical answers to the question, 'What do you like about working in a group?' were:

'We help each other.'
'We share.'
'We help each other and cooperate. Yes, when you're stuck they might know what the answer is and tell you. And if they don't know the answer you can tell them. You get your work done quicker then.'

The three teachers who used the new techniques, also reported that they were increasingly committed to using cooperative group work approaches. They felt positive about the impact of the methods on the children in their classes.

We were generally pleased with the results from this one-year study in so far as they suggested that children's ethnic attitudes and preferences could be changed in a more positive direction. However, we were cautious about drawing firm conclusions for a number of different reasons. As we have seen, not all of the results were statistically significant. Moreover, the teachers were not selected randomly for the cooperative group work and control classes. In each school, the teacher that used the cooperative group work methods was suggested to us by the headteacher as being someone who was actively committed to them. While this may also be true of many other teachers, it would certainly not be true of all of them.

Planning the second study

Given the promising findings but also the limitations of the first study, we undertook another study. Again, we were fortunate in getting funding from the E.S.R.C. for this project, entitled 'Prejudice, isolation and bullying: Intervention in ethnically mixed classrooms'. The main findings of this project are discussed in the rest of the book.

The second project built on the first in several respects:

(1) a larger sample of classes was used;
(2) the teachers receiving cooperative group work (CGW) training were more representative of junior-school teachers, not having been especially interested in CGW prior to the project;
(3) some 2-year longitudinal data was obtained to look for longer-term effects;
(4) we included measures of bully–victim problems, as well as many of our prior measures of friendship, and of ethnic relations and attitudes. This was because we had become increasingly aware of the importance of bully–victim problems over the prior two years, and had been carrying out parallel research on this topic (see also chapter one).
(5) supported by comments from referees of the research proposal, we decided to make more use of qualitative as well as quantitative data in our assessments.

The design of the project

The schools

We first approached the three schools which had taken part in our first study, to see if they would like to continue the use of CGW methods with a larger number of classes and teachers. Two of the schools were willing and interested – we call these schools B and C. In both cases we decided to continue the policy of matching a CGW class with an N.C. (normal curriculum) class in the same year group. This design allowed for the clearest inferences as to the impact of CGW, and these schools were happy to enter into this arrangement and had teachers who were willing to be trained (for CGW classes) or to continue as usual (for N.C. classes).

We also approached a new school, called here school A, to see if they would also like to take part. This school was selected because again it was ethnically mixed and from a fairly disadvantaged area of the city. The headteacher was interested and the research team went to talk to the staff, after which the school expressed its willingness and interest in participating. In this school, which was smaller than schools B and C, classes were sometimes mixed across year groups, and it was not feasible to match CGW and N.C. classes within a year group. We thus went for a different design, having only CGW classes in this school. Because of constraints of staff taking time off for training, only three classes could take part in the CGW training; but the intention was that these teachers could, if they wished, share ideas amongst themselves and with colleagues.

Although this 'all-CGW' design lost the advantage of control class matching, it was felt that it gained in another respect. It allowed the CGW trained teachers to support each other and to be uninhibited in talking with colleagues about their approach. In effect, CGW was given a 'freer rein' in its application. In schools B and C we had to ask the CGW trained teachers not to discuss ideas too much with the N.C. teachers – a somewhat unnatural constraint.

By embodying both approaches in the project, we hoped to be able to draw on the strengths and limitations of each.

All three schools, A, B and C, were innercity middle schools when the project started in summer 1990. The project ran through to 1993, but the work with the schools finished in summer 1992. As discussed more fully in chapter five, school C decided to withdraw at the end of the first year (summer 1991). In part, this decision was precipitated by the need for the school to make staff cuts and the difficulties allowing time for in-service training. However school B was willing to increase the number of classes participating, so that we continued with just schools A and B in the second year. In the second year (1991-92), at school A the middle school amalgamated with the local first school, to form a new primary school. The first school head was appointed headteacher of the new school and fortunately was keen to continue involvement with the project.

All the schools supported the general anti-racist policy of the Sheffield L.E.A. The L.E.A. was fully informed of this project, as they had been of the first study and were supportive of it.

The children and the classes

Some children participated in the first year only, some in the second year only and some were involved in both years. Over the two years some classes took part in cooperative group work intervention (CGW) and other classes were matched controls continuing with their normal curriculum (N.C.).

In the total sample, the children's ages ranged from 7 to 12 years and there was a roughly equal mix of males (56 per cent) and females (44 per cent). The main ethnic groups were White (53 per cent year 1; 39 per cent year 2) and Asian (28 per cent year 1; 39 per cent year 2). There were also some children from Afro-Caribbean and mixed race backgrounds (18 per cent year 1; 23 per cent year 2). The Asian children were mainly from Punjabi, Urdu and Gujerati speaking backgrounds.

Table 4.1 shows details of the classes taking part (the numbers in the right-hand columns are of pupils actually assessed, with actual class

Table 4.1 Summary of the schools, classes and teachers taking part in the project in years one and two.

	School	Year	Teacher	Class	n (T1)	n (T2)
YEAR ONE	A	5/6	Margie/Jane	CGW.1	21	17
	A	4/5	Tom	CGW.2	22	20
	A	4/5	Pat	CGW.3	22	18
	B	4	Sally	CGW.4	21	19
	B	4	Kay/June	N.C.1	22	19
	C	6	Ann	CGW.5	23	22
	C	5	Judy	CGW.6	20	20
	C	6	Lorraine	N.C.2	21	20
	C	5	Roy	N.C.3	21	19
	School	Year	Teacher	Class	n (T3)	n (T4)
YEAR TWO	A	6	Pat	CGW.1	19	16
	A	5	Jane	CGW.2	18	17
	A	5/6	Margie	CGW.3	18	17
	B	5/6	Sally	CGW.4	27	27
	B	4	Joe	CGW.5	26	26
	B	5/6	Kim	N.C.1	26	24
	B	4	Kay/June	N.C.2	24	22
	School	Year	Teacher	Class year one	Class year two	n
FOLLOW-THROUGH CHILDREN	A	5/6	M+J/Pat	CGW.1	CGW.1	11
	A	4/5	Tom/Jane	CGW.2	CGW.2	16
	A	4/5	Pat/Margie	CGW.3	CGW.3	15
	B	4	Sally/Sally	CGW.4	CGW.4	15
	B	4	K+J/Joe	N.C.1	N.C.1	18

sizes being slightly larger). In year 1 we worked with nine classes in the three schools. In school A three classes participated: two mixed year 4/5 and one mixed year 5/6. All were CGW classes. In school B two classes participated: both year 4 classes, one CGW and one N.C. class. In school C four classes participated: two year 5, and two year 6, each year with one CGW and one N.C. class. Of the total sample of 193 children at the beginning of the year, 20 children left or were not available for interview at the end. The final sample for analysis was 173 (CGW=115; N.C.=58).

In year 2 we worked with seven classes, in schools A and B only. In school A three classes participated: one year 5, one mixed year 5/6 and one year 6. All were CGW classes. In school B four classes participated: two year 4 and two mixed year 5/6, each year with one CGW and one N.C. class. Of the total sample of 158 children at the beginning of the year, 9 children left or were not available for interview at the end. The final sample for final analysis was 149 (CGW=103; N.C.=46).

Some children were followed through both years: they came from school A, the three CGW classes, and school B, year 5/6 CGW and year 5/6 N.C. (total CGW=57; N.C.=18). Only one of these five classes remained with the same teacher throughout years 1 and 2. The children from the other four classes were split up into different classes in year 2 from where they had been in year 1. What did remain constant over the two years, however, was the type of class the children were in. Children who had been in a CGW class in year 1 went to another CGW class in year 2 and the children in the one N.C. class in year 1 went to another N.C. class in year 2.

The in-service training in CGW

The teachers in the CGW classes received in-service training in CGW methods before the start of the first assessment phase, beginning with days on methods and resources and followed by separate days where they came together to share and evaluate experiences. The initial objective for these teachers was to use CGW techniques for at least one hour, each day. These in-service sessions were backed up by further training days, during which aspects of CGW methods and their implementation were discussed more informally. The second year of training took a different format: as some of the teachers were now more experienced, it was appropriate to give them more control to express their needs and request training or time together to share ideas. The details of the training are given in chapter five.

The cooperative group work intervention

The CGW techniques used were developed further from our earlier study (Smith, Boulton and Cowie, 1993). Cooperative group work sessions generally started with a trust-building exercise, followed by group activities such as problem-solving tasks for which each child would hold a different source of information, brainstorming, cooperative games, role-play activities, and discussion groups. An essential part of the process was debriefing (discussion by the teacher with group members of any difficulties such as non-cooperation that have arisen in the groups).

The experience of the teachers was that it took time to develop skill and confidence in the use of CGW techniques, but that they *could* be used successfully with 8- and 9-year-olds (Cowie and Rudduck, 1990). In particular the debriefing activities were crucial in consolidating the potential gains in understanding on the part of the children brought about by CGW activities. Furthermore, the teachers also benefitted from the feedback and shared experience provided by the in-service days.

The CGW/N.C. distinction whilst affecting the organisation of lessons, had little effect on the content of lessons, which were geared to the incoming National Curriculum.

Fuller descriptions of the CGW activities are given in chapter five.

Diary records

Diary records were kept by all the teachers through the year to ascertain how much time children were spending in cooperative group work and other kinds of activities, and check that CGW was used much more in the CGW classes than in the N.C. classes. The categories, developed in collaboration with teachers in our previous study (Smith, Boulton and Cowie, 1993) were: whole-class teaching, whole-class activity, independent work, small-group work, cooperative group work, and other. Fuller details are given in chapter six.

Quantitative assessments

The main quantitative measures were of ratings of liking; sociometric status; bully–victim scores; bully–victim status; ethnic preference; stereotyping; and prejudice. These were obtained by individual interviews with children. Full details of these are given in chapter six.

Interviews were carried out at four time points, the beginning and end of the first academic year (October and June/July, times 1 and 2) and at the beginning and end of the second academic year (times 3 and 4). Each interview lasted approximately 30 minutes.

Qualitative data

Semi-structured interviews were carried out with class teachers, with some individual children and with children in their CGW groups.

The teachers were interviewed at the beginning and end of each year. They were asked to talk about relationships between the children in their class and to identify those they considered to be popular, controversial, rejected, neglected, prejudiced, bullies and victims. The CGW teachers were also interviewed about their feelings and attitudes towards CGW groups, and about the impact they thought it would have had.

The individual child interviews focussed on a sub-group of children who were of particular interest: children who were prejudiced, those who were popular or controversial, those who were rejected or neglected, bullies, victims and bully-victims. Selection criteria were based on peer nominations but where possible children were chosen when peer and teacher nominations agreed. We aimed to choose from each class one of each of the children from the eight categories above, though this was not always possible. The interviews, which lasted five to ten minutes, were carried out in the middle of the year. They covered the child's perceptions of their social relationships with others in the class.

The children in CGW classes were interviewed in their working groups at the end of each year, about life in the classroom generally, how they felt about working in cooperative groups and also about their relationships with other children. These interviews were also used quantitatively to score each child's feelings about CGW on a 5-point scale from +2 (very favourable) to -2 (very unfavourable).

The qualitative data are used more fully in chapters five and seven.

Academic performance

The academic performance of the children was measured to check on any relative changes in academic attainment over the two years. Each school provided test scores from reading and mathematics tests given at Easter each year. Schools A and C gave the Profile of Mathematical Skills and the Macmillan Group Reading Test; school B gave the Richmond Test of Basic Skills.

Ethical issues

The consent of headteachers and school staff was obtained for the project, and parents were informed of the nature of the project through Newsletters and parents' evenings. The assessments were all agreed with the headteachers and class teachers in each school.

Two of our assessments did raise ethical issues, which were thoroughly discussed in the research team, with the departmental ethical committee and with the schools. Sociometric status testing requires nominations of classmates 'liked least'. This could lead to negative consequences for children labelled this way. However, evidence to date (Hayvren and Hymel, 1984) suggests that there is no evidence of negative effects resulting from this procedure, which is widely used.

The stereotypes test raised the possibility of assigning negative traits by race (Carrington and Short, 1993). We did consider the use of this test carefully, but decided to retain it since, in our first study, it had yielded clear evidence of stereotypical attitudes (Boulton and Smith, 1992) and, it had also proved sensitive to change (Smith, Boulton and Cowie, 1993). In using the test we were careful not to label the different groups by ethnic or racial terms, and the possibility of using the 'Nobody' box was made very explicit.

Methodological issues: qualitative and quantitative methods

Sociometric techniques and their associated quantitative statistical procedures, have been challenged by some on methodological grounds. In one study, Denscombe (1983) noted that many teachers were sceptical of the validity of research findings that showed that a substantial proportion of pupils strongly favoured classmates that were of the same race as themselves when it came to friendship choices (see chapter two). The teachers were of the opinion that children were generally unbiased in terms of their friendship choice. Denscombe set out to compare the results obtained with sociometric/statistical approaches with an 'interpretative' stance that involved looking at the pattern of results obtained, in some cases from individual children. He concluded that

> interpreting the data, rather than relying on quantitative measures, revealed that a significant majority of the pupils . . . included members of the other ethnic groups amongst their friends despite the opportunity to select others from the same group . . . Quite contrary to the quantitative analysis, this would suggest a definite absence of ethnic bias as the basis for friendship

choice – or at least its relative lack of significance compared with other personal factors affecting friendship choice. (p.189)

We believe Denscombe's work is helpful in so far as it encourages us to look closely at the data rather than simply at the output of statistical tests that have been carried out on those data. Denscombe has clearly demonstrated that any general patterns of preferences that emerge from studies based on sociometry can obscure the fact that a substantial proportion of children do not fit this pattern. Nevertheless, we also think that sociometric methodology should not be abandoned because it is so good at highlighting these general trends. With respect to racial bias in friendship choice, it is clearly important to know that some children do choose friends from other ethnic groups; it is just as important to know that the majority of children also tend to name more own-race than other-race classmates as friends.

Ashley (1992) has also questioned the validity of sociometric methods. He examined the extent to which sociometric test results matched observations of children's social behaviour during playtimes. In particular, the correlations between how often children were named by their classmates as one of their three preferred play partners and (i) how often they interacted with other pupils on the playground (total contacts) and (ii) how many different pupils they interacted with on the playground (range of contacts), were computed. The correlation between sociometric choices and range of contacts was low at -0.17, a finding which prompted Ashley to state that 'sociometry does not necessarily indicate the reality of friendships' (p. 152). However, a high positive correlation of 0.64 was found between number of sociometric nominations received and total contacts on the playground. This finding does suggest that the sociometric data were tapping some useful elements of the children's level of participation within their peer group.

Troyna and Hatcher (1992) have also questioned the usefulness of sociometry and other quantitative approaches to the study of children's ethnic perceptions and preferences. Their arguments would also be relevant to the study of many (if not all) aspects of children's (and adult's) social relationships. Troyna and Hatcher argue that quantitative methods are of little use in revealing why children behave as they do or hold a particular constellation of attitudes. To this end, they advocate the use of qualitative methods. We share their belief that qualitative approaches can yield insights that would probably be missed if only quantitative methods were employed. Nevertheless, we feel that this point, along with the other shortcomings of quantitative methods, should *not* mean that quantitative approaches should be abandoned altogether. Hammersley (1992) argued that

> it is necessary to apply the same sceptical approach to qualitative research findings . . . They must not be treated as the products of some distinctive way of knowing whose reliability is beyond question. (p. 176)

It is our belief that neither quantitative nor qualitative approaches are 'better' than the other in any absolute sense. Rather, each approach has its own strengths and weaknesses which must be recognised when results are being considered and conclusions drawn. Qualitative and quantitative approaches complement each other in the sense of providing different kinds of data on a topic – individual perspectives and overall trends – and it can be especially useful to contrast or 'triangulate' data from both sources, not to attempt to denigrate one kind of insight, but rather to get a more complete picture of what is really going on in the situation one is studying. We felt strongly that the foci of our own project should be investigated by using both approaches and planned accordingly.

CHAPTER FIVE: In-service training and support

Introduction

From the beginning, the members of the research team shared their belief in designing an in-service training and support programme which reflected the values of cooperation which, it was hoped, the teachers would promote in their classes. So, although the team began with clear ideas about how they wanted to heighten awareness of CGW and create opportunities for the practice of the skills of cooperation, they were also in agreement that they wanted the teachers themselves to be actively involved in designing the activities, in evaluating them and in forming support groups for one another.

The teachers using CGW in this study were selected by the headteachers and by the research team partly to meet consistency of school organisation and research design; they were then invited to take part. The teachers from school A were Margie, Jane, Pat and Tom; those from school B were Sally and, later, Joe; those from school C were Judy and Ann. Unlike the teachers in the first study, they were not volunteers with a strong initial commitment to CGW. Although most of them would claim that CGW was a part of their normal repertoire, there was a sense in which CGW was viewed as a set of useful techniques which could be added on to their existing skills. There was also a willingness to try out something new and to enhance existing teaching strategies. As one said in the initial stages of the project: 'It's probably the way I want to work anyway, so it just sort of gives me that extra push.' With the exception of Judy, each of these teachers had been trained and experienced in teaching *World Studies*, a curriculum project which incorporates CGW methods and principles. Nevertheless, they saw the CGW intervention as 'innovative' and expressed the view that it might 'conflict with their normal way of teaching'. Common to the teachers was a readiness to try something different, a motivation to take risks and move from a traditional pedagogy to one where CGW was central.

This was expressed in their general willingness to take part in the project since it gave them 'permission' to attempt methods which in normal circumstances they would not have used.

Teachers and their pupils, like everyone else, need to go through particular stages when they try out something new. The research team recognised that it would be easy for teachers to become discouraged when trying to introduce unfamiliar procedures into their classrooms. It was felt that, if there is understanding and support in the early stages of trying out an innovation, then the transition to working in new ways will be easier. Previous experience had shown that it was helpful for teachers to work collaboratively with colleagues over the period of the transition to CGW.

Cowie and Rudduck (1990) viewed the process of transition to more democratic, participatory styles of teaching as a sequence of four stages in a cycle of change.

In stage one there is a need for *orientation* or preparation for change. The teachers are open to the idea that there are likely to be changes in pupil behaviour as they make the transition but they are not particularly experienced in facilitating cooperative group work activities in the classroom. This had to be taken into account when planning the initial training days so that the teachers were given first hand experience of CGW in action and a pack of materials with specific activities to try with their classes.

The second stage involves a period of *experimentation* where both teacher and pupils are feeling their way. At this point it may be difficult for the teacher to let go of traditional controls. There may also be anxiety as pupils too show insecurity about the new and unfamiliar responsibilities which are being handed to them. This is the stage when support from colleagues can be most useful. In the in-service training there was to be scope for the teachers to share feelings about the experiences – good and bad – of trying out this approach with their pupils. There would be practical sessions on common problems and how to resolve them. The teachers would be encouraged to build on the support of colleagues by forming their own network of support within the school. The team would build on earlier experiences of sharing in the process of designing their own CGW lessons. Pooling of ideas would be encouraged. A framework for doing this was found in Bennett's three models of CGW.

In stage three, the time of *adaptation* to the new way of working, the 'survivors' of the process are beginning to find CGW normal rather than innovative. They experience satisfaction at achievements and pleasure in the progress which has been made. Both teacher and pupils

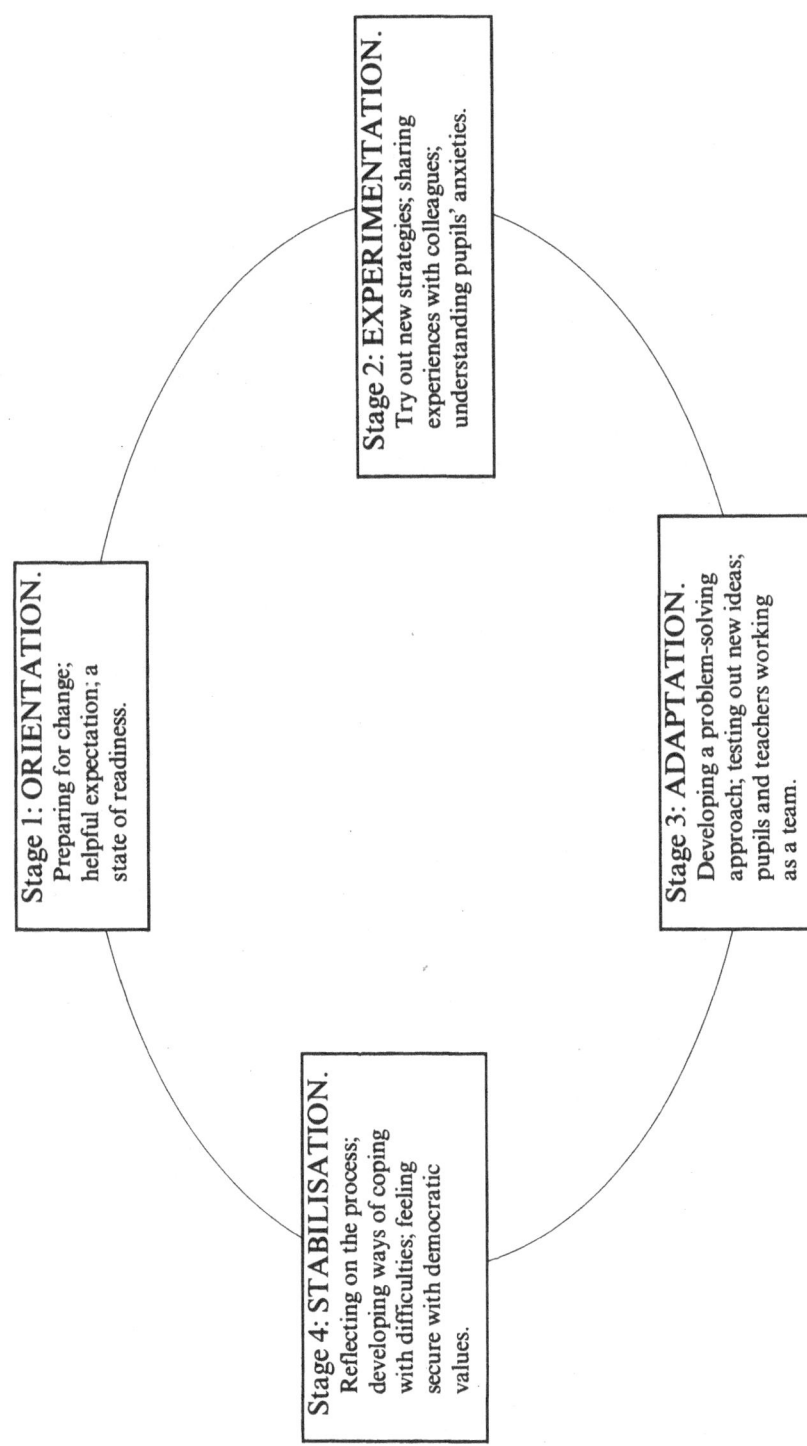

Figure 5.1 The cycle of change

are likely to be more tolerant of any difficulties which may arise. This is a creative time as pupils and teachers begin to devise new ways of working themselves. Even setbacks are problems to be solved rather than personal failures.

Finally, in stage four there is a period of *stabilisation*. The essential features of the cooperative process are being formulated and refined. The teacher is reflecting on the process, being more precise about which strategy matches which activity and is more at home with procedures for making it all run smoothly. This stage may lead on to a new cycle of change and it is useful to consider that the transition to CGW contains opportunities for personal and social change, including the acknowledgement of understandable feelings of insecurity and anxiety. Paradoxically this is likely to be a time when those involved begin to feel safe in acknowledging the polarities of values within themselves.

Teachers, it was expected, would move through the cycle at different rates and in different ways. But the in-service training was designed to provide support for the teachers, especially at transition points in the cycle when workshops and peer-support would give the kind of 'scaffolding' necessary to guide each participant through his or her Z.P.D. (see chapter three). Although in the first study we had found that the three experimental teachers moved quite quickly through the first three stages of the cycle, we were aware that many teachers find CGW threatening (as we saw in chapter three). Although they had all been trained in the *World Studies* project which relies heavily on CGW methods, it was possible that at critical points in the cycle some might find that the cooperative approach did not suit them and would either limit the amount of CGW which they did or even consider dropping out of the project altogether.

In-service training

As in the first project, the teachers were introduced to a variety of CGW strategies, were encouraged to adapt these methods to suit their own classroom needs and to share their ideas with the other CGW teachers; in all the CGW classes the teachers were required to create frequent opportunities for their pupils to work outside friendship groups.

It had been decided that the CGW techniques were to cover a variety of methods, including trust-building exercises, problem-solving groups, role-playing, discussion groups, report back sessions and debriefing. The aim was to enable children to express their own point of view and to recognise that of others in a shared task. Debriefing sessions were important opportunities for the teachers and children to discuss difficulties or conflicts, and try to resolve them. Three people were involved in the training: Helen Cowie, a member of the project team, who had designed the in-service training for the first study; and John Allen and Jim Lewis, teachers from the first study who were both very experienced in using CGW methods with their primary classes. The teachers' perceptions of the training and support were elicited through debriefing immediately after each training day and through in-depth interviews carried out regularly in school.

The training fell into four main time phases, each characterised by a distinctive training focus. A summary is given in table 5.1.

Phase one: June to July 1990

In the summer term before the intervention began, the teachers were given a block of training in CGW – a two-day intensive workshop in June 1990, a period of one month in which to try out the methods and a follow-up one-day workshop designed to consolidate what they had learned and give them a forum for sharing difficulties and celebrating successes. There was full attendance for all of the training days with the exception of Ann who missed the second training day in phase one.

In the intensive two-day workshop we wanted to demonstrate the importance of building up trust in the group in the initial stages, and to show a range of CGW activities, based on the pack (table 5.2) in action.

They were given experience of *trust-building exercises* (self-introduction in pairs and fours, non-verbal birthday line-up, guided fantasy); *group discussion* (preparing issues for a reporting-back session, discussing the definition of CGW), *problem-solving tasks* (*Seven Evil Dragons, Rabbits*); *group projects* (making a badge, designing a poster for a film, photographs); *simulation and role-play* (*The Trading Game*); *cooperative games* (the rain dance, circle games); and *debriefing* (telegrams, smiley faces, sentence completion, *The Wall*). There were opportunities for sharing feelings and for exploring anxieties and reservations about the method. (It is important to note that all of the sessions were closed to outsiders, apart from the first day. Outsiders who had shown interest in CGW were invited to the first session because we wanted to give the teachers the experience of participating in a simulation, *The Trading Game*. To do this effectively, we needed around 20 participants.)

The teachers responded positively to this training. Typical comments were:

Table 5.1 Summary of the four phases of in-service training

Phase 1: June to July 1990. (Training focus: input on CGW by research team.)

In the summer term prior to the intervention, the teachers were oriented to CGW methods by trialling the approach of their classes. The training began with a two-day workshop on a range of CGW methods, followed by four weeks' practice of the method and a final one-day workshop at the end of term. Each in-service training day was planned so that the teachers would experience CGW for themselves and would be given ideas on how to adapt specific strategies for the children in their classes. There was also to be time for reflection and sharing. Each teacher was given a pack of CGW materials (table 5.2) to give them a starting point. However, all were encouraged to develop their own ideas. It was stressed that CGW applies to all aspects of the curriculum.

Phase 2: September to December 1990. (Training focus: input on CGW by research team and peer support.)

The teachers were asked to introduce CGW methods to the experimental classes. Pupils were to work in heterogeneous groups for a minimum of one hour each day. Members of the training team offered support and modelling of the methods where appropriate. Two workshops in October and November also supported the intervention. The teachers were encouraged to move beyond the CGW pack and to devise their own activities. Bennett's three models of CGW were presented as a useful framework for extending CGW to all areas of the curriculum.

Phase 3: January to July 1991. (Training focus: supervision by research team and peer supervision.)

The teachers' problem-solving approach based on Bennett's three models of CGW was developed. Teachers were asked to keep children in heterogeneous home groups for longer periods of time, preferably for a half-term block. In-service training days focussed on particular issues as they arose, for example dealing with conflict within groups, exploring the values of CGW.

Phase 4: September 1991 to July 1992. (Training focus: peer supervision and input by trainers in school.)

The teachers asked for in-service time to be used by them to work collaboratively with one another to produce materials and share ideas on practice. Both children and teachers now expected there to be regular sessions of CGW each day. The children were to work each day in the same heterogeneous groups for half-term blocks. Most of the teachers reported that CGW had become integrated into normal practice and was no longer seen as an extra intervention.

'I feel that this session was fun.'

'I can imagine using the ideas – some directly, some with adaptations. I can see the value of all the language work but would like to see it more related to learning in geography, science, etc.'

'It has been very enjoyable. I am looking forward to more strategies and concrete class-related work.'

'It was relaxing, well-organised and fun.'

'Useful good ideas. Thought provoking.'

'It was useful for self-discovery and also for realising the value of team work and the way the ideas shape and form.'

But some comments indicated the underlying anxiety with which the training had been approached:

'Much more enjoyable and non-threatening than I expected.'

'It was less embarrassing and more fun than I expected.'

'It has been enjoyable. I'm always apprehensive about this type of work with adults (not children) but I like getting new ideas to take back to the class.'

'It has been very interesting but I haven't always been able to say what I think and feel because some other people seem to take charge! I don't always feel it's worth the hassle objecting to that (in this short period).'

All agreed to try out the methods regularly with their classes over the next four weeks. The final one-day workshop provided a forum for sharing experiences and exploring difficulties which had arisen during the practice period.

This was planned as a day in which we would enable the teachers to debrief on their experiences of doing CGW during the previous month. We were to look at common problems and share highlights. The day was to end with the question 'Do you really want to continue?' We went on to say 'If not, this is the time to drop out.' Each teacher brought a successful example of CGW which they had done with their class. One of the teachers (Judy) had also brought a video of herself in action which she was prepared to show to the others for commentary. This indicated the extent of the trust which had already built up within the group. These examples of CGW in action in the classroom gave varied opportunities for the teachers to contrast positive and negative aspects of CGW.

On the positive side they all found that CGW had facilitated opportunities for children to work outside friendship groups. Boys worked with girls; White and Asian children worked together. The variety of

Table 5.2 The range of activities in the CGW pack

In-service day 1

The Wall What is CGW? Participants are given sheets of paper on which to write answers to the question; these responses are put up on the wall.

Making a badge Participants collect badges on which they write their name and use an image to illustrate their mood at that moment in time.

Introduction to the project The aims of the project are outlined.

Self-introduction Participants in pairs tell three interesting things about themselves (in one minute) to their partner. Then in fours each person introduces his/her partner to the group.

Circle games Participants form into a large circle and are introduced to the idea of 'getting to know you' games. They have the right to 'pass', of course, if they do not want to contribute at any time. They use the daisy chain exercise to reinforce names, share adjectives which describe their feelings at that point and throw a ball (or teddy) to one another by name.

Non-verbal birthday line-up

Forming groups using coloured stickers

Five evil dragons A problem-solving task in which each group of four is asked to come to a solution.
Reporting back Groups compare answers at the end in the plenary. The solution is that there is no one 'right' answer!
Debriefing Groups are given two questions: how we arrived at an answer; how well we worked together.

Group poster In the same groups participants work collaboratively to plan the poster of the film *The Five Evil Dragons*. They are asked to rename the cast, design the poster, write rave reviews.
Present posters Who did what? How did you cast it? How did you design the poster? How did you decide on the captions?
Individual debrief Each participant writes a telegram anonymously completing the sentence 'For me this morning has been . . . ' The telegrams go on the wall for everyone to read.

Circle games Raindance; forming groups using random numbers.

The Trading Game A simulation which highlights inequalities in trading policies and practices between groups.
Plenary The winning group is announced.
Debriefing In two groups, each representing two nations, participants share what happened for them, how they felt, what they learned, how well they worked together.

Reflection During a minute's silence participants reflect on the day. They are asked to think back, to think of something positive about themselves or others to take away with them. They share this in a few words in the circle.

Table 5.2 (continued)

In-service day 2

Talk on sensitivity to others and the ways in which we can develop skills to enhance it.

Breathing and relaxation exercise Participants listen to a sound in the room. Imagine sounds in the room at night. Visualise the room at night.

Active listening with a partner (*or* Telling your problem.) Participants share images from the previous exercise with a partner.

Creative visualisation with a partner They are asked to visualise their partner: when very young; when very old; as a flower; as an animal; as a bird. Again share the images with the partner. Then share in the group.

Beyond the frame Participants select two photographs of people representing contrasting emotions. They answer questions on that photograph – How did you choose the photograph? They share these questions with another pair. The photographs are mounted on the wall for group sharing.

Rabbits A group problem-solving task designed around jigsaw pictures of a rabbit; carried out in silence. The rule is 'you can give but you cannot take'.

Debriefing Rabbits How it felt, what we did, how difficult was it to accept and give help?

Discussion Evaluation of the two days: what we tried to do; how you experienced it. What, if anything, would you take back to the classroom? Did you feel threatened, challenged, empowered?

Activity sheets Would you be prepared to run the activities with a group of children? [Responses were mainly positive, although there were some reservations about less familiar activities such as the photographs exercise.]

---

the activities had demonstrated that children react in different ways to CGW and that there is no one type of CGW. Furthermore, they had found that on the whole children like having rules in their cooperative activities and enjoyed the structure.

Overall, there was agreement that, in the words of one of the teachers:

> It gives us an opportunity to develop important things – getting on with others; working together; exploring processes rather than focussing on products.

Teachers reported back on how the children had responded to the regular experience of CGW outside friendship groups. Examples of typical comments are shown in table 5.3.

Table 5.3   Teachers perceive positive aspects of CGW

CGW engages the interest of the children.

I heard one child say, 'That was good and we didn't do any work either!'
They got very excited and I thought they were finding the activity too difficult but everyone enjoyed it.
The children do not look on CGW as work but as a game.
I found that some children responded well to CGW activities who had not previously shown interest in class. The greater involvement in class continued in other lessons
I found that generally children enjoyed the tasks they were being asked to do.
Feedback from the parents is positive. The children talk to them about what happens at school.
It can be used in all subject areas.

The children are being more friendly and supportive of one another.

The children are beginning to help each other.
Group dynamics is an important consideration.
Children are very relaxed about moving desks around the class as they can now work with a larger group of friends. I want to encourage this more in the future.
CGW is a way to help shy, quiet children to join in.
I found that the children had to listen *to each other* to complete a task. I was surprised that a class I think of as having lots of problems of relationships between children worked cooperatively in groups for quite long periods.
CGW brought on children who were not responsive in other lessons.
I was surprised that children I thought of as very quiet, even withdrawn, spoke out about their feelings. Some loud, leader types were very self-conscious about this.
I found that some children worked extremely well with others that they would normally have little to do with.
I found the children were more aware of what other children were feeling, for example if they were upset.
I was really surprised and glad at just how honest some children are.

However, there was also agreement on some common problems which regularly arose. There were practical difficulties in rearranging the furniture in the class. The resulting noise and confusion encouraged some children to be disruptive and this, it was feared, could invite the condemnation of colleagues and the headteachers. Major issues which recurred during the discussion are shown in table 5.4.

Table 5.4   Teachers perceive negative aspects of CGW

CGW is noisy

The children are not used to working in this way – unless the rule is silence. But it will be better next year.
I found at first I was always shutting the classroom door and telling the children to be quiet.
Noisy groups worked too quickly.

Children disagree and argue more outside friendship groups

I wish everyone would get on and stop arguing.
I wish they would give those who are less assertive the chance to speak.
Some didn't like working in a group they didn't choose.
I found working in groups made me aware of the uncooperativeness between genders.
I found I had negative feelings about uncooperative children.
I found that CGW seems to cause more problems than it appears to be solving.
I found that most children are uncooperative.

Children are competitive

I've found that during CGW the groups will work well together because their aim is to beat other groups. It has led to rivalry between groups.
Children begin to cooperate more if it meant their team would win.

Individual children can disrupt CGW

I have found it difficult to deal with a giggler in an otherwise quiet and cooperative group.
Unfortunately, some children use CGW to gain attention in a negative way.
My class are quite immature and extremely fussy. It takes a long time to explain each activity because they keep interrupting and then they usually do the activity wrong because they are impatient.

The teachers were asked to collaborate in suggesting solutions to the most difficult problems which they had encountered in implementing CGW. A major concern was the 'lack of motivation to cooperate with the teacher'. At this stage, the teachers did not seem to consider that this might be an issue for the debriefing session. Rather, a suggested solution to this problem was to provide *external* motivation in the form of incentives – praise, team points, a tick chart – and a consistent policy to highlight the positives and ignore/play-down the negatives. The essence of the teachers' concern was 'losing control' and 'feeling left out'.

A second concern – that 'some children use CGW to gain attention in a negative way' – focussed on the dynamics of the group but revealed a worry about failure to manage the children firmly enough and reflected the teachers' ambivalence about the power of the group to negotiate roles and relationships.

The suggested solution used *external* reinforcement in the form of 'lots of positive feedback from the teacher to the individual children in their groups'. The ultimate sanction, they concluded, was to exclude the disruptive child from group work altogether, while explaining to that excluded child why this course of action had been taken. At the same time, they also stressed the importance of 'calling regular debriefing meetings in which the children evaluate how well they had worked together', indicating some willingness to involve the groups themselves in addressing interpersonal difficulties within the group.

The teachers were still very much in the orientation stage of the cycle of change. The negatives seemed to outweigh the positives and we were anxious to give them the opportunity to drop out of the project if it seemed too difficult at this stage.

However, when the teachers were asked if they were sure that they wanted to continue, all said that they were definitely committed to the method and would begin to apply the CGW method with the new intake in the autumn.

Phase two: September to December 1990

The teachers were asked to introduce CGW methods to their new classes – the experimental groups – right from the start of the new academic year for a minimum of one hour each day. It was felt that it would be useful to use trust-building from the first day of term as a way of beginning to form the groups. They were initially to base these activities on the CGW pack but were asked to begin to think about developing their own cooperative strategies and activities. This intervention was reinforced by two further training days in October and November 1990 designed to facilitate the sharing of ideas with peers; to develop a readiness to accept comments from peers and to acknowledge anxieties on the part of the teachers and pupils in the face of unfamiliar methods. Two major themes were covered during this phase: *experimenting* in the development of new activities and considering Bennett's three models of CGW as a template for further work on all aspects of the curriculum; *sharing common problems*, in particular on dealing with conflict within groups.

All of the teachers had found it difficult to introduce CGW to a new class. Activities which had been introduced with confidence at the end of the summer term were viewed with some suspicion when it came to integrating children at the beginning of a new academic year.

Ann noted that 'with CGW the children actually teach each other a lot more than I do – but I'm spending my time trying to solve arguments more!' The conflicts within groups caused her to experience strong feelings of anxiety. Her reluctance to allocate the children to groups emerged early and was to remain a pattern throughout her involvement in the project:

> I often let *them* sort their groups out, knowing that they would work a lot better if *I* sorted the groups out.

Margie was also ambivalent, but in a different way. Unlike Ann, she did not experience CGW as disruptive, but she was sceptical of the value of it as a teaching method:

> It's a very pleasant, nice way of spending the afternoon but fifty per cent of the energy is wasted because you might as well have been learning something – something 'schooly'.

It was understandable that she was wary of introducing a seating arrangement which might disrupt a teaching style which she had spent much time and energy in building up. At a practical level, Margie had found that, in group work, she preferred to have the children 'sitting in rows' to avoid situations where 'children have to twist round uncomfortably when I use the blackboard'. She was aware of the value of language in learning but had many reservations about CGW as a means of enhancing productive talk. She introduced the CGW activities very cautiously in the early stages and it was some time before the children were placed in heterogeneous groups.

Judy, by contrast, plunged in right from the beginning with circle games, cooperative writing groups and problem-solving groups. She instigated *The Wall* with empty speech bubbles where children could anonymously write comments on their relationships with others in the class, so long as they were not hurtful or unpleasant. The outcomes were positive:

> Two children wrote that they were scared at home time as someone was threatening to thump them . . . I didn't know who they were. We discussed the problem and everyone thought they should tell the teacher. I said I hoped the people who felt threatened would do something now – but they haven't approached me yet.

The statements written in the bubbles formed a basis for discussion in the class and the children had found it a useful forum for sharing problems.

Judy's most ambitious project was to facilitate the children in forming cooperative writing groups in which they designed books similar to *The Jolly Postman* (Ahlberg and Ahlberg, 1986). The children wrote a narrative which allowed them scope to enclose a letter, card or message on each page. Since she was unsure about how well the children would work together, she kept them in friendship groups. Even so there were arguments:

> One of the girls' groups had a row because they both wanted to do a telephone bill as one of the letters and they had both gone ahead stubbornly and done it. I said they couldn't have two so there were arguments there – not very cooperative!

Judy was also finding it hard to challenge the racism which can be perpetuated by overreliance on friendship groups. When it came to forming groups she met with resistance:

> There's only one Asian girl in the class and last year she apparently sat with her cousin. I asked her this year if she wanted to sit with him or with some girls and she said, 'With the girls.' The seven girls in this group are not working as hard as they should so I keep saying, 'I'll have to divide you up into two groups' and not one of them seems to want to be with her.

Judy was aware of the difficulty but was trying to overcome it through random grouping, a method which seemed to go some way to solving the problem:

> You see I haven't tried to mix them much but when I mixed them for the cooperative rabbit game they were quite happy. They didn't complain . . . If you do it according to some criteria like birthdays, they don't mind, but if you just pick groups, they start complaining . . . They pull faces and moan.

Pat was honest about some really 'awful' experiences of experimenting with CGW and admitted that she had found it much more difficult than she had during the summer term with her previous class. She had kept to friendship groups while she tried out the method since with some children 'if they're not with their friends then that causes a lot of problems'.

A major difficulty was with the disturbed behaviour of a small number of children whose fights and tantrums threatened the easy creation of cooperative groups. There were also difficulties in crossing race and gender barriers when Pat attempted to form heterogeneous groups:

> I don't think that the Asian boys and girls want to sit together because of their upbringing and how they view it... I noticed that I have two half-caste [mixed-race] children who sit together and two Asian children who sit together... Delroy is Afro-Caribbean so he seems to want to be friends with them... I think it's maybe because of the colour. Maybe he relates to them because they are Afro-Caribbean-looking even though they are half-caste. I have another boy who is half-caste who's not got Afro hair so maybe he sort of relates to them because he's sort of on his own and they sit together. Maybe he wants to mix with them.

Pat's solution was to move towards mixed groups very gradually.

Tom too started gradually because 'he was trying to get the children to come in and be wanting to work for themselves before they work for other people'. His initial experience with circle games was very disappointing:

> In the *Magic Microphone* they were very reluctant... They weren't very open and I felt that things they said about their first week back at school weren't really honest comment. They were things they thought I wanted to hear.

Strangely enough, he had not actually shared this perception in the circle. When he did try putting the children into mixed groups he had some negative reactions. One Asian girl was so upset about being placed in a group that she stopped coming to school:

> There's one Asian girl that's very upset that she wasn't with her friends in another class and I had to come to a compromise because she wasn't coming in and I put her with another girl whom she wanted to be with... We haven't had a lot of time yet to really get going because we are still getting to know the children.

Sally was equally cautious at this stage of the intervention:

> We haven't had a lot of time yet to really get going [with CGW] because we are still getting to know the children.

Again, the CGW intervention was viewed as something separate from helping the children to form into a well-functioning class group. Like Tom, Sally saw CGW as coming later and considered that cooperation with the teacher was a prerequisite for cooperation with peers. She had only done a few circle games which ended when 'we all fell about laughing':

> ...we all fell about laughing. We ran out of time and it just deteriorated. They were giggling and all sorts. We couldn't get round the circle at all, so we packed it in and I said we'd have another go, but we haven't had time yet.

A compromise was to start with work in pairs because:

> It's actually a bit difficult to try and decide on who's working with whom. I will decide whether they are capable of doing the work that I'm actually giving them and at the moment I still don't know what they can do.

In her class, boys worked with boys and girls with girls.

By the time of the two in-service days in October and November there was some shift towards experimentation with CGW methods. The teachers brought their own examples of CGW which showed that they were not short of ideas for developing new strategies.

There was a growing sense that the teachers were trying to understand the processes which are involved in group work. For example, there was a shift away from stressing external constraints on children who sabotaged the work of the group to giving the groups opportunities to explore what had gone wrong and take some responsibility for change. The teachers were now saying things like:

> 'We should encourage not force.'
> 'We should work towards understanding why a particular child won't join in.'
> 'We should try to understand why children with special needs are sometimes left out of the activity by the group. This is unfortunate because the low-attaining child can gain in confidence through the achievement of working productively in a group.'

Physical factors like the moving of chairs or the layout of the classroom were now seen as less of a threat. The teachers and the children were now seeing this reorganisation as a common experience in the classroom.

There was a growing recognition of the value of debriefing and a willingness to use the power of the group to challenge dominant children. Bennett's three models were introduced at this point, using a handout as in table 5.5. This helped to emphasise that teachers were not simply to follow ideas from the pack but to begin to apply CGW to lessons across the curriculum. We looked at ways in which they were applicable within the National Curriculum.

The three models were outlined with specific examples drawn from classroom practice. The teachers were then asked to design a topic web or plan of work to last for half a term showing examples of CGW drawn from the three models. They were asked to choose one of the following topics – water, friends, Vikings, building, festivals, books and to make a series of lesson plans bearing in mind the attainments targets of the National Curriculum.

Phase three: January to July 1991

In this phase, the teachers were encouraged by the research team to continue to develop their own cooperative activities using Bennett's three models as a guide. The pupils were to work for longer periods, preferably lasting for a half-term, within heterogeneous groups. During the summer term, the children were to be given the opportunity to write letters to children from another class. This was to culminate in a whole day of cooperative games and a simulation (*Rafa Rafa*) in June when all the experimental classes would meet and work together.

From January 1991 through to the end of July 1991 the in-service days and visits to the schools were designed for support and sharing in order to enable the teachers to develop a sense of achievement in the art of CGW and a problem-solving approach based on the three models of CGW. Ideas were to be pooled and solutions to difficult problems shared. During this phase, the teachers continued to work productively on developing CGW ideas to incorporate into the normal work of the classroom. Model one had continued to provide a background of support within the groups whatever they were studying.

Pat and Tom had found model two to be very useful in their project work on 'Invaders and Settlers'. The method of working in cooperative groups had helped 'keep up the momentum for the children' when covering a long time period (e.g. the Romans or the Vikings) with many aspects to be studied. Sally had created her own version of the Rabbit game using a design of the mosque to coincide with a visit from an outside speaker who was to talk to the class about religious customs.

Table 5.5 Bennett's three models of CGW

MODEL 1: working individually on identical tasks for individual products

• = children a = task

```
                    •
                    a

              a           a
              •           •

                    a
                    •
```

On the surface, this model does not look like a cooperative group structure, for individuals are asked to provide individual products. Yet, when children in a group are working on the same task it is possible for them to share the experience and contribute to each other's interest, motivation or understanding. Their talk may influence each other's actions, ideas and the quality of the end product. But it is unlikely that this will occur unless the teacher specifically demands and encourages this kind of behaviour. Since children are asked for individual products, the task does not in itself demand cooperation.

Example 1

The teacher introduces the task and emphasises that the children are working as a group, not on their own. He or she could introduce the CGW aspect in these words:

> You are working as a group, not on your own. Everyone must join in and you must help one another. Try to solve any problems within your group. I will be available for any problems which your group cannot solve.

Example 2

Children who have been working individually consult one another after a given time. In story-writing, where each child produces his or her own piece, children share as they go along or consult one another about difficulties which have arisen or evaluate different possible endings to the story. In technology (e.g. building a wall or bridging a gap) children are encouraged to share solutions or ideas. Questions posed by the teacher might be: 'Is this your own idea or did you borrow it?'; 'What did you like about it to borrow it?'

Example 3

The children are given sufficient time at the end of an activity for debriefing, either about the task which they have just done or about the way in which they have worked together, or both.

Table 5.5 (continued)

MODEL 2: working individually on 'jigsaw' elements for a joint outcome

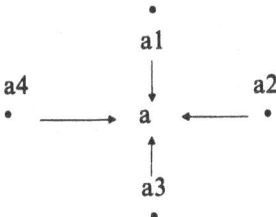

In this kind of task, there are as many elements to the task as there are group members. Each child works on one element and the task is divided in such a way that the group outcome cannot be achieved until every group member has successfully complete their piece of work. At this point the 'jigsaw' can be fitted together. Cooperation is thus built into the structure, as indeed is individual accountability. It is difficult in this type of group task for a child to sit back and let others do all the work, especially since group members are likely to ensure that everyone pulls their weight.

Example 1

The task can be literally a jigsaw, as in the *Rabbits* problem-solving activity, where the task is not complete until each member of the group has finished his or her part. In P.E., children may be given different pieces of apparatus to put together in order to form a game.

Example 2

Another task could be the production of a group story or newspaper. This can cater for a range of contributions. Non-readers can use drawing; non-English speakers can contribute in their first language and interpreters found from within the group.

Example 3

In technology (for example, building a land-yacht) there are three expert groups who have already been tutored in specific skills – making wheels, making a sail, making the base. The experts (in pairs if necessary) tutor the others in their home group.

Example 4

In a topic (for example, the Celts) the children find out about different aspects of the everyday life of that period – being a serf, being a woman, being a noble. They become experts within these groups and then return to their home group to create a short role-play showing aspects of Celtic life. This can also be done with the dramatisation of narrative poems, for example *The Pied Piper of Hamelin*.

Table 5.5 (continued)

MODEL 3: working jointly on one task for a joint outcome

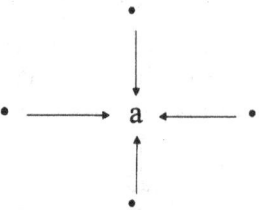

For this type of task, children will need to work cooperatively since only one product will be required of the group. Activities will therefore have to be coordinated and it is possible that a group leader will emerge, or could be selected, in order to create the necessary organisation. Each individual's work will have an impact on the group product but will be worthless until it becomes part of that product.

Example 1

Brainstorming can be used to generate ideas for a new task. This is the best-known and most frequently used procedure to stimulate creative thinking. During brainstorming sessions you can employ four basic ground rules:

(i) Criticism is ruled out – no evaluation at this point; discussion is not allowed as this usually raises doubts and qualifications.

(ii) Free-wheeling is welcomed – the wilder the idea the better. It is easier to modify ideas than to think up new ones.

(iii) Quantity is wanted – the more ideas the more likelihood of an original one coming up.

(iv) Combination and improvement are sought – members are encouraged to build on one another's ideas and to combine them to form new ones.

Example 2

Problem solving in technology and in construction tasks requires collaborative endeavour for the group to succeed. Learning to negotiate becomes an important part of their understanding.

Example 3

Whole-group discussion. For example, the children could read a story and then, in groups of four, make a critique of it. Alternatively, after reading a poem, children in groups make posters to illustrate aspects of its meaning. Children can share posters with other groups and challenge one another about the ways in which each group has interpreted the poem.

adapted from Dunne and Bennett (1990)

Margie had used model three to enable the pupils to work collaboratively in order to produce a play for assembly around the theme of a court scene. This was empowering to a normally shy girl, Shamina, who made 'a very good judge' so that, to Margie's surprise, 'the others shut up when she said, "Silence in court!"'. Jane had used brainstorming and diamond ranking to help children clarify their ideas on fundamental human rights. Tom had designed his own *Sector Games* where children collaborated in groups to design their own games with particular rules.

Children in small groups went round the school examining different areas and identifying what they were used for, looking at 'busy places' and 'quiet places'. This produced map-work and plans which were tied to an on-going concern about areas in the school where bullying might take place.

Judy continued to develop her writing projects and found that CGW could be used at all stages of the writing process – planning the story, proof-reading, checking spellings and designing illustrations.

Ann had done some work on bullying using statements which had generated discussion, first in small groups and then in the circle. In their groups, the children had designed cartoon stories depicting bullying incidents from their own perspective.

All the teachers collaborated during this time to set up a letter-writing activity in which children wrote to a child from another class. Their pen-friends were selected randomly to ensure that race and gender barriers would be crossed. The children were asked to write to a person (unknown to them initially) describing themselves, their class and their friends and asking for information about that person's interests. They were told well in advance that a cooperative day was planned in which they would have the chance to meet with their pen-friends and work in groups with them.

The research team was also aware of the problems which the teachers were encountering in handling children's relationships while developing CGW. The teachers were dealing with children, many of whom came from difficult backgrounds. Conflicts were frequent and tempers often ran high. Some children threw regular tantrums in the classroom and fights were common. To offer constructive support on this issue, the in-service day in early March focussed on coping with conflict – its causes and strategies for resolving it. The team examined three major causes of conflict – shortage of resources, personal needs not being met and clashes of values. Influenced by Kreidler's (1984) work, we also examined patterns in the escalation and de-escalation of conflict (table 5.6).

Table 5.6 Factors which influence conflict

Conflicts are likely to escalate if . . .

i) there is an increase in expressed emotion, especially anger;
ii) there is an increase in perceived threat;
iii) more people get involved;
iv) the children are not friends;
v) the children do not have peace-making skills.

Conflicts are likely to de-escalate if . . .

i) they are encouraged to focus on the problem rather than the people in conflict;
ii) there is a decrease in expressed emotion and perceived threat;
iii) the children are friends;
iv) the children know how to make peace.

adapted from Kreidler (1984)

The teachers found it helpful to share their experiences in this challenging area, particularly where an episode in the playground had spilled over into the classroom.

Pat, for example, discussed how she had been able to use CGW strategies to deal with a fight between two boys. The conflict could be traced back to a clash between the two families, but she felt that she could still deal with it in class.

Tom pointed out how play-fighting was a common way of bonding between boys. However, it often led to conflict. He suggested the development of alternatives, for example cooperative games and drama. He made good use of humour and tried to defuse arguments rather than escalate them. He was very aware of his role as a mediator and the influence which this could have on the children.

However, CGW strategies did not always work. Judy had found that, where the parents were not supportive of her, it was very difficult to resolve conflicts between children which took place outside school.

Ann argued that when conflict took place outside the class it was 'nearly impossible to resolve' and suggested that CGW was not 'a transferable skill'. She still considered CGW to be 'more sort of games and puzzles and discussions rather than book work'. Though she conceded that cooperative *games* could be used as a way of defusing anger she had not yet integrated CGW into the mainstream daily work of the classroom. A major factor was, in her opinion, the social background of the pupils:

> Especially in this school there are a lot of social problems. This way of

working CGW is extremely important for them but it should be started a lot earlier in the school. By the time they get here, they've a lot of in-built aggression and hatred of one another and it's hard to get them to cooperate.

Despite the continuing concern about the interpersonal relationships within the groups, by the end of phase three the teachers had definitely moved out of the *orientation* stage of the cycle of change and had tried to experiment with their own forms of CGW. As we had predicted, this was a difficult time. Innovation can be stressful and the teachers' comments indicated that their initial enthusiasm was being tested severely at times.

Sally had still found difficulties in establishing a cooperative ethos in her class. Gender barriers persisted; some children continued to be left out or discriminated against:

> Some of the girls won't work with the boys and they're not all that keen on working with some of the girls either because they are very shy... Farana tends to be left on her own. She's very shy, very quiet and finds it difficult to work with other people. But Farana is coming out of her shyness a little more. She will now sit with Bushra (a new girl) rather than cling to her cousin.

However, some changes were occurring in her view. The children liked to work in small groups, usually pairs, so it was hard to get them to work individually. This became especially noticeable when a student-teacher was placed in the class at the end of the summer term. The student-teacher – trained and experienced in Pakistan and updating her qualifications – had been 'a disruption', particularly as she was used to a very formal, didactic style:

> She was expecting the children to sit and listen and do as they were told and I think it was a bit of a shock when they didn't.

Sally had also noticed that Douglas, a previously rejected child, who used to 'fly off the handle and have tantrums in the middle of assemblies', had settled down a lot. Though he was left out sometimes, he was not so rejected, and had actually begun to make friends with new children who came to the class. Hafeez, after a block of time in Pakistan, found it hard to do CGW:

> He'd been to school in Pakistan and in the schools in Pakistan it's a case of 'Sit down and do as you're told'... Or they, you know, beat them, which he told me as soon as he walked through the door.

However, by sharing her concerns with his parents and through their commitment to supporting her way of working with the children, Sally was more optimistic about him. She had stabilised in her work and was adapting to a level. However, it was mainly work in pairs. She was honest about her inability to facilitate CGW in larger groups:

> I find it very difficult to do large group work with younger children ... even working in fours and fives ... I think the children are too young to actually get very much out of it. I've done a lot of pair work. They're that much older next year so hopefully they should be able to do more work.

This had solved the problem of free-riders: 'if you've got them working in pairs at least there's a bit more chance that they're working'.

Yet she had found that the children got much nicer 'from being a horrible class'. Relationships had improved and colleagues who had formerly been sorry for Sally at having such a difficult class were now commenting on how well they behaved. Sally was to continue with the class during the next academic year but was to acquire about ten new children. This concerned her, and again it did not seem to occur to her that CGW could be used as a way of integrating the two groups of children:

> I'm a bit concerned about how it is going to work. I don't want it to be 'them and us'.

She did not spontaneously consider that the team-building activities might be appropriate for re-forming the class. This paralleled the attitudes of most of the teachers at the beginning of phase two.

Judy was discouraged, especially over the continuing barriers of gender and race in her class:

> Sarya – no one wants anything to do with her. There is an undercurrent of this. She is shy. Ali has gone – he used to go around accusing everyone of being racist. With Kelash there are no barriers. Samira does not mix – she's just back from Pakistan – but she is not shunned. She has friends from elsewhere. Barbara and Lee, the two mixed-race children are accepted. Ruth is racist – she was very distressed about having a Pakistani boy as a pen-friend [in a letter-writing exercise]. There is a bad attitude between boys and girls.

In general, Judy admitted, she was not doing as much CGW as she had at the beginning. One attempt to do a simulation had failed:

In the groups, they each had a different role – interviewer, environmental expert, spokesperson for poverty – and they had collected together the information and they had one rep who appeared on a T.V. documentary. But it didn't go well because there was a lot of arguing. Where it's discussion I find it to be chaotic; where they have to get together and produce a piece of written work, then it tends to work well.

She had also found that some children took advantage of CGW to opt out of working. Her impression was also that relationships had not improved since 'freedom is a difficulty'. She had eliminated 'the CGW that was causing chaos' and replaced it with 'lots of structure'.

Judy had been one of the most innovative of all the teachers and was evaluating from an informed knowledge of what worked and what did not. Unfortunately, the conflict and tensions within the class seemed to have made her become very discouraged.

Pat highlighted the interpersonal problems in her 'very difficult class'. There were particular problems for children with special needs

> in evaluating what the children were getting out of it. In some groups there were children with special needs and they need to be encouraged in anything they do, and sometimes they couldn't find anything easy in the task . . . These children complained that they didn't have anything to do since the group had taken over and had left them out.

When she tried to explore this in debriefing sessions, she found:

> It was very delicate [hard to confront]. They said, 'Well, they didn't do anything' and often they were right because that child just sat there doing nothing. It was low self-esteem but the other children just saw it as not joining in.

However, she had found that, when peers said this rather than the teacher, it could have more of an impact:

> They were more tactful, which was surprising. They didn't say anything as direct as 'You were rubbish' or 'You didn't help'. These children knew it was aimed at them. They just said, 'I don't care anyway' or 'I didn't want to learn that' – but you could see that they did.

Eventually, in her view, the message got through from other members of the group that it was important for everyone to join in. As the year wore on, the children became more independent and, in Pat's view, they changed. She had noticed how much more effectively the children were communicating with one another since she had created opportunities for this to happen. There were fewer 'free-riders' and she herself had more opportunity to stand back and observe the interactions.

Margie spoke of racism in her class. Sam had sat next to an Asian girl at the beginning of the year and referred to her as 'that girl I sit next to', never by her name. But there had been some positive changes:

> It was Asian girls mainly who were encouraged to go to Whirlow because they miss out generally on field trips and residentials, but we didn't get twelve so we had to pick six white girls or Afro-Caribbean girls, and Laura was one that we deliberately picked because of her [negative] attitudes [towards Asian girls] . . . The field trip really transformed her relationship with Farana . . . They are very good friends now . . . and Laura seems more relaxed.

Jane was very grateful for Margie's support in implementing CGW:

> Without Margie I wouldn't have survived. It's been difficult. If you'd asked me in April, I'd have said I'd been really pleased with the CGW but, you know, towards the end of term it has been hard. There are so many extra things, different things, especially this year when circumstances are so strange [i.e. with the change to the new headteacher]. But I'm really looking forward to doing it next year. I'm happy about this. I like the fact that you can do quite normal things but instead do them as a cooperative group.

Jane was convinced that she was now able 'to do normal things but cooperatively' and that this resulted in more learning for the children.

Tom said:

> I think there's still some reluctance and some racism in this class, and it's sort of hidden . . . They're very keen on helping Amin and Raj and I wondered if sometimes they've not got some doll status. They're treated like toys by some of the kids rather than as people. But if you look today when *they've* chosen groups, they've drifted back into gender and racial groups.

Tom found that if *he* assigned the children into groups they would accept it. He had discussed it with the groups and when he said 'Some people say that boys and girls don't work well together' the pupils said 'that's silly'. They were adamant that there was no problem. Some children had been unkind when Sajid came back from a long stay in

Pakistan. Despite these setbacks, Tom had, in his view, got to the stage where CGW was becoming a normal part of his teaching. He did not need to think consciously about it. Some children 'moaned about model one' - they hated having to help one another. (These were all domineering children.) They used the CGW system to get the right answer and then to sit back and chat. But in his view, relationships had definitely improved.

Ann had not found that her interventions made any difference. But then she had not really implemented it since 'boys and girls don't like to mix'. She found that they had settled into a pattern which was hard to break. The letter-writing project had not been well received by children in her class. Kathy had been 'upset' to receive a letter from an Asian girl in another school. Overall, she had found it hard to get the children to work in the CGW way, for example, 'If Jake doesn't like someone he will be racist.' She took the easier option of allowing the children to do group work with their friends, rather than challenging the gender and race biases in her class. She admitted that she would have appreciated more help from the project team in the classroom and, with hindsight, perhaps did not appreciate that the researchers' role was evaluating the CGW intervention rather than taking on the role of support teacher.

The teachers were still in the experimentation stage and most had adapted to a level which suited them. For Sally this meant that pair work was the most adventurous thing she did. For Margie there was a strong ambivalence and a tension between formal seating arrangements and group work. Jane was trying it with growing confidence. Pat was having great difficulties with a turbulent class but persisted in her idealistic approach. Tom was very committed. Ann seemed not to be doing it much and there was a great reluctance on the part of her class to cross gender barriers (there were few Black children in her class). Judy was gifted at thinking up new ideas but was losing confidence as pressures in her school grew.

Despite the continuing concern about the interpersonal relationships within the groups, the teachers continued to work on developing CGW ideas to incorporate into the normal work of the classroom. We had come to the end of the first year of the intervention. Overall, despite the difficulties, evaluations of the experience of working in the project were, for the most part, still positive. Typical responses by the teachers to the question 'What have you learned most through using CGW?' included:

'Everything can be done in a cooperative way.'
'It doesn't matter if activities do not go as planned – during debriefing you

can always discuss why something happened.'
'Giving people the chance to express feelings in a safe way."
'It is not a package but an approach.'
'It should be practised from a very early age – but it's still worth doing with older children.'
'It creates a certain atmosphere in the room – different from that in other rooms.'
'It can be used on any topic; children will become involved and you don't need lots of resources; children help and learn from one another.'

The teachers had also liked the training sessions and particularly valued the three models which helped them to rationalise what they were doing. It gave them a framework for their thinking and planning. They also valued the opportunities to learn from one another and to share their own expertise in this area. However, many of the problems of relationships among the children seemed to remain unsolved. In answer to the question, 'What is the main problem with CGW?' they replied:

'Some children rely on others too heavily and do very little work.'
'Freeloaders are a problem! I have problems with individual children – what do you do when they won't cooperate?'
'Very shy children who won't join in.'
'Children who exploit the situation to the extreme of spoiling it for everyone else.'
'It is hard work on the emotions. One needs support.'

The theme of support recurred. Despite the in-service days and the frequent visits of members of the research team to the schools, there was a longing for even more support ('We would have liked the research team to come in more and participate in CGW activities.'). The CGW method was proving to be very taxing for the teachers and demanded a lot of them at a time when they had many other pressures to contend with. There was also a concern that, when they were away at training days the children were very uncooperative with the supply teachers! This was especially a problem in school A where four teachers would be out of school on any given in-service day. At this point, we offered them the opportunity to use the in-service days to collaborate among themselves in the second year of the project – in other words, to have more control over how they spent the time in planning or sharing what they were to do cooperatively. This offer of peer-supervision and support within school was eagerly accepted and formed the backbone of the in-service training in the following year.

Sadly, at this point School C pulled out of the project. It seemed that there had been some confusion in their minds about the functions of the dual roles of researcher and trainer so that when project team members came into school simply to interview or test the children this was perceived by the headteacher as unsupportive when, in his view, the teachers were giving so much to the project. The headteacher summarised this feeling as 'resentment':

> The teachers [Judy and Ann] felt they'd done all the work which they didn't mind doing because it was valuable to the children. They'd put extra effort in and then there was a lack of continuity on the other [the project] side . . . Otherwise we might have carried on [into the second year].

Yet when pressed on this point, he expressed appreciation of the in-service training days and the ideas which the experimental teachers had gained. The problem was that the threat of redundancy or redeployment had been hanging over the teaching staff throughout the year with an understandable drop in morale. Furthermore, the school had become involved in another project which offered some immediate financial benefits and a ready-made behaviour policy for dealing with bullying and other difficulties. Unfortunately, the headteacher had not been able to make links in his own mind between the aims of the two projects and had considered that he must make a choice between them. One year after the end of the project, Judy wrote to say that, in fact, she regretted the school's decision to withdraw from the project. She valued the training in CGW methods and will, in her own words, 'continue to use the skills and ideas the project allowed me to develop throughout my teaching career'.

Phase four: September 1991 to July 1992

The second year of the project began with two schools only – A and B – since school C had withdrawn from the project. All but one – Tom – of the teachers from school A were to continue, that is Jane, Margie and Pat, though the children were formed into different classes. In school B, Sally remained with the same children, now in year 5, but, because of school administrative reorganisation, had an additional 10 children from year 6 to integrate into the class. Kim remained with the same control class. There were two further classes in school B, one experimental (Joe's class) and one control (Kay and June). Joe was the only experimental teacher who had not been through the initial training in CGW although he was experienced as a teacher of *World Studies*. He was given time with a member of the research team to go through the CGW pack and an orientation period in which to familiarise himself with the method and practise with his class. As deputy head and a teacher of long standing in the school it was felt that he would be able to find his feet fairly quickly.

At the end of the first year of the project, the teachers had expressed the wish to have more say in planning their own training and support. A major reason for this request was that the children reacted very badly to an unfamiliar adult in their class. This was a particular difficulty in school A where three supply teachers were required each time there was an in-service training day. Although members of the research team visited the schools regularly to offer support and collaboration in attempting new activities – Jim Lewis, for example, demonstrated the range of cooperative activities which could be done with parachute games – the teachers' request seemed to be a reasonable one. Since they had already taken on a peer-supervisory role during the in-service days in the first year of the project, the research team agreed to build on this experience and to give them the opportunity to work collaboratively, within their own school settings on new ways of working cooperatively in their classrooms.

In school B, Sally agreed to work closely with Joe, to share ideas with him and to be supportive if there should be any difficulties, especially in the early stages of introducing the intervention. Later in the term, Sally and Joe visited another school to try out CGW activities with children who were less turbulent and presented less of a challenge in terms of discipline. The planning days shared by Sally and Joe were productive and helped to allay some of his anxieties. The most positive aspect was, in their view, having time to sit down, reflect on what they did and explore ways in which they could enhance the cooperative nature of their teaching. In Joe's words:

> We sat down and wrote a list of the sort of activities we do, that we felt could be classed as cooperative activities and I actually went through my record book in order to do that. And when we had done that, it transpired that I had actually done more than I thought I had done. So I was quite pleased with that.

In school A, Margie, Jane and Pat used the in-service time to plan a range of visits and cooperative activities which were to be shared among the three classes. Margie saw the advantages of teacher cooperation:

> It's really important to work with other people. I didn't find it easy. But I do think, as an adult and as a teacher, that people don't really share enough of their ideas ... It is a real saving of your work load for one person and it means that the quality of the work that's produced can be that much bigger ... People have got different skills. It's nice how we all got on together and trusted each other so that we could each do as much as we could ... When we've organised trips (for example when we went to the Woodhall Centre for the week) and I organised quite a lot of it and I was asking Pat to do things and I was worried because it seemed bossy for me to be asking her to do things and she said 'no, it's fine' just like she trusted that I would be pulling my weight.

The time for planning was greatly appreciated. Jane, too, appreciated the opportunity to prepare group work activities:

> It was wonderful that time we had to prepare group work here [in school]. That was excellent because it really gave you time to sit back and think about it with all the things you need to hand.

She felt more 'in control' and 'that I was doing something constructive'.

> We circulated round each other's rooms and it's interesting to see other children doing the same work that you have done with your class.

As the headteacher at school A said:

> The staff have felt able to spend time to do certain things and to be able to develop CGW. I think that's given them an extra boost.

However, as in the early stages of the first year of the project, there continued to be difficulties as the teachers and children adjusted to their new classes. Joe found it very difficult to use a CGW approach, despite his experience of *World Studies*. He accepted that:

> the ethos was there as I did *World Studies* for two years, but it fades. This project has jogged me into thinking about it again but I am also under pressure from the National Curriculum.

He had found an initial hostility by the class to CGW: 'Some are intolerant of interference or infringement of their desks.'

Left to themselves the children did not usually cross gender and race barriers. When he set up a discussion, he noticed a lot of competitiveness between groups and 'hoots of laughter' when certain individuals formulated a point of view. He concluded that 'the children are not quite ready for CGW yet – perhaps in two or three weeks. I don't want it all negative.' However, after some time he had been very pleased with a session on 'ourselves' when children shared something exciting that had happened to them with a partner. Then in fours the partners shared this information with the group then reported it back to the whole class. Joe described this activity as 'a small step into a more demanding kind of activity' but one that was 'very successful'. It led him to think of ways in which he could 'perhaps integrate CGW into what exists rather than append it'. In the summer term, Joe asked for some support. He had decided to use the *Rainbow Game*, a *World Studies* approach that demonstrates the need for different countries to share or trade by creating a situation where, in order to complete the colouring of a picture, groups of children need to negotiate the sharing out of coloured pencils. Joe integrated this game with his project on transport and, with the support of Jim Lewis, videotaped the children as they engaged in the task for reflection in small groups after the event. Jim Lewis also co-facilitated a session on parachute games at the end of the day.

Sally had difficulties at the beginning of the year in integrating one of the new children into her class. Keith, who found CGW very unfamiliar, had been calling the other children by racist names. The others had quickly indicated to him that this was an unacceptable way of behaving. She had noticed lots of cooperative behaviour in general. The new children were quickly adjusting to her way of working:

> Since I've moved them so they are now sitting in their teams I've noticed a lot more cooperation between children that aren't particularly friends . . . Yesterday I noticed one of the boys with Bushra and they were helping each other which is unusual as she is fairly quiet and she doesn't tend to have an awful lot to do with the boys.

The new children had been split up among the groups and had integrated very easily. In fact, they seemed to have contributed a liveliness and a willingness to challenge. The children had a team as a base:

> They're all in teams, all mixed up – mixed ages, mixed ability, mixed races – seven in a team. That has made it easier for the register. And they are actually getting things done instead of coming in and carrying on with their conversations. Yes, it's what we did last year. We had a base in the teams but for a lot of the lessons they were allowed to sit with other people . . . they're quite capable of getting on without me a lot of the time now. They

appreciate that, if they are working in a group, then they're supposed to ask everyone in the group before they come and demand help from me.

She was finding that group products, for example designing a poster, making tallies, collaborating to produce a graph, were 'worth looking at . . . and everyone, even the pains, joined in'. However, she admitted that she was not doing as much 'interactive' work within the groups as she would have liked since her numbers were much bigger:

> I'm definitely not doing the amount of discussion work I ought to be doing . . . because we've spent so much time just getting things sorted out . . . And the *My Body* project is so vast that I've had little time to spare with, you know, days and days just finishing things off.

Again Sally had not made the connection between CGW and the *My Body* project work:

> I've not felt that I have been able to say, 'Right, pack away. I'd like to talk now.' We're all doing different things as well so it's difficult to pull something together at the end of the lesson and talk about it.

It was clearly very much model one with hopes that at some point 'I will be able to get small groups out and talk to big groups'. As before, and like a number of the other teachers, she found it hard to challenge the children's reluctance to work outside their normal friendship groups:

> When I move their places you've got 'the moan' but it wasn't a big moan because they know what's coming. And they have had a little say about where they sat on the big table so on two of the tables we had one side with girls and one side with boys, so I could move the tables round so it wasn't so split . . . and there's not been any bother about people helping one another at a table and they're quite happy to work with whoever's sitting next to them or on their table.

Jim Lewis spent time supporting Sally in her classroom by co-facilitating a simulation and enabling some useful debriefing activities to take place. This support was appreciated by Sally and by the class. However, by the spring term Sally was again feeling very pressurised. The time of Ramadan posed particular problems for her:

> They're not having enough sleep, they're up at all hours . . . Some of the

children are very tired and it rubs off on the White kids and the Black kids... They seem to have gone overboard this year. Usually they've chosen one or two days a week to have a go at it because they're not old enough to do it all the time. This year, some of the children have been fasting almost all week... This year they've been bringing notes to say, 'My child can't go swimming, can't do P.E. because they're fasting.' And there's been a strange attitude to it this year that's been different from other years... Suki (the community teacher) is of the opinion that the children should do swimming and P.E. and that they should not really be fasting on those days.

Sally was feeling the strain and unable to maintain the cooperation which, in her view, had been well-established during the previous term. She was feeling 'very negative' about everything and really looking forward to Easter. By the end of the year she was saying:

To be honest, at the moment I don't actually feel as if I'm doing it properly. I seem to spend so much of my time sorting out.

At the beginning of the year, Margie was feeling more positive about CGW and considered that 'it has become more part of my teaching now – and it is more genuine CGW'. She had been struck by the 'calmness' of the children at the beginning of the year and had noticed a much greater readiness to work. There was trust among the children and a readiness to help one another. They 'moved around sensibly' and 'argued constructively'. She was highly motivated by having control of her own training time and played a leading part in organising the in-service days within school A. This form of peer support had been chosen by all the teachers at school A in preference to in-service training at the university. However, by the end of the year she admitted that the CGW had somewhat lapsed:

I did change the groups at the beginning of this half-term. We only had two or three group-work sessions.

To an extent she blamed the method itself:

There were some that seemed to cope with class work and when they came to do their exams have not done very well and I think it's because they relied on other people to sort them out instead of sorting them out for themselves.

Margie confirmed that she found it 'a hassle to keep remembering "Oh no! I'm supposed to be doing cooperative things." No matter how valuable they are, I suppose it still doesn't come naturally.'

Pat was aware of difficulties, especially between boys and girls:

> They groan when it is CGW and they're not with their friends . . . Some don't contribute well in groups; some opt out.

However, overall she claimed that it was not 'such a problem as last year' and she noticed that the groups were more likely to take responsibility for telling group members if they were not sufficiently involved in the task. Pat was very positive about CGW by the end of the year. She felt that the class had really 'gelled' and that the class generally were very supportive of one another. The big problem in the class was Sean. Yet she felt that the other children had become more assertive and able to challenge his domineering behaviour:

> Some of them look after each other and do things for each other more. There are certain people who've really taken that on board and done the same things for each other. It's good.

Jane had found initial difficulties. For example, Beth had complained about her team 'They're dipsticks; they're not clever and they're all Pakis.' But she had found over the year that most of the children accepted that they would do quite a lot of work in their teams. Jane was discouraged at points in the year by the resurgence of racism and intolerance in the class:

> We've had a lot of unpleasantness concerning a new little girl. I did wonder whether it was because they'd got into being quite a cohesive little group and that other people they'd rejected in the beginning they were now more accepting of them . . . She came late and she wasn't used to this way of working and she doesn't belong anywhere.

She recognised that 'the biggest part of life here is continually trying to make people cooperate with one another instead of conflict with one another'. Yet, overall, she was able to conclude at the end of the year that there had been real progress and that it had proved to be a method which she would continue to use after the end of the project:

> It has been real pleasure to see children working together and cooperating pleasantly together which I'm sure they've done more in working in a group way than they did previously.

The teachers had found the process of transition to CGW a difficult one. Despite their early enthusiasm about the in-service programme and their expressed commitment to this more participatory style of teaching, the experience of putting the ideas into practice over an extended period of time had turned out to be much more demanding than any of us had predicted. The teachers had engaged willingly in the orientation and experimentation stages and had responded well to opportunities for sharing and pooling ideas. Support from colleagues was highly valued, as was the opportunity during the second year of the project to be given time to work and plan together.

Two teachers – Judy and Ann – left the project at the end of the first year because of school reorganisation, though, as we have seen, they had mixed feelings about this decision. Tom was willing to continue but, because of school amalgamation, was given a younger class to teach and so could not be involved in the second year. Joe, an experienced senior teacher, willingly entered the project in its second year. The 'survivors' were Margie, Jane, Pat and Sally, each of whom arrived at the adaptation stage of the cycle in her own way. Each of the teachers had mixed feelings about the effectiveness of the method and had experienced difficulties in its implementation. In chapter six we see in some detail how they coped and how they felt day by day about using CGW with their classes.

CHAPTER SIX: The effects of cooperative group work on social relationships

Introduction

The principal aim of the study was to establish whether or not CGW had a positive impact on the social relationships of the children in the schools and in the classrooms that we worked in. In order to assess social relationships we felt it crucial to employ both qualitative and quantitative methodologies. The qualitative assessments took the form of in-depth semi-structured interviews with the teachers and children. The children were interviewed both in their groups and individually and asked how they felt about working in CGW groups and about their relationships with other children. The teachers were asked about their feelings and attitudes towards the CGW groups; they were also asked to discuss the children in their class and talk about the relationships among them.

In this chapter we mainly consider the quantitative data. We aimed to assess quantitatively several aspects of social relationships. Firstly, we wanted to know how much the children liked the other children in their class; in particular, how much children from different ethnic backgrounds liked one another. We also targeted the sociometric status of the children by examining how often a child was picked as 'liked most' or 'liked least' by classmates.

A second aspect concerned the levels of bullying and victimisation in each class, as perceived by the children. From this information, we assigned each child to certain categories – bully, victim, both a bully and a victim, or none of these.

A third aspect concerned the extent to which the children said they liked to do activities with peers from different ethnic origins (ethnic preference), and how much stereotyping and prejudice there was of other ethnic groups in general.

The process of carrying out the assessments

The assessments were made at the beginning of the academic year, and again at the end. In the first year of the study this was October 1990 (time one), and then June/July 1991 (time two). In the second year of the study the times were the same, October 1991 (time three) and June/July 1992 (time four). In these assessments, each child was interviewed individually for about half an hour; the child was asked to accompany the researcher into either another spare empty classroom or at least to a reasonably quiet place where they would not be disturbed and where the child would be at ease. Care was taken by the research workers to get to know the children by spending some time in the classroom before these assessments were made.

Most children seemed to enjoy their assessment session. For one thing it meant being taken out of class for half an hour. Often, the children would be more than ready to go when they knew it was their turn and other children would ask if it was their turn next. However, some children were quieter than others during the sessions and seemed a little nervous, looking around at any indication of the presence of other children.

The assessments demanded intense concentration from the children at times and some children found the sessions taxing towards the end. The assessments were scheduled to run outside the children's breaktimes and every attempt was made to keep to this. However, there were times when the assessment ran over a little into breaktimes and on these occasions the children usually offered to stay and finish the assessment.

The measures we used

Liking

The researcher showed each child head and shoulder photographs of the other members of their class and asked him or her to identify them. The child was then asked to place each photograph on one of three piles, depending on whether they liked them 'a lot', 'a little' or 'not at all'. These ratings were scored 3, 2 and 1 respectively. A mean liking score was then calculated for each child from the liking ratings received from all classmates.

Sociometric status

The same photographs were used as above but this time the child was asked to select only six people, the three that they liked the most and the three that they liked the least. It was then possible to classify each of the children into one of the six sociometric status types by employing the procedures of Coie et al. (1982). The six status types were 'popular' (several like most, few like least); 'controversial' (several like most and several like least); 'neglected' (few like most and few like least); 'rejected' (few like most, several like least); 'average'; and 'other'.

Bullying and victimisation

The children were introduced to the topic by the researcher commenting that sometimes children got bullied at school. They were asked what they thought being a bully meant, which the researcher usually confirmed if reasonably accurate and added: 'yes, someone who picks on other children or who hits them for no reason'. The children were then asked to use the same photographs of classmates and to place them into two groups, one for children who bullied others and one for children who did not bully others. The 'bully' score for each child took the form of a percentage obtained from the proportion of classmates who nominated them as a bully.

The same assessment and scoring procedure was repeated for victims of bullying. The definition of a victim was 'a child who gets picked on or bullied for no reason'. A 'victim' score for each child was obtained in a corresponding way.

This assessment identified who were the bullies and who were the victims in the classroom, from the point of view of classmates; the children sometimes nominated a class member as both a bully and a victim.

We defined categories in terms of cutoffs of 33 per cent and 50 per cent (in general, we found that mean scores were around 33 per cent, with 50 per cent being about one standard deviation above the mean). If a child received 50 per cent or more of bully nominations and less than 33 per cent of victim nominations from the other members of their class then they were assigned to the 'bully' category. Conversely, a child receiving a score of 50 per cent or more victim nominations and less than 33 per cent of bully nominations from the rest of the class was assigned to the 'victim' category. If a child received 33 per cent or more of both bully and victim nominations from their classmates, then they were assigned to the 'bully-victim' category. If a child received nominations from their classmates which scored less than 33 per cent for both bully and victim then they were used as a control child. Finally, an 'other' child was someone whose bully and victim scores placed them outside any of the above four categories (in other words if they received less than 33 per cent in one category and between 33 per cent and 50 per cent in the other).

Social preference

The Social Preference Test was based on the procedure of Wilson (1987). The researcher presented each child with a selected set of six head and shoulders photographs of unknown children who were around the same age and the same gender as themselves. The photographs were similar facially and in what they were wearing and consisted of a female and a male child from each of Asian, White and Afro-Caribbean ethnic backgrounds. Each child was then asked to rate the children in the photographs on how much they would like to participate in certain activities with each of them on a scale of 'a lot', 'a little' and 'not at all'; these responses scored 3, 2, and 1 respectively. The activities that they were asked to consider were: 'sit next to in class'; 'ask them to help with their school work'; 'have them in their team for a game'; 'invite them home to their house'; and 'play with them in the playground'. By totalling the rating scores given by the children for each photograph from all the activities a social preference score was obtained.

Stereotyping

This was based on the work of Davey (1983). The researcher presented each child with three different sets of photographs of Asian, White and Afro-Caribbean boys and girls whom they had never seen before. Each child was asked to assign five positive traits: 'works hard', 'is friendly', 'is truthful', 'clever' and 'clean'; and also five negative traits: 'is lazy', 'tells lies', 'is stupid', 'is dirty' and 'argues', each written on a card, to one or more of the sets of photographs that they felt it best described. There was also a box labelled 'nobody' which they were very clearly told they could put cards into if they felt that the trait did not suit any set of photographs.

To obtain a score for stereotyping, the number of negative traits was subtracted from the number of positive traits that a child gave to each set of photographs. Thus, each of the ethnic groups would have a stereotype score which could range from +5 to -5.

Prejudice

Using the Stereotypes Test, we made an operational definition of a prejudiced child as 'one giving either of the other two ethnic groups who were different from themselves at least three more negative than positive nominations, while at the same time giving his or her own ethnic group at least as many positive as negative traits'. For example, a White child who assigned five negative traits and one positive trait to Asian children, and two positive and one negative trait to White children, would be prejudiced on this definition.

How the data were analysed

Our main interest was to see if changes occurred over time, and whether the CGW and N.C. classes differed in this. To examine these questions, scores from the assessments were analysed using a range of statistical tests. Analysis of variance tests were run to measure the changes in the levels of liking, bullying, victimisation, social preference and stereotyping in each of the classes. For the categorical data which came from the sociometric status, bully and victim, and prejudice assessments, chi squared analyses were carried out.

Although we used three ethnic groups in our assessments – White, Asian and African-Caribbean – there were rather few African-Caribbean children in the schools we were working in. The main ethnic groups could broadly be characterised as White and Asian. Therefore, we restricted analyses using race of child, to these two groups.

Findings

Table 6.1 summarises the results of the main analyses of variance on our assessment measures. It shows the condition x time interactions, that is, whether the CGW classes or the N.C. classes diverged over time, with one or other showing greater change or improvement. In our first analyses we entered all the classes: six CGW and three N.C. in Year 1; five CGW and two N.C. in Year 2. These analyses are shown as 'All Classes' in table 6.1. Using results from all the classes maximises the sample size, but the CGW and N.C. classes differ partly by school and age group. However, we could also match pairs of classes for age level and school, in schools B and C, in Year 1 (three matched pairs of classes); and in B only in Year 2 (two matched pairs). It seemed worth doing the analyses on these matched pairs as well and these are labelled as 'Matched Pairs' in table 6.1. The analyses are shown for Year 1, Year 2 and for those follow-through children who stayed in the project for both years (15 in CGW, 18 in N.C., all in school B).

Table 6.1 Summary results for condition x time interactions

		YEAR ONE	YEAR TWO	FOLLOW-THROUGH
OVERALL LIKING	All Classes	$F_{(1,172)}=0.31$ n.s.	$F_{(1,147)}=0.33$ n.s.	–
	Matched Pairs	$F_{(1,116)}=1.72$ n.s.	$F_{(1,97)}=1.89$ n.s.	$F_{(3,93)}=4.31$ $p<.01$
WHITES LIKING ASIANS	All Classes	$F_{(1,48)}=1.85$ n.s.	$F_{(1,56)}=3.85$ n.s. ($p<.06$)	
ASIANS LIKING WHITES	All Classes	$F_{(1,90)}=0.07$ n.s.	$F_{(1,57)}=0.28$ n.s.	–
BULLYING	All Classes	$F_{(1,172)}=0.69$ n.s.	$F_{(1,147)}=0.04$ n.s.	–
	Matched Pairs	$F_{(1,117)}=0.15$ n.s.	$F_{(1,97)}=2.08$ n.s.	$F_{(3,93)}=1.31$ n.s.
VICTIMISATION	All Classes	$F_{(1,172)}=1.14$ n.s.	$F_{(1,147)}=4.42$ $p<.05$	–
	Matched Pairs	$F_{(1,117)}=3.75$ n.s. ($p<.06$)	$F_{(1,97)}=0.74$ n.s.	$F_{(3,93)}=3.38$ $p<.05$
SOCIAL PREFERENCE	Whites view of Asians	$F_{(1,78)}=0.52$ n.s.	$F_{(1,56)}=0.53$ n.s.	–
	Asians view of Whites	$F_{(1,43)}=0.43$ n.s.	$F_{(1,60)}=0.01$ n.s.	–
STEREOTYPING	Whites stereotyping Asians	$F_{(1,81)}=0.65$ n.s.	$F_{(1,56)}=0.92$ n.s.	–
	Asians stereotyping Whites	$F_{(1,40)}=0.38$ n.s.	$F_{(1,60)}=0.03$ n.s.	–

Most of the results in table 6.1 are not significant (n.s.). This means that CGW did not appear to have had a major impact in changing or improving social relationships; at least, it did not differ from N.C. appreciably in this respect. We will examine each set of results in some more detail, in tables 6.2 to 6.8. In these tables, mean scores are given at the four different time (assessment) points (T1, T2, T3 and T4). The CxT (condition x time) interaction is repeated from table 6.1 and these remain the most interesting results from our perspective. In addition we give the main effects for C (condition) and T (time). A significant result for C means that the CGW and N.C. classes differed consistently all the time, probably because of differing class compositions. Fortunately, very few of these are significant. Rather more significant effects are found for T, meaning a general trend upwards or downwards found in most or all classes, irrespective of whether they are CGW or N.C.

Liking

Fuller results for the liking scores are given in table 6.2. During year one there was little change, though the trends slightly favoured the CGW classes. In year two, there was again little change, though now the trends slightly favoured the N.C. classes. There was a significant finding for the children who were followed through both years, with liking increasing in the N.C. classes but decreasing in the CGW classes; this finding was of course against our predictions. The effect, however, appears mainly due to the change from year one to year two (T2 to T3) when some changes in class composition did take place.

Liking by race

Here we considered White children's liking of Asian classmates and Asian children's liking of White classmates. Fuller results are given in tables 6.3 and 6.4. In year one the White children's liking of Asian classmates changed only marginally with a slight decrease in the CGW classes and a slight increase in the N.C. classes. In year two there was a nearly significant interaction with the White children's liking of Asian classmates, with the increase in liking in the N.C. classes greater than in the CGW classes (table 6.3). The Asian children's liking of White classmates decreased slightly (not significantly) over both year one and year two in both the CGW and the N.C. classes, the sharper drop being in the CGW classes in year one but the N.C. classes in year two (table 6.4). On the whole these results suggest that White children's liking of Asian classmates stays fairly constant, but Asian children's liking of

Table 6.2 Summary results for overall 'liking' scores

		T1	T2	T3	T4	C×T	C	T
YEAR ONE	All Classes CGW	1.97	1.95			n.s.	n.s.	n.s.
	N.C.	1.95	1.91					
	Matched Pairs CGW	1.91	1.93			n.s.	n.s.	n.s.
	N.C.	1.95	1.91					
YEAR TWO	All Classes CGW			1.97	1.97	n.s.	n.s.	n.s.
	N.C.			2.00	2.03			
	Matched Pairs CGW			2.00	2.03	n.s.	n.s.	$F_{(1,97)} = 6.93$ $p<.01$
	N.C.			1.91	2.00			
FOLLOW-THROUGH	CGW	1.91	1.89	1.78	1.79	$F_{(3,93)} = 4.31$ $p<.01$	n.s.	n.s.
	N.C.	1.81	1.79	1.85	1.91			

Table 6.3 Summary results for Whites liking Asians

		T1	T2	T3	T4	C×T	C	T
YEAR ONE	CGW	1.81	1.75			n.s.	$F_{(1,48)} = 3.96$ $p<.06$	n.s.
	N.C.	1.52	1.60					
YEAR TWO	CGW			1.81	1.78	$F_{(1,56)} = 3.85$ $p<.06$	n.s.	n.s.
	N.C.			1.66	1.80			

Table 6.4 Summary results for Asians liking Whites

		T1	T2	T3	T4	C×T	C	T
YEAR ONE	CGW	1.92	1.84			n.s.	n.s.	n.s.
	N.C.	1.90	1.85					
YEAR TWO	CGW			1.87	1.85	n.s.	n.s.	n.s.
	N.C.			194	1.86			

White classmates decreases. There is no significant difference in the impact of CGW and N.C. curricula.

Bullying and victimisation

In these analyses we used the 'bully' and 'victim' scores received by each child. Fuller results for these scores are given in tables 6.5 and 6.6. So far as bullying scores were concerned, there was little change in year one; in year two, however, there were quite large (and significant) increases in bullying, which occurred equally in both the CGW and the N.C. classes (table 6.5).

Results for victimisation scores are shown in table 6.6. In year one there was a decrease in victimisation in both the CGW and N.C. classes, with a trend to greater decrease in the CGW classes; although this did not reach significance, when the classes were matched by pairs this did verge on a significant interaction, with a larger decrease in victimisation in the CGW classes. In year two, there was a significant increase in victimisation in both the CGW and the N.C. classes. However, the increase in victimisation was slight in the CGW classes but substantial in the N.C. classes, giving a significant interaction.

There was also a significant interaction for the children who were followed through both years. Levels of victimisation dropped in both CGW and N.C. classes overall, but there was a large initial increase in victimisation in the N.C. classes occurring between times one and two.

Social preference

We examined here the social preference scores received by Asian children from White children and by White children from Asian children. Fuller results for these scores are given in table 6.7. There was not much change in these scores over time, in either year one or year two. None of the condition × time interactions approached statistical significance.

Stereotyping

Fuller results for the stereotyping scores are given in table 6.8. Again, we focussed on the extent to which White children stereotyped Asian children and Asian children stereotyped White children. In year one, both of these changed only marginally. There was a slight increase in the amount of stereotyping from the White children in the CGW classes and a very slight decrease in the N.C. classes. This marginal change was reversed with the Asian children's stereotyping of White children

Table 6.5 Summary results for overall bully scores

		T1	T2	T3	T4	C×T	C	T
YEAR ONE	All Classes CGW	29.2	29.6			n.s.	n.s.	n.s.
	N.C.	33.1	31.5					
	Matched Pairs CGW	30.4	27.6			n.s.	n.s.	n.s.
	N.C.	33.1	31.5					
YEAR TWO	All Classes CGW			25.8	33.6	n.s.	n.s.	$F_{(1,147)} = 40.0$ $p<.001$
	N.C.			24.3	31.5			
	Matched Pairs CGW			23.7	31.2	n.s.	n.s.	$F_{(1,97)} = 37.8$ $p<.001$
	N.C.			24.0	36.0			
FOLLOW-THROUGH	CGW	30.6	43.8	30.0	37.4	n.s.	n.s.	$F_{(3,93)} = 5.67$ $p<.005$
	N.C.	38.8	42.1	31.8	35.0			

Table 6.6 Summary results for overall victim scores

		T1	T2	T3	T4	C×T	C	T
YEAR ONE	CGW All Classes	36.4	32.1			n.s.	n.s.	$F_{(1,172)} = 5.38$ $p<.05$
	N.C.	35.9	34.7					
	CGW Matched Pairs	34.6	26.7			$F_{(1,117)} = 3.75$ $p<.06$	n.s.	$F_{(1,117)} = 6.98$ $p<.01$
	N.C.	35.9	34.7					
YEAR TWO	CGW All Classes			32.4	35.3	$F_{(1,147)} = 4.42$ $p<.05$	n.s.	$F_{(1,147)} = 10.1$ $p<.005$
	N.C.			24.8	35.4			
	CGW Matched Pairs			24.8	35.4	n.s.	n.s.	$F_{(1,197)} = 20.1$ $p<.001$
	N.C.			24.7	31.9			
FOLLOW-THROUGH	CGW	44.0	38.3	36.7	34.9	$F_{(3,93)} = 3.38$ $p<.05$	n.s.	$F_{(3,93)} = 8.28$ $p<.001$
	N.C.	39.0	46.1	34.4	29.8			

where the slight increase was in the N.C. classes and the slight decrease in the CGW classes. In year two, there was an increase in stereotyping from the White children in both the CGW and the N.C. classes, but with a trend to a larger increase in the N.C. classes. The Asian children decreased their stereotypes of White children during year two, in both the CGW and N.C. classes.

In general, these changes were slight: the CGW and N.C. curricula had no significant effects on stereotyping, either by White or Asian children.

Categorical data

We carried out a number of tests using the categorical data, although as expected these largely replicated the findings from the data just reported.

SOCIOMETRIC STATUS
We looked to see if more children changed in to, or out of, the rejected and neglected status categories, in the CGW or N.C. classes. We found no significant differences, either in year one or year two.

BULLIES AND VICTIMS
We looked to see if more children changed in to, or out of, the bully or victim status categories, in the CGW or N.C. classes. We found no significant differences in year one. However, in year two we found a greater improvement in the CGW classes: this was because a greater proportion of victims and/or bully-victims in these classes moved out of either victim status by the end of the year. This confirms the significant finding from analysis of variance referred to above.

PREJUDICED CHILDREN
We looked to see if more children changed in to, or out of, the prejudiced status category, in the CGW or N.C. classes. We found no significant differences in year one or year two.

Academic Performance

Using A.N.O.V.A. analyses, we looked for condition by time interactions for the scores from school B and school C. At school B, there were no such significant effects on any of the Richmond scales (vocabulary, reading, language skills, work study skills, mathematics). As expected, this suggested that there was no impact of CGW, one way or the other,

Table 6.7 Summary results for social preference test

			T1	T2	T3	T4	C×T	C	T
YEAR ONE	Whites view Asians	All Classes	CGW	17.8	17.3			n.s.	n.s.	n.s.
			N.C.	15.9	16.2					
	Asians view Whites	All Classes	CGW	19.9	20.6			n.s.	n.s.	n.s.
			N.C.	19.7	19.5					
YEAR TWO	Whites view Asians	All Classes	CGW			17.3	17.7	n.s.	$F_{(1,56)} = 3.85$ $p<.06$	n.s.
			N.C.			19.0	20.2			
	Asians view Whites	All Classes	CGW			19.6	19.9	n.s.	$F_{(1,60)} = 3.82$ $p<.06$	n.s.
			N.C.			21.6	22.1			

Table 6.8 Summary results for stereotypes test

			T1	T2	T3	T4	C×T	C	T
YEAR ONE	Whites view Asians	All Classes					n.s.	$F_{(1,81)} =$ 6.67 $p<.05$	n.s.
		CGW	0.54	0.93					
		N.C.	−0.52	−0.67					
	Asians view Whites	All Classes					n.s.	$F_{(1,40)} =$ 4.49 $p<.05$	n.s.
		CGW	2.12	2.04					
		N.C.	0.53	0.88					
YEAR TWO	Whites view Asians	All Classes					n.s.	n.s.	n.s.
		CGW			0.02	0.39			
		N.C.			−0.59	0.53			
	Asians view Whites	All Classes					n.s.	n.s.	n.s.
		CGW			1.88	1.71			
		N.C.			2.33	2.05			

on academic performance. At school C, we only had data from the first year, and unfortunately could not get data from one of the N.C. classes. The analyses did indicate a greater improvement in the one remaining N.C. class than the two CGW classes, on the Macmillan reading and mathematics scores.

Summary

Our analysis of the quantitative data gave results which were, on the whole, rather disappointing. Our previous study had suggested that CGW could be successful in improving some aspects of social relationships in the classroom and had led to an expectation that this project might give similar, if not better, outcomes. But for the most part, and with the important exception of 'victimisation' scores, the quantitative results did not justify this expectation. It seems that CGW had not had much impact on peer social relationships within the classroom. Nor did there appear to be any cumulative effects across the two years. This appeared to be in some conflict with the qualitative data from the interviews, both with the teachers and the children. What might explain these findings?

Could it be that there were changes in other aspects of social relationships which were omitted in our assessment measures? Although possible, this is unlikely as not only do the measures which were used seem to be quite fundamental ones, they and some similar ones were used in our previous study which had produced promising results.

Another possibility would be that the measures themselves were unreliable. But, peer nominations are usually reliable, and given that the main quantitative measures were based on the nominations received from each child for each of the other members of their class, this explanation also is unlikely.

The length of time allowed to measure changes in the study could be a factor in CGW not appearing to be effective. Was enough time allowed? But the minimum time the children were measured over was one year and the follow-through children over one further year. This would be considered by most people to be a sufficient length of time from which to draw reliable conclusions from the results.

We felt that further investigation of what was going on in the classroom was necessary in order to find other possible causes for the seeming failure of CGW. One necessary factor for any success of CGW must be that it is actually put into practice. How much time was spent on it by the teachers involved and how strong was their commitment to the principles of CGW? It is also possible that there could be other adverse factors intrinsic to the classroom, some of which are explored below.

'Difficult' children

If a class has a number of particularly disruptive individuals then this could make it problematic for the teacher to implement CGW in effective ways. We decided to define a 'difficult' child as one who had a 'bully' score exceeding 50 per cent, and a mean liking score from classmates of less than 2.0. This selected those children who were 'bullies' or 'bully-victims', and who were also not especially liked or actively disliked by classmates. It excludes any 'popular' and most 'controversial' bullies, but includes the 'rejected-aggressive' children who appear to be most problematical (see chapter one).

Altogether, there were 40 such children in year one (35 boys, 5 girls) and 27 in year two (25 boys, 2 girls). The numbers of 'difficult' children in each class are shown in table 6.9.

Also, some children may respond positively to CGW whereas other children may respond more negatively. The mean CGW liking score in each class is also shown in table 6.9. We explore the relationship between child characteristics and CGW liking further, in chapter seven.

Diary records

The teachers had been asked to keep diary records throughout the whole of each year. This was to ascertain what kinds of activities they engaged in with their pupils and how much of their classroom time the children were actually spending in CGW activities as opposed to other kinds of activities. The list of activities had been developed in collaboration with the teachers who had participated in the previous study. They covered: *whole-class teaching*, which entails most or all of the children in the class being involved in some sort of sedentary listening activity; *whole-class activity*, during which all of the children may be involved in a discussion or music lesson; *independent work*, where the child works alone in their own time; *small-group work*, which entails the children working in groups without necessitating real collaboration; *cooperative group work*, which entails collaboration between pupils for a common goal; and *other* activities which fall outside the previous categories, such as class visits or registration periods.

The diaries enabled us to check that CGW was in fact used more in the CGW classes than in the N.C. classes, as was expected. Table 6.9 shows the percentage of time spent in each of the activities, according

Table 6.9 Percentage of time spent in various classroom activities, from diary records and number of 'difficult' children, and mean CGW liking score, in each class

School/class	Teacher	Number of teaching hours reported	Whole-class teaching	Whole-class activity	Independent work	Small-group work	Cooperative group work	Other	Number of 'difficult' children	Mean CGW liking score
YEAR 1										
A/CGW 1	Margie/Jane	316	13.8	19.4	29.6	14.6	12.2	10.3	5	4.18
A/CGW 2	Tom	-	-	-	-	-	-	-	2	3.67
A/CGW 3	Pat	366	3.8	7.7	35.3	8.7	28.7	15.8	5	3.20
B/CGW 4	Sally	253.5	8.5	14.2	20.5	24.5	16.5	15.7	7	3.00
C/CGW 5	Ann	179	2.2	5.9	8.9	32.4	42.4	8.1	7	4.70
C/CGW 6	Judy	540.5	7.3	10.1	17.0	7.3	42.0	16.3	2	3.86
B/N.C. 1	Kay/June	647	13.9	15.4	15.4	34.0	8.6	12.5	3	-
C/N.C. 2	Lorraine	358.5	18.1	20.4	27.9	13.9	13.4	6.3	5	-
C/N.C. 3	Roy	-	-	-	-	-	-	-	4	-
YEAR 2										
A/CGW 1	Pat	75.2	3.0	7.0	46.2	4.0	27.9	12.0	5	2.76
A/CGW 2	Jane	108	7.4	13.2	18.0	14.6	28.5	18.3	3	3.75
A/CGW 3	Margie	115.5	11.5	12.3	40.5	12.1	12.5	11.0	4	4.29
B/CGW 4	Sally	105.5	5.9	11.4	15.2	37.9	14.9	14.2	4	3.57
B/CGW 5	Joe	146	14.0	14.7	26.2	17.0	21.7	6.3	3	3.64
B/N.C. 1	Kim	101.2	13.6	13.8	37.3	11.8	6.7	16.8	7	-
B/N.C. 2	Kay/June	94.2	11.7	24.7	26.5	14.3	7.9	14.8	1	-

to the teachers in each class (note that it was not possible to obtain diaries from the CGW2 teacher in year one). Generally, there was considerably more CGW activity in the CGW classes (range 12 per cent to 42 per cent) than in the N.C. classes (range 8 per cent to 13 per cent), though it is also clear that some CGW classes did not do as much as was hoped for – at least one hour per day, which would be about 20 per cent of time.

The teachers were invited to write in the diaries about their experiences of CGW, for example, after a particular session, how it had gone, whether they felt that it had been successful or not, any problems that arose with particular children which made it difficult for CGW to operate well.

Now, a further examination of the diary records that the teachers had filled in could be used in an attempt to shed some light on the findings and hopefully provide answers to some questions concerning them. Did the CGW classes really differ from the N.C. classes in their curriculum content? And if they did differ, was CGW implemented effectively in the CGW classes? Had the school classes changed in any way over a full school year? We look next at profiles of each class, drawing on the diary records. We also refer to tables 6.10 and 6.11, which indicate for each class, in year one (table 6.10) and year two (table 6.11), whether the change in each assessment measure was in a positive (+) or negative (-) direction.

Class profiles

There was wide variation in the quality of the written records that the teachers gave about their experiences of implementing CGW, and their own personal feelings about its effectiveness. Some teachers were able to give detailed and descriptive information about particular incidents, both positive and negative; diary records from other teachers, however, were somewhat sparse.

Year one: school A

From school A two of the three teachers from year one were able to fill in their diary records in some detail.

CGW 1: JANE AND MARGIE
Jane and Margie shared a CGW class. Out of their total teaching time, the time that they spent in CGW activities was quite low, at 12.2 per cent (see table 6.9). Apart from the 'other' category the next least time

Table 6.10 Increases (+) and decreases (-) on the main assessment measures in each class: year one (times one and two)

School	Class	Whole-class liking	Asians view of Whites	Asians view of Asians	Whites view of Asians	Whites view of Whites	% Bullying	% Victimised	Asian stereotype Whites	Whites stereotype Asians	Prejudice
A	CGW 1	-	+	-	+	-	-	-	+	-	-
	CGW 2	-	-	+	=	+	+	+	-	+	+
	CGW 3	-	+	+	+	-	+	+	-	-	-
	CGW 4	-	+	-	-	-	+	-	+	-	+
B	N.C. 1	-	-	-	+	-	+	+	-	+	=
	CGW 5	-	+	+	-	-	-	-	-	-	-
C	CGW6	+	-	-	+	+	-	+	+	-	-
	N.C. 2	-	+	+	-	-	-	+	=	+	+
	N.C. 3	+	-	-	+	+	-	-	-	-	-

Table 6.11 Increases (+) and decreases (-) on the main assessment measures in each class: year two (times three and four)

School	Class	Whole-class liking	Asians view of Whites	Whites view of Asians	% Bullying	% Victim-ised	Asians stereotype White	Whites stereotype Asians	Prejudice
A	CGW 1	-	-	+	+	+	-	+	+
	CGW 2	+	+	+	+	-	+	+	+
	CGW 3	-	-	-	+	-	-	-	+
B	CGW 4	+	+	-	+	-	-	+	+
	CGW 5	+	-	+	+	+	-	-	+
	N.C. 1	+	-	+	+	-	+	-	+
	N.C. 2	-	-	+	+	+	-	-	=

was spent in CGW activities. They spent the largest amount of their time doing independent work.

Jane and Margie saw some good results for their class on the assessment measures (see table 6.10). Over the year there was a slight decrease in the amount of liking across the whole of the class, but across racial groups, liking had increased over the year, both for the White children liking Asian children and the Asian children liking White children.

The levels of bullying and victimisation also found a positive direction over the year in this class. There were fairly good decreases in the prevalence of both.

The optimistic pattern was upheld in the stereotyping results, with the White children's stereotyping of Asian children also seeing quite a decrease, but, sadly, there was a fair increase in the amount of stereotyping from the Asian children towards the White children. At the first phase of assessment there were three prejudiced children in their class. By the end of the year, this had reduced to none.

On the whole then, Jane and Margie had quite positive results despite the little time they spent doing CGW activities. On examination of their diary records, however, it seems that there may have been other factors at work in this classroom which served to increase the positive impact of CGW.

The experiences of implementing CGW were described by Jane and Margie in a very positive manner. Their records for the initial few weeks were non-committal, but as the year progressed their comments became increasingly more enthusiastic about CGW. They alluded to positive experiences:

> During an informal chat with Farana she said there was no longer any racist problem with Debbie. I asked what had solved the problem and Farana said that it was working in a group with Debbie the previous day.

Weeks later:

> a small group of children who would normally *hate* to work together [i.e. one child would complain vehemently] chose to cooperate on a joint project.

Many comments like the above were found in the records. An occasional negative comment arose about particular disruptive children, but these were far outweighed by positive ones.

Jane and Margie had their share of 'difficult' children, five of whom were identified using agreed criteria (see chapter eight). It could be then that their positive attitude to the value and effectiveness of CGW was indeed a factor in the promising changes in the social relationships within their class. The quality of the CGW activities may be another factor. The diary records cite a wide range of CGW activities that the children were involved in. Cooperative group work was used in the more academically taxing sessions such as sciences, mathematics, computers, understanding graphs, practical problem-solving activities such as designing machines and making hovercrafts. It was also employed in fun and art types of activities such as games, stories, music and dance. Other activities included deciding on a Diwali picture and a *Five Evil Dragons* type activity about road safety.

Margie commented that 'The children all enjoyed the work and concentrated well.' And later, 'Children [i.e. *a* child] spontaneously commented that they'd enjoyed the group work and I felt they'd worked hard.' Another factor here, then, seems to be the positive attitude of the children themselves. The average liking score for cooperative group work was, in fact, quite high in Jane and Margie's class: at 4.18 it was the second highest score in any of the classes (see table 6.9).

CGW 3: PAT

Pat spent the largest amount of her total teaching time on independent work, 35.3 per cent, but she did spend her second largest amount of teaching time, 28.7 per cent, on CGW activities.

On the whole, the results from the assessment measures were not very promising for Pat's class. There was a slight decrease over the year in the amount of liking going on across the whole of the class, although there were increases in both the Asian children's liking of White children and the White children's liking of Asian children. These were also quite substantial increases.

The levels of both bullying and victimisation were on the increase too in this class. The increase in the amount of victimisation was very slight, but the levels of bullying in Pat's class increased quite dramatically and was, in fact, the largest increase found across all the classes.

The positive trend in inter-racial liking *was* reflected in the amount of racial stereotyping occurring in Pat's classroom; she had a decrease in stereotyping for both the White children and the Asian children.

Pat also had a slight positive decrease in the numbers of prejudiced children over the year, coming down from four at the first assessment to three by the end of the year.

Pat's poor results on these assessment measures were unexpected given that she had spent quite a substantial amount of time in CGW activities. She, too, had quite a positive attitude towards CGW, but probably less so than Jane and Margie. Some of Pat's comments about the effectiveness of CGW were positive, such as: 'Children filled in a cooperative survey. They all helped each other and all the time sat together with very little fuss', and 'Thelma went into a group which did not have her main friends in for the first time'; but these were counteracted with others such as 'Cooperative group work very poor. Children really clash in group A. Delroy is so aggressive' and 'Two children suspended for aggressive behaviour on Tuesday.'

The type of CGW activities that the children in Pat's class engaged in encompassed quite a range. Her class employed CGW in science experiments and mathematics, games, arts, dance and drama activities, such as treasure hunts, making mosaics, and book reviews. Pat's class also engaged in group discussions about different types of food, issues about causes of famine and poor people in western society. Other activities included a cooperative survey and making informative posters. Many debriefing sessions were also documented.

So, if CGW, of the right kind and amount was implemented in this class, could there be other factors that militated against the effectiveness of CGW on social relationships? Pat had five 'difficult' children also in her class and it would appear from the records that some of these children were quite disruptive. They may, therefore, have had an impact on the poor results.

Did the children have a positive attitude towards CGW? From the comments the class seemed to have mixed feelings. One child was quoted as saying 'I'm glad all groups worked well', but another child said 'I'm sick of doing everything in a group. Can't I do one of my own?' One of Pat's final comments had a very mixed message: 'Children have started to say "I like my group" or "my group worked well", which is a good position to be in at last. *But* I feel they are only saying it because they think I want to hear it, even if their group hasn't got on well.' The average liking score for CGW in this class was the second lowest at 3.2.

Year one: school B

Both the teachers taking part in the project at school B were able to fill in their diary records.

CGW 4: SALLY
Sally spent her third largest amount of time on CGW activities, at 16.5 per cent. Most of her time was spent on small-group work and independent work. This was also a CGW class which came out with mixed results on the assessment measures (see table 6.10).

Over the year there was a slight decrease in liking across the whole of the class. The White children's liking of Asian classmates also decreased, although Asian children's liking for White classmates had increased by the end of the year.

The levels of bullying in Sally's class increased quite dramatically, the second largest increase in bullying across all of the classes. On a more positive note, victimisation levels saw a reasonable decrease by the end of the year.

Racial stereotyping in the class did not see a similar trend to liking scores, with the White children having a decrease in the amount of stereotyping of Asian children and the Asian children stereotyped White children more over the year.

Another poor result for this class was a large increase in the numbers of prejudiced children. At the first assessment, not one child had been identified as being prejudiced, but by the end of the year, the numbers had reached seven.

These were disappointing outcomes for Sally's class. Although the results were mixed there were more negative results than positive ones and they were of a more disturbing pattern.

On examining Sally's diary reports and her comments, it became quite clear that there were a number of factors influencing the shape of her results. The kinds of CGW activities that Sally's class engaged in were equally as varied as Jane's and Margie's class and Pat's. There were lots of science and art activities mentioned, problem solving with computers and graphs, a range of games which included circle games, 'magic microphone', jigsaws and P.E. activities. Others mentioned include making pakoras, building a mosque, brainstorming transport words, traffic surveys and playing with a parachute.

What emerged most clearly from Sally's diaries was the almost impossible time she was having trying to implement CGW in an effective way. There were some positive comments made at intervals, for example 'quite good at swapping pens during "rainbow" game' and 'cooperative "clown" game very good'. On the whole, however, Sally's diary records read like a running commentary of sometimes daily and weekly incidents of fighting and arguing in the classroom, lack of cooperation and other general difficulties. She comments 'Am finding it difficult to fit in the required amount of cooperative work as children are not getting their work done – it takes them so long to settle down and listen that we are wasting a lot of time – also children do not really listen to me explaining things as a class – they wait until we start and then come and ask me to explain it to them individually.' On another occasion she comments, 'Friday was an appalling day. Class would not cooperate with me at all.'

The fighting and arguing incidents were many and they tended to be with the same children. Sally shared (with CGW 5) the highest number of 'difficult' children, seven. This large number of disruptive children is more than likely to be a factor affecting the effective implementation of CGW.

The prevalence of these incidents, it could be argued, may also reflect the attitudes of some of the children in the class towards CGW and their willingness to engage in it. Positive recordings from the children about CGW were virtually absent from the diaries. Sally's class in fact had the lowest average liking score for CGW in that year. Both this and the diary information serve to reinforce each other.

N.C. 1: JUNE AND KAY

June's and Kay's class was required, being an N.C. class, to spend much less time in CGW activities than the CGW classes. They did, in fact, spend the least amount of their total teaching time doing CGW, at 8.6 per cent. They spent the largest amount of their time in small-group work.

June and Kay had consistently poor results on the assessment measures. The amount of liking amongst the whole class decreased slightly over the year. There was a reasonable increase in the White children's liking of the Asian children, but there was a decrease in the Asian children's liking of the White children. The White children's increased liking of Asian children was the only positive result for June's and Kay's class.

Bullying and victimisation also increased in the class. The rise in bullying was modest but the rise in victimisation was considerable, the largest increase in the prevalence of victimisation out of all the classes.

Stereotyping had increased, also, quite substantially in the case of White children's stereotyping of Asian children. But, for the Asian children's stereotyping of the White children, there was a slight decrease.

One measure of social relationships that remained stable was the levels of prejudice in the classroom. At the first assessment the number of prejudiced children was three and it remained as three at the end of the year.

These results were particularly poor even though some amount of CGW was implemented in this class. What were the factors in this class that were militating against the effectiveness of CGW? Were they similar to the ones in the CGW classes so far or were they perhaps different ones?

In terms of the type of CGW activities that the children in June's and

Kay's class were engaged in, again there was much the same variation, although obviously less of it – science, computer activities, maths and graph activities, which included graphing personal data. The rainbow game cropped up again and many other games involving numbers, measurements and words. Other CGW activities included music, problem-solving activities, reading, listening and discussing stories on tapes, working on the nativity play, mosque game and testing cars.

June's and Kay's diary records were detailed. However, they offered descriptive ones rather than interpretations, good information about what activities the children did in their groups, but little information on feelings associated with how well it had gone.

An occasional comment was documented which highlighted both positive and negative incidents. It was commented, 'One group of four worked very well together' and 'Class cooperation much better.' An encouraging comment was made about an activity involving measuring fingers, 'This seemed to work quite well with children helping each other, except for one group...'

On a negative note, 'joint games activities with 4B is proving difficult. There seems to be friction between certain members from each class resulting in aggressive behaviour.' The cited class 4B is Sally's class which serves to reinforce further her diary experiences. Another comment about particular children went 'Rebecca and Carl could not cope. After fifteen minutes Carl joined in, Rebecca refused.'

Finally, a comment was made which perhaps did reflect a certain reticence about the effectiveness of CGW or a low level of commitment on their part. It concerned the activity of brainstorming ideas on water, whereby one child acts as 'scribe' and the others offer information 'Whenever this type of group work is undertaken there are *always* those who will not "fit in" any of the groups.'

The number of 'difficult' children was low at 3, so it seems unlikely that the poor results were a consequence of this. Possibly, a larger amount of time spent in CGW would have helped improve relationships in this class.

Year one: school C

Three of the four teachers from school C were able to fill in their diary records, two CGW classes and one N.C. class.

CGW 5: ANN
Ann reported spending most of her time, 42.4 per cent, in CGW activities.

Some positive and negative results were found in this class. Liking across the whole of the class decreased slightly over the year. The amount the Asian children liked the White children did show a slight increase by the end of the year, but the White children's liking of the Asian children showed a slight decrease.

This class had good results on the bullying and victimisation measures; it had the greatest decreases in the prevalence of both bullying and victimisation out of all the other classes.

The results for stereotyping were encouraging. The White children's stereotyping of the Asian children decreased slightly, but there was a much greater decrease in stereotyping of White children by the Asian children.

Another good result was the reduced level of prejudice in the classroom. The numbers of prejudiced children had dropped from five at the initial assessment to only two at the end of the year.

Ann spent a great deal of time working in CGW groups. On examining her diary records it was also clear what a variety of activities her class had been involved in. Her diary records were extremely detailed, each activity or session of CGW being described clearly. Her sessions included numerous games, adjective name games, alphabet games, science activities including one about floating and sinking, art activities, dancing, P.E., making story wheels, designing Joseph's coat, activities about safe driving, safety signs and the Green Cross Code, maths games, making bar charts, designing posters, brainstorming, and many discussions and debriefing sessions.

Her recordings were very descriptive and there were few comments about how things had gone, but it was quite clear that Ann had gone about implementing CGW in her classroom in a very serious and committed way. She made very few comments about negative incidents, but she did have a bad time in a country dancing session when she comments, 'Awful, will not hold hands!!!'

The children themselves seemed to respond positively to the CGW activities and games. They appeared particularly to enjoy the maths games and Ann comments 'Maths games – variety of number-based games. Very popular. If a group thinks they are missing games they become very argumentative.' Further comments about the children's feelings were found in a debriefing session where she comments, 'talked about why they were working in groups and how they felt about it. Concentrated on the negatives although there weren't many. Most of the class thought group work was a good idea. After that continued with story wheels. Class worked 100 per cent better than day before.'

Generally Ann had a reasonably good experience with little disruption or confrontation. Given that she had seven 'difficult' children in her class, one might have expected a much more negative response to CGW, making it difficult for Ann to implement it effectively and possibly leading to poorer results. There was no sign of this from the diary recordings; also, the average liking for CGW was at its highest in this class at 4.7. It would appear that the amount of time spent in CGW and the commitment with which it was implemented were positive factors, which might have had greater positive impact on social relationships in this classroom had there been fewer 'difficult' children.

CGW 6: JUDY

The total amount of classroom teaching time which Judy spent in CGW activities was 42.0 per cent. This was the largest amount of time that she spent in any of the activities.

There was a substantial increase in the amount of liking across the whole of the class. For the White children, the amount that they liked the Asian children increased quite well over the year. Amongst the Asian children, however, their liking of the White children saw a similar sized decrease.

The levels of bullying in Judy's class had decreased quite substantially over the year. Victimisation did not follow the same pattern, however, with a marginal increase.

On the stereotypes measure, the extent to which the Asian children stereotyped the White children increased quite considerably; for the White children, their stereotyping of the Asian children decreased slightly over the year.

The prevalence of prejudice saw a positive trend with the numbers of prejudiced children being two at the initial assessment and only one at the end of the year.

Judy's results on the whole were promising. On examining her diary records, it would seem that the CGW activities that she engaged her class in covered quite a varied range. They included science experiments and maths games, quizzes, games such as *Rabbits*, coo-ee and the Perfus exercise, problem-solving tasks, arts and dance, P.E., activities of expression, for example 'I just want to say.' The parachute game cropped up again and so did circle games.

Further examination of her diary records showed that Judy had a reasonably positive attitude to CGW. Although occasionally she would report that a particular activity had not gone so well and described arguments and clashes with particular children, most of her comments are about positive outcomes of CGW. She comments 'The children seem to be getting better at co-op games, although Dean is still frequently silly and is excluded.' Her succession of comments thereafter give an impression of increasing cooperation. Comments such as 'The children have worked well this week with no "incidents" I can recall. I think this is probably due to the fact that the groups have been self-chosen' and 'The children are getting more used to helping each other.' In reference to a particular child she comments 'Anna seems to have settled down to work and is far less disruptive now than I ever imagined possible.' She did hit a bad patch subsequently where for about two weeks she seemed to spend most of her time rearranging the groups. One of her final comments, however, concluded her diary reports on a hopeful note: 'Group work does still appear to be working well but only when avoiding personality clashes.'

Throughout the diaries there are few reports of negative responses to CGW from the children themselves. The average liking score for CGW, at 3.86, was around average (table 6.10).

It would seem that for this class one influential factor could be the amount of time Judy spent in CGW activities. Also, Judy had only two 'difficult' children in her class, so maybe she also found it relatively easy to implement CGW effectively. But it is also clear that she avoided too many 'problems' by sometimes allowing children to choose their own groups, which, if done often, would defeat the objectives of CGW.

N.C. 2: LORRAINE

Lorraine was the N.C. class teacher at school C who was able to offer detailed diary reports. Again, not expecting her to have spent very much of her time in CGW activities, this was verified with only 13.4 per cent of her total teaching time being spent in CGW. (Though this did exceed the amount in Margie and Jane's class in School A!)

The average liking for Lorraine's class showed a marginal decrease by the end of the year. The Asian children's liking of the White children showed a slight increase over the year, but the White children's liking of the Asian children showed a decrease of a similar size.

The bullying and victimisation levels in Lorraine's class did not change dramatically over the year. The prevalence of bullying in this class did decrease slightly and there was a marginal increase in the levels of victimisation over the year.

There was a reasonable increase in the level of stereotyping of Asian children by the White children over the year. The levels of stereotyping of White children by Asian children remained constant at both assessment times. However, the prejudice levels in this class also increased over the year. Lorraine had three prejudiced children in her class at the initial assessment but this had doubled to six by the end of the year.

It was difficult from Lorraine's diaries to get a reasonable picture of what was going on in her classroom. Her diary recordings were extremely sparse. Although she would write in the number of hours she had spent in different activities any particular week, often there was no entry in the comments section.

There were a small handful of CGW activities recorded. Computers were mentioned, P.E., activity games, science experiment and a decision about chips in a jar. These activities were not broken down any further. Lorraine did spend 13.4 per cent of her time in CGW activities so there must have been others which she did not record.

There were five 'difficult' children in Lorraine's class. She did make a few comments about particular children in her class who were quite disruptive, in particular, Tariq, Jack and Darren. She comments that they found it difficult to concentrate and twice mentioned that their behaviour involved spitting, flicking heads and flicking plasticine. Also, Tariq had a tendency to run out of school and head for home from time to time. These incidents must have made it difficult for Lorraine at times to work on social relationships in her classroom.

Year two: school A

The three CGW classes from school A were all able to fill in their diary records, again some in more detail than others.

CGW 1: PAT

Pat spent a reasonable amount of her total teaching time doing CGW activities, 27.9 per cent, the second largest amount of time she spent in any activity. But again in this second year she did not see very good results on the assessment measures for her class (see table 6.11).

The amount of liking across the whole class decreased by the end of the year. There was also a substantial decrease in the amount that the Asian children liked the White children, although the White children's liking of the Asian children did show a slight increase.

The changes in the levels of bullying and victimisation in this class were also disappointing. By the end of the year there was an increase in the prevalence of bullying in her class and also a considerable increase in levels of victimisation.

The racial stereotyping results in Pat's class were mixed, with a slight decrease in the amount the Asian children stereotyped the White children, but a slight increase in the amount the White children stereotyped the Asian children. At the time of the first assessment Pat had two prejudiced children in her class and by the end of the year this had doubled to four.

On examining Pat's diary records it was clear it was not easy to use them to clarify these poor outcomes. There was an absence of positive or negative comments about incidents which occurred as a consequence of implementing CGW, or the attitude and feelings of herself and the children in her class. However, in the previous year's diary records Pat's attitude came across as fairly positive towards CGW and spent a good amount of time in a varied range of CGW activities. Possibly because the teachers were required to fill in their diaries less often in the second year, the more limited recordings did not reflect what she actually did in a particular week.

There were five 'difficult' children in Pat's class again which may have militated against her results, but, also, the responses of some of the children towards CGW may not have been favourable. Although the diary records cannot corroborate this, Pat's class score for liking of CGW at 2.76 was the lowest of all the classes, in both years, and indicates an overall dislike for CGW.

CGW 2: JANE

Whilst most classes had either poor or mediocre results on most assessment measures, Jane's class did very well. She spent most of her total teaching time in CGW activities at 28.5 per cent.

Liking increased in Jane's class, both amongst the whole class, slightly, and between racial groups. The White children's liking of Asian children increased only slightly, but there was quite a big increase for the Asian children's liking of the White children.

There was an increase in levels of bullying by the end of the year, but this was slight. However, there was a decrease in the levels of victimisation which was quite substantial, being the largest out of all the classes.

The positive trend, however, did not continue in Jane's class with the stereotyping data. There was a slight increase in the amount that the White children were stereotyping the Asian children and a substantial increase in the amount that the Asian children stereotyped the White children. There was also an increase in the number of prejudiced children from four to eight.

Jane spent a reasonable proportion of her teaching time implementing CGW activities, which would be one factor influencing her promising results. Were there any others which could be gleaned from her diary records?

The diary records certainly describe a good range of CGW activities being engaged in. Jane involved her class in experiments designing cogs and belts, lots of games including maths games, quizzes, puzzles, a snakes and ladders game based on ordnance survey signs on maps, word games, lots of model making, geographical exercises which included making a group booklet on a chosen country, video and discussion sessions, and cooking in groups. Also trips to the Botanical Gardens which involved identifying flowers and plants, and painting and sketching areas.

Although Jane's diary records were descriptive rather than analytic about the CGW activities, it would seem that most of the children responded positively to CGW. Jane comments 'Trying to finish "Jolly Christmas Postman" in groups. Still not quite finished but children still enjoying the activity.' Also, the average liking score for CGW was the second largest at 3.75 in this class. The occasions when she mentioned a problem involved particular children and were not aggressive incidents. For example, she comments 'Charles refused to join group' and 'Alan unwilling but eventually joined in.'

On the whole Jane appeared to have a relatively good experience with implementing CGW activities. There is little evidence to the contrary. The number of 'difficult' children in her class was low at three, which would have helped activities to run fairly smoothly.

CGW 3: MARGIE

Margie spent only 12.5 per cent of her total teaching time in CGW; most of her time was spent doing independent work (table 6.11).

The results for her class were generally discouraging. Liking across the whole class decreased slightly by the end of the year; so, also, did White children's liking of the Asian children, if only marginally, and Asian children's liking of the White children.

The levels of bullying increased in Margie's class, although only slightly. However, by the end of the year there was an appreciable decrease in the levels of victimisation within her class.

The amount of racial stereotyping decreased over the year; marginally for the Asian children stereotyping White children but more markedly for the White children stereotyping Asian children. At the beginning of the year the number of prejudiced children in the class was only one but by the end of the year it had increased to four.

Margie filled in her diary records in quite a detailed way, describing both the CGW activities her class engaged in and associated incidents. She described a reasonable range of activities, although perhaps not as extensive as that of teachers in the other CGW classes. These included maths, learning times tables, interviewing in groups, making sculptures and 3D models, making booklets, quizzes, various games, working out a music rhythm and working on an accompaniment to a song, and also various discussions entailing decisions and solutions.

It is quite possible that the small amount of time that Margie spent doing CGW could be one militating factor in its lack of effectiveness on social relationships in her class. Margie's approach to CGW and its principles seemed on the whole fairly positive from the comments in her diary records. She began one entry with 'Felt pleased that the group work was easier going than last year' and, later on, 'With my next group I am thinking: it's good to have an introductory activity to "bond" the group. It's good to have lots of opportunities for them to take pride in their groups achievements.' It would appear, also, that most of the children in Margie's class liked doing CGW as she had the highest average score for liking of CGW out of all the other classes.

However, it is also true that Margie had some problematic children and she had troublesome incidents to deal with. She commented very early on in the diaries: 'A dreadful day! All tired and fractious. Children tipped over tables/chairs, etc. Horrible atmosphere and no co-op feelings even though we played a few class games together.' A little later 'Thelma "blew" upturning tables, chairs, steel drums, etc. and the class stayed very calm but showed their upset by very unco-op behaviour towards each other and me in the afternoon.' Margie had four 'difficult' children in her class and her records illuminate the impact that they can have on the whole class at times.

Year two: school B

All four classes at school B were able to fill in their diary records, although the teachers from the two CGW classes recorded much more detailed information about the activities they engaged in and the experiences that they had in implementing CGW.

CGW 4: SALLY

Sally had a CGW class again in year two. She spent a little less time engaging in CGW activities than she had done in year one. She spent the largest part of her total teaching time in small-group work and teaching time in CGW was her third largest amount at 14.9 per cent.

Sally's class results were again quite mixed, seeing both positive and negative outcomes. Liking across the whole class increased slightly by the end of the year. The amount the Asian children liked the White children increasing slightly, but the amount the White children liked the Asian children decreasing slightly.

The bullying levels in this class were not altogether encouraging either. By the end of the year the prevalence of bullying increased considerably. However, the victimisation levels in Sally's class had decreased substantially by the end of the year.

In the stereotyping results, the Asian children were stereotyping the White children less by the end of the year and the White children were stereotyping the Asian children more, although both were only slight changes. As in the previous year the number of prejudiced children increased in Sally's class, this time from six to eleven.

Sally's experiences with implementing CGW seemed much the same as the year before, although not quite so fraught with continuous negative incidents. Her references to the actual CGW activities that were engaged in were not abundant. The few that were mentioned included drama, games, spelling workshop, throwing and tennis, and matching pictures or signs to speech bubbles which was a kind of verbal communication exercise. One comment that she made early on reflected both the difficulties and her feelings towards them: 'Class are being very awkward at moment. They are extremely uncooperative with me e.g. lining up for assembly, putting things away. I must sort this out. I am not in the right frame of mind for cooperative work at moment – the class is irritating me. Nobody does anything drastic but it is not good at moment.' She did also mention an occasional good experience: 'Cooperation going on most of the day by some of class. Lots of cooperating to get work finished before holidays' and, a few months later, 'Much of work is now done cooperatively in Maths and other subjects although it is not specifically set up like this . . . more difficult to get individual work from them now.'

There was little reference to how the children on the whole responded to CGW in this class. They had a mean score for liking of CGW of 3.57, a fairly average score.

On the whole Sally's most prominent difficulties seemed to be with particular disruptive children. She had four 'difficult' children in her class whom she referred to from time to time: 'Jonah has been in trouble again this week. He hit Lara during craft work.' Even outside the classroom, 'Keith, Hafeez, Douglas and Jonah in bother with dinner lady in games room', and 'Child in Joe's class reported that Douglas had put a coat down a toilet last week. [The head] confronted Douglas about this and he admitted five other occasions.'

CGW 5: JOE

Joe spent most of his time in individual work, but a substantial amount, 21.7 per cent, of his teaching time was in CGW activities. However, there was not much impact on social relationships, the class results being quite mixed.

Across the whole of the class the amount of liking increased slightly, as also for the White children's liking of the Asian children. However, the Asian children's liking of the White children showed a slight decrease at the end of the year.

There were poor results for bullying and victimisation levels in this class. There was the largest increase in bullying out of all the classes, almost doubling by the end of the year. The increase in levels of victimisation was also substantial, more than doubling by the end of the year.

There was a marginal decrease in the amount the White children stereotyped Asian children and a slight increase in the amount that the Asian children stereotyped White children. The number of prejudiced children in the class was stable, starting the year with seven children and ending it with seven.

Joe was able to complete lengthy and detailed diary records. The range of CGW activities that he covered in his class was quite impressive. After one weeks detailed listings of CGW sessions he comments 'What a lot of CGW! Is this just an anomaly or is it becoming truly co-operative?' His class activities included maths and maths games, making tally charts and graphs from personal information, various science experiments, singing rounds, using percussion instruments, drama, P.E. including game skills, team games and a 'blindfold trust game' around obstacles, story sequencing, brainstorming words and putting together an oral story, group comprehension, survey and research work, problem-solving activities, and building models. They also engaged in discussion and report back sessions.

So, with a reasonable amount of time spent in CGW and a good range of CGW activities being implemented there must have been some other factors militating against it having a positive impact on social relationships. Did Joe implement CGW in an effective way?

In terms of Joe's approach to CGW he seemed quite positive on the whole, but also very realistic about some of the restrictions he was facing. He comments: 'Finding it quite difficult to find time to plan specific CGW activities within day-to-day class work except in areas like P.E., drama, music. Other activities are more likely to be *ad hoc*, "on the spot" ideas. Hopefully a day can be arranged soon so that Sally and I can get together to plan a little more coherently. Supply cover availability is a major problem.' A comment he made about one negative incident when playing team games also reflected this awareness. The incident involved a considerable degree of intolerance by the children with team members who made mistakes and opponents who acccidentally clashed or bumped. On discussing the issue with the children, Joe comments 'I see a long road ahead.'

As far as the children's attitude was concerned there were quite a few comments about them enjoying certain activities. Comments were documented such as 'Parachute hugely enjoyed and very effective' and about a team game involving passing a ball through the legs and over the head: 'Group ethic began to develop – desire to "do it properly" was evident.' There were negative comments also. About a task which involved building a vehicle Joe comments about a particular group, 'Try to work together but can't' and a comment about the make-up of free-choice groups, 'All other groupings were single sex and racial groupings also very obvious.'

This class had an average liking score for CGW of 3.64: the median score out of all the classes in this second year. There were three 'difficult' children in Joe's class which is not many. There were few comments about particular children being problematic.

It is difficult to see what could be a major factor in the poor assessment results in this class. Given Joe's initial comment about the difficulty in planning, one explanation could lie in the issue of quality of CGW and not necessarily in its quantity.

N.C. 1: KIM

Kim spent only 6.6 per cent of her total teaching time in CGW, the least time in any activity. Most of her time was spent in independent work.

The assessment results were not especially encouraging. By the end of the year liking across the whole of the class had decreased, albeit slightly. There was a slight increase in the amount that the White children liked the Asian children, but a slight decrease in the amount that the Asian children liked the White children.

The bullying and victimisation results were also mixed. By the end of the year levels of bullying in Kim's class had increased slightly, but victimisation levels showed a slight decrease.

The degree to which White children stereotyped Asian children showed a slight decrease. But unfortunately the Asian children's stereotyping of the White children showed a good increase. However, there was a large increase in the numbers of prejudiced children over the year, starting with three and finishing with nine.

Kim hardly provided any comments in her diary records. However, she had seven 'difficult' children in her class, a large number: this would surely contribute to difficulties in improving social relationships.

N.C. 2: JUNE/KAY

In year two June and Kay taught an N.C. class again. This year they spent 7.95 per cent, slightly less of their total teaching time engaged in CGW activities than in the previous year. The assessment results from this class proved to be generally poor.

The overall liking in June and Kay's class showed a slight decrease at the end of the year, as did the Asian children's liking of the White children; however, the White children's liking of Asian children did show a slight increase.

The prevalence of bullying and victimisation was also greater by the end of the year. There was a substantial increase in bullying in the class, the second largest in the year. The prevalence of victimisation in this class showed a very large increase from 16.6 per cent to 44.3 per cent, the greatest of all the classes.

Both the White children's stereotyping of the Asian children and the Asian children's stereotyping of the White children saw good decreases by the end of the year. The levels of prejudice in this class were stable with the number of prejudiced children starting at four at the first assessment and remaining at four by the end of the year.

The diaries that June and Kay kept were slightly better documented than Kim's although virtually all entries were about the activities they engaged in and not about their experiences. The few documented activities in these diaries included, rehearsing for the Nativity play, a trail at the Botanical Gardens, which entailed children in groups being given photographs and a map and they had to find out where the photograph was taken and mark it on the map, sending messages and communications, finding routes by road, sea and air, from Sheffield to Karachi, writing about photographs from Pakistan, colour mixing, 'rainbow' game, computer activity called 'through the dragon's eye', and deduction activities.

One comment seemed positive but had conflicting messages. Three boys, Ricky, Hassan and Nick, were playing on a karate computer game, by choice, one lunchtime. They had had trouble working out which key to use for kick, jump, punch, left, right, etc. They were working together and helping each other, then one of them commented 'We know how to fight!'

There was only one 'difficult' child in this class, the lowest number of all classes in both years. It is certainly possible that more CGW might have had a positive impact on the very negative outcomes of this class.

Conclusions

By and large, the quantitative assessments did not reveal significant effects of the CGW curriculum on our measures of social relationships, as compared with the N.C. classes. Specifically, there was no clear impact on helping rejected or neglected children, or improving the behaviour of bullies, or reducing stereotyped attitudes or ethnic prejudice. There was, however, some indication, especially in year two, that the CGW curriculum had helped some children, perceived as victims of bullying by classmates, to escape from this status; and that this was more marked than in the N.C. classes.

Why had there been this general lack of impact? In certain cases – for example Margie in both years one and two – a teacher did not spend as much time as hoped implementing CGW activities. These hesitations and reservations were also documented in chapter five. Another factor may be the number of 'difficult' children in many of the classes, whose resistance to CGW compounded the difficulties which these teachers – less experienced with CGW work than those in our first study – were finding in trying to use the procedures. We look further at the responses of individual children to group work, in the next chapter.

CHAPTER SEVEN: Individual differences and case studies of children

In this chapter we take a closer look at the children's perceptions of CGW. First, we listen to children as they recount their experience of and express their opinions on CGW. From this we gain access to the inside perspective on CGW from the point of view of those who took part and we hear, in the words of the children, how it may have affected their relationships in the class. Second, we present case studies of children who are experiencing particular interpersonal problems at school. The focus here is on children who bully, children who are victimised and children who are not involved directly in bullying.

These were difficult classes and with a number of quite disturbed children. This could make cooperation outside normal friendship groupings very demanding and could undo some of the anticipated benefits. The children were interviewed in groups of their own choice at the end of the two years about their experience of CGW and how they valued it in terms of learning and in terms of enhancing relationships within the class. Varying as they did in their opinion of CGW, the groups were categorised as follows – those who were unconditionally in favour; those who liked CGW but only within same sex or same race groups; and those who disliked it.

Children who liked CGW

George, a White boy, Arthur, a mixed-race boy, Jilly, a White girl and Sita, an Asian girl formed a very cohesive mixed-gender, mixed-race group who had become friends through being placed together by Sally, their teacher. It was clear that relationships were good within the group, expressed through friendly banter and good humour. They were all enthusiastic about their experience of CGW which they liked because:

> 'There are a lot of laughs.'
> 'We work well as a team.'

They were united in the view that their teacher had done the right thing by deliberately mixing up the groups in a way that crossed barriers of race and gender and they all said that she should adopt the same policy next year. As Arthur said: 'If I were a teacher, I'd mix them up.' Sita confirmed this through her own personal experience:

> 'I am the only Indian in this year group...so for me it has been important to make friends and to learn about other people.'

A friendship group of Asian boys expressed the same approval of Sally's policy. They were open about the fact that, by working in this way, they had had to come to terms with working with people whom they would not normally have chosen: 'Some people you might not like. I don't like Hafeez but I have to work with him.' In fact, they had found: 'It's all right when you work with other people. When you get used to them they are all right.' There had been conflicts in their group but they agreed that it was important to stay with them and try to work through them. Racism was hard to deal with and they were aware that it could be difficult to change entrenched attitudes:

> *Nadeem:* Sometimes there are people who are racist who say 'Nigger!' in the groups. If they're not racist and if they work properly, then that's all right.
> *Helen Cowie:* Might some of the racist children learn to be different if they worked in groups and got to know you?
> *Nadeem:* No, because they're nasty.

Despite such difficulties they were strongly in favour of working outside friendship groups and had developed a supportive stance amongst one another. They had no difficulty in offering positive comments towards one another.

Another group of boys stated that CGW had strengthened their friendship towards one another. They had also got to know other children very well and they spontaneously mentioned both boys and girls as friends who were Asian, Afro-Caribbean, White. They admitted that conflicts arose during CGW and that, if the task was not challenging enough or where there were too few aspects to the task for everyone to be engaged, then CGW could be frustrating. At the same time, they were unanimous in the view that it is important to work outside friendship groups in order to get to know a wider range of children: 'It's like teacher is making everybody be friends.' They also made the point that, if a person has a talent, they will be in demand: 'We don't care if they're Black or White!'

Similarly, Jason (mixed race), Jay (White), Cecile (African-Caribbean) and Sorbia (Asian) were extremely positive about CGW:

'You get to work together a lot.'
'You can concentrate better.'

They were adamant that CGW had an important part to play in enhancing friendships within the class:

'Yes, it works. It [CGW] has helped us to work together better.' (Sorbia)
'You're learning to work with other children.' (Cecile)
'Yes, we mix in.' (Jason)
'Because it's like any coloured children are just the same as any other person. It's just that they are another colour. They are just the same as White.' (Jay)

There was a friendly atmosphere in this group and they found it easy to give and take feedback from one another. They were comfortable about sharing positive things about one another and each child seemed confident in his or her abilities.

Another group of friends – Elijah (African-Caribbean), Nathan (White), David (African-Caribbean) and Hannah (White) – who had got to know one another through CGW praised the method highly:

'It's a good way to communicate.'
'We can get our work done a lot quicker.'
'You can put two brains together.'

They were aware of the conflicts that can occur in groups and did not like the 'fighting, punching and kicking' which could occur in groups but saw CGW as a way of helping people to work through differences. Within their own group they had no difficulty in finding supportive and positive things to say about one another:

'She tells you the answer.'
'She will pass the ball to you.'
'He is kind and thoughtful.'
'He is a good friend.'
'He smiles and plays with people.'

They affirmed the value of the friendships which they had formed through the process of working together and, as a group, they expressed their outrage at the bullying which they had observed in other classes.

This view was also shared by four girls – Nadine (Asian), Cath (White), Janice (White) and Nimo (Asian) – who liked CGW because 'you learn a lot' and 'you get on with each other'. They were aware of the arguments which sometimes occur but seemed to think that they had learned to work through these conflicts and that they were less frequent: 'We are better at dealing with them.' They noted a particular benefit to Nimo, a newcomer to the class, who had found it easy to make friends and said that 'it was a good thing that teacher [Jane] had mixed up the groups'. Janice listened and said thoughtfully:

> Most times when you've got White children in with other White children they tend to fight [with newcomers like Nimo] but if you've got others mixed they don't tend to fight. They just try and learn what the others do.

Cath added:

> There's a lot of Muslim children and White children and Yemeni children in the year fours and year fives, and if they're all mixed together they *can* make friends with each other.

Finally, Yussef, Alex and Jamie – three friends – expressed their enthusiasm for CGW:

> 'We got to know people in us groups a bit better – people we didn't know very well.'
> 'We learned about how they liked to work and whether they liked to work in groups.'

They were aware of some bad things about working in groups:

> 'Sometimes people beat you up and call you names.'
> 'Some groups don't work very well.'
> 'Some people won't do any work. No, they leave it for other people to do.'
> 'If someone wants to do work and they don't want to, they leave it to the person who wants to work.'

They thought that this would be less likely to happen in groups where people are already friends and who would be more likely to share things out. However, they agreed that they had actually become friends with people whom they would not otherwise have had the chance to get to know well. When they reflected on working with girls they cautiously admitted that 'some girls' can be good as group members. They had begun to like Mandy 'a little bit' and Sofina was useful because 'you can ask her for words'. They all agreed that it was good to mix children of different ethnic backgrounds and proudly shared their own different origins:

> *Yussef:* I'm part Scottish, part Irish, part Arabic.
> *Jamie:* I'm part Scottish.
> *Alex:* (whispers) I'm half-caste.
> *H.C.:* (softly) You're mixed-race . . .
> *Alex:* (in a louder voice, smiling) I'm Jamaican.

They ended by affirming their feelings of regard for one another.

Children who liked CGW but only within certain groupings

Saima, Sofina, Shabina and Nazia (Asian girls) were very friendly with one another outside school and formed a close-knit group in school. Outside friendship groups they said:

> 'You act mardy and you scribble on your work. You argue with the boys and they get right cross.'
> 'When the boys tell you what to do, you've got to put up with it.'

They missed the support of their friendship group and had not found that they made special friends. Sofina's statement 'I don't like boys' was echoed with approval by all the other members of this group.

However, very cautiously they admitted that they had got to know some girls through the CGW policy and they did recommend that their teacher (Sally) do the same again next year. The impression from this group of friends was that the personal qualities which they valued – 'being shy and kind', 'being friendly', 'being helpful' – could be overshadowed in some groups. They seemed to rely very much on the support of their own friendship groups and would need help in gaining the confidence to branch out into new kinds of relationships in groups.

In the same way a group of Asian boys preferred to work with one another. They too were a close-knit group who played together, liked to work together, met at break time, went to the same mosque and lived near one another. Two of them (Kelash and Saleem) came from neighbouring villages in Pakistan. They were nervous of the conflicts and about the fact that 'other people do not always listen to your ideas'. They had particular difficulty in working with girls: 'You can't talk with them because you get teased by your friends.' The only solution to this problem that they could see was 'You don't sit with them!' But with boys they were more at ease and in that case welcomed the opportunity to work outside friendship groups. As Kelash said:

> 'I made friends with George. Now me and George work together in Maths.' (Later this led him to defend George when a fight broke out in the playground.)

They certainly liked the values promoted by CGW and were cautiously in favour of it.

Nasreen, Shaista and Shabina made a similar point. They liked group work but only when in their own friendship groups because: 'You always got your best friend to rely on. I don't like it if she's not here.' In CGW groups they were not happy because: 'It's not really good without your best friend.' They would consider working with some other girls – Cath, Janice and Nimo – but they did not like working with boys:

> 'Not unless they're sensible like Phillip. But they're really noisy. All the boys are not really bothered.'

However, they did say that they had made friends through CGW. One said:

> 'Girls are normal, boys are funny. I've got used to Black people. Before I was used to White and Asian.'

Children in this category tended to be in same-race, same-gender groups. There were shy children who were understandably nervous about working closely with other children who could domineer or be nasty to them.

Children who did not like CGW

Most of the groups with a strong antipathy to CGW were made up of boys, often very domineering or aggressive boys. In one group of boys – Delroy, Seth and Joshua – they were very conscious that they were all Afro-Caribbean. On balance they did not like CGW:

> 'I don't like it when I'm not with my friends. I'm bored.' (Joshua)
> 'When you've got other people it gets on your nerves. You've got other

people you don't play with. We're really good friends so we like to be together, we like to sit together, we like to work together, we like to do all sorts together, we're best friends ... When teacher picked groups we can't pick groups. She picks groups. She like gives us White people and when teacher picking groups she never picks me and Joshua ... She picked me to be really last. She always puts me with other people who I don't like but she won't put me with my best friends. She says I'll mess about.' (Delroy)
'When Miss was picking groups I said to go with Joshua and Delroy and Miss changed it and I were put with Katy and Ralph.' (Seth)
(*H.C.:* Do you think that by working with White children and Asian children you actually get to know them better, get to like them?)
'There's only two White people I like in our class. Two White people in our class.' (Delroy)
'I like only one.' (Joshua)
'These are all the friends we like. We like Seth, we like Joshua, we like Olivia, you know.' (Delroy)
(*H.C.:* Well, so that's who you are most friendly with, with Black children. Is that what you mean?)
'Most of our friends are Black.' (Joshua)

Should your teacher work in this way next year?

'No!' (Joshua)
'I think we should pick who we want to sit with.' (Delroy)
'I think we should pick who we want to be with.' (Seth)
'We're all Black people; we're cast as one.' (Delroy)

Brian and Sean, both White boys, expressed a strong dislike for CGW, in particular because it involved working in multi-ethnic groups.

Brian: (contemptuously) Pakistanis!
Sean: They're Charlies, Pakistanis. You get 'em, you pick 'em up, you put 'em there. Get Black people, put 'em in there (gestures); get White people, put 'em there (gestures). Give 'em a stir; put them in groups, then chuck 'em in the air. [inaudible comment] We've not got a Black person in our group!
Brian: We have! Alex! [a mixed-race boy]
Sean: It's all right working Black and White, but not Pakistanis.
Brian: Looks like White people have been in the sun a right long time and Black people, they're like White people who's been in t'oven. [laughs]
H.C.: What do you mean?
Sean: What we're trying to say is get the charlies, put 'em on your foot and kick 'em back to cha-cha land. [he and Brian laugh uncontrollably]

Which children like and which dislike group work

Our qualitative data on feelings about group work led us back to some further quantitative analyses. We decided to look further at children's liking of CGW and its relationship with bully or victim status and with sociometric status. Most of the children in the CGW classes (85 in year one and 93 in year two of the project) were interviewed individually at

Table 7.1 Percentage of boys and girls of different sociometric status types, by different degrees of liking for CGW

BOYS YEAR 1	POPULAR (n=10)	AVERAGE+ OTHER (n=18)	REJECTED+ CONTROVERSIAL (n=15)
dislike a lot	10	6	27
dislike a bit/ neutral	30	11	20
like/like a lot	60	83	53

GIRLS YEAR 1	POPULAR (n=12)	AVERAGE+ OTHER (n=18)	REJECTED+ CONTROVERSIAL (n=12)
dislike a lot	0	6	0
dislike a bit/ neutral	42	22	42
like/like a lot	58	72	58

BOYS YEAR 2	POPULAR (n=11)	AVERAGE+ OTHER (n=22)	REJECTED+ CONTROVERSIAL (n=22)
dislike a lot	18	27	50
dislike a bit/ neutral	0	5	23
like/like a lot	82	68	27

GIRLS YEAR 2	POPULAR (n=11)	AVERAGE+ OTHER (n=18)	REJECTED+ CONTROVERSIAL (n=9)
dislike a lot	18	11	0
dislike a bit/ neutral	18	28	22
like/like a lot	64	61	78

the end of each year about their liking of CGW. Their answers were rated on a 5-point scale from 1 (dislike a lot), 3 (neutral) to 5 (like a lot). Table 7.1 shows that most children like CGW (65 per cent for the first year and 60 per cent for the second year) but a clear minority strongly dislike it.

Who dislikes CGW most? The figures in table 7.1 are also broken down by the main sociometric status types, comparing popular children, average plus other, and rejected plus controversial (there were very few neglected children – four in the first year, two in the second year), so these are not included here. As can be seen, popular children tend to be more favourable to group work, and rejected and controversial children less favourable; but this generalisation is much more true of boys, than of girls. On an analysis of variance, the interaction of gender with sociometric status on liking scores, while not significant in year one, is significant in year two, $F_{(2,89)}=4.8$, $p<.01$.

We found a very consistent trend for both years when we compared children who bully others a lot (bullies and bully-victims) with the rest (children not often involved in bullying) Whereas most children like CGW, some bully and bully-victim children dislike it strongly (on chi-squared tests, first year $X^2=12.0$, $p<.005$; second year $X^2=5.67$, $p<.06$; see table 7.2).

The negative effect which some children perceived as bullies could have on cooperative groups came out strongly from interviews: Lianne, a bully, had nothing good to say about CGW: she disliked it and she

Table 7.2 Percentage of bully and bully-victim children (those who bully others) compared to the rest (those who do not bully others) by different degrees of liking for CGW

YEAR 1	BULLY OTHERS (n=26)	THE REST (n=59)	TOTAL (n=85)
dislike a lot	23	2	8
dislike a bit/ neutral	15	32	27
like/like a lot	62	66	65

YEAR 2	BULLY OTHERS (n=39)	THE REST (n=54)	TOTAL (n=93)
dislike a lot	33	17	24
dislike a bit/ neutral	21	13	16
like/like a lot	46	70	60

did not think that her teacher should use it in the following year. Her peers in the group found it a trial to cope with her because 'she always fights with everybody and she thumps'. Sarah, a bully, said that she disliked CGW because 'it is difficult if you have to work with people you're not used to'. Yasser pointed out that CGW was a good way of working except when you had Sean, a bully, in your group. 'He is bad in a group. He kicks you under the table. Everybody's scared of Sean because he beats them up.' Sean was even more critical of fellow members of his group. 'They smell! This kid Jamie that I work with, he spoils ozone layer. He don't brush his teeth. I don't like him.'

Some of the bullies seemed to resent the fact that they had no say in selecting the working groups.

> 'When teacher picks groups *we* can't pick groups. *She* picks groups. She gives us White people and when teacher picking groups she never picks me and N . . . She always puts me with other people who I don't like but she won't put me with my best friend. She says I'll mess around.'

Brian, a bully, had little to say about CGW except that 'It stinks!'
Some bully-victims also disliked CGW:

> 'I don't like it. You can't concentrate and people don't always listen. I hate girls and I don't like mixing.'
> 'I don't like CGW. I like working with my friends.'
> 'CGW causes fights when girls are in the group.'

This contrasted with the views of victims who often reported positive feelings about CGW:

> 'It's better because you get further with your work and more brainy people are there to help you.'
> 'You learn a lot.'

We found that girls generally, and popular boys, also liked CGW:

> 'It doesn't matter what colour children are. They all play together otherwise some would be left out and would be on their own.'
> 'CGW stops racism!' (said with feeling by a mixed-race boy)
> 'You get on with each other.'
> 'We work well as a team.'
> 'It's important to make new friends and to learn about other people.'

Case study reports

The following ethnographic reports use interview data gathered from the children themselves, their peers and their teachers. We also asked the children to do three tests: the F.A.S.T. test, the P.S.Q. test and the Separation Anxiety Test (Smith, Bowers, Binney and Cowie, 1993).

The F.A.S.T. test is a family sculpt task, in which children place figures representing their family on a squared board. Figures can be placed on rectangular blocks to make them higher. It measures affiliation and power in the family. For further details see Bowers, Smith and Binney (1992).

The P.S.Q. (Parenting Style Questionnaire) test measures warmth, over-protection, accurate monitoring, punitiveness and neglect. Children post cards with items representing these qualities into boxes labelled 'a lot like my mum (dad)', 'a bit like my mum (dad)' and 'not at all like my mum (dad)'. For further details see Bowers, Smith and Binney (1994).

The Separation Anxiety Test assesses aspects of security of attachment to parents using six photographs of family separation scenes: for example, mother going into hospital or the child leaving on a school camp for a week. The child is asked how the child in the photograph is feeling, why, and what he or she is going to do about it. Children were shown photographs appropriate for their sex and main ethnic group.

Graham: a victim of bullying

(time 1: 50 per cent; time 2: 13 per cent; time 3: 58 per cent; time 4: 33 per cent)
At the beginning of the project, Graham was a quiet child, easily overlooked in class. When the teacher asked children to choose partners for an activity, Graham was seldom chosen; at breaktimes he was often alone. His sociometric status was neglected. His experience of peer relationships seemed to be largely a negative one and the reasons which underlay his role as victim seemed to have more to do with his introverted personality and his lack of opportunity to develop appropriate social skills. His perception of the children in the class was that 'they are always fighting'. He could name two children who would sometimes play with him. He said that he liked them but added, 'Probably they are the only people (in the class) who want to play with me.' Graham was not a popular choice when it came to taking a partner because he was so shy and unforthcoming. Other children did not find him fun to be with.

As Ann, his teacher, said: 'He's very withdrawn. He doesn't give much to other children unless he is in a good mood... He is just a very introverted, withdrawn person.' Graham was vulnerable to attack in the playground simply because he was so often on his own. He was also excluded from many activities by his peers, especially the prestigious football activities which play such an important part in the lives of boys in his age group. Probably the most alarming aspect of Graham's experience of peer relationships was that, although he is perceived as a victim by classmates, he himself did not consider that he had been bullied. Difficult as he found it to talk about his loneliness and lack of contact with friends, the overriding impression was that he blamed himself for his isolation.

During the first year of the project it seemed that CGW was not having much impact on Graham and by the beginning of the second year he was still nominated as a victim. However, with his new teacher and in the safety of his new group which was a very supportive one, Graham began to change. A significant move came when he began to feel free to talk within his group – Shoukat and Rafiq (both victims), Claire and Tracy – about how he felt; members of his group were also able to give him some honest feedback about his lack of involvement at times:

Graham: I'm spoilt in this group.
H.C.: Why?
Graham: Because I don't do any work.

At this point, members of the group pointed out that they could help him:

Claire: We could encourage Graham to do more.
Graham: Treat me nice. Sometimes you bully me.
Claire: Only when your chair leg gets on mine.
Graham: That's not my fault. It's the chair's!
H.C.: Others would appreciate it if you put more effort into things. Does that seem okay?
Graham: (in a relaxed tone of voice) Yes.

The others responded to Graham in a kind way but firmly indicated to him that they would appreciate it if he put more effort into his work in the group. Tracy said:

He's all right. Do you know, the other week we were playing that balloon game and he was starting to win.

This interview was in marked contrast to a similar one in the first year of the project when Graham had been almost totally overshadowed by other members of his group.

By March 1992 Graham was becoming much more outgoing. He conceded that he was still being bullied by some children ('They take rulers and papers off me sometimes.') but was also describing the support which he got from other children in the class:

> I get on with Raj a lot ... and with Phillip and Giles ... Sometimes no one plays with me but now Phillip plays with me and Giles.

By the end of the project, Jane, his teacher, was able to report a dramatic change in Graham:

> Things have changed for Graham ... He is more at ease with himself and therefore people are at ease with him. ... He has gained in confidence. He can now read and that has helped. It has given him some confidence ... He is very bright in some situations and so in a group there have been things that he has been able to do.

There were home circumstances which contributed to Graham's isolation and a visit from the Educational Social Worker had highlighted some problems over personal hygiene which the other children had noticed and which had made them, in the words of his teacher 'shy away from him'. The F.A.S.T. test showed him as a rather sheltered child. He scored high on over-protection on the P.S.Q. Support to the home coupled with a sense of security within his group at school had a strong impact on Graham's sense of self-worth. That in turn enabled him to make a few friends which shielded him to an extent from more domineering children. In turn his work began to improve and that too increased his confidence in himself. By the end of the project, Graham was clearly a much happier, livelier boy who was even able to be slightly cheeky to adults.

Mark: a bully

(time 1: 65 per cent; time 2: 88 per cent; time 3: 65 per cent; time 4: 38 per cent)
At the beginning of the project, Mark was 9 years old, tall for his age and physically fit. One of his hobbies was practising karate. It seemed that he tended to view the world as a threatening place and thought it necessary to be ready to defend himself. In his words:

Karate is defence, so if someone came up to you and hit you, I've got licence even to kill. You know, if you killed someone doing karate, yeah, you can't get done because it [the licence] tells you that you're doing it for self-defence.

Mark's parents are perceived by him as somewhat punitive and they scored high on neglect in the P.S.Q. test. From Mark's perspective, his mum and dad are both high on warmth but, at the same time, they both:

have locked me in my room for punishment;
make a fool of me in front of other people;
call me nasty names.

His dad in particular:

often threatens to punish me;

and his mum:

doesn't mind where I go;
lets me stay up as late as I want;
doesn't mind if I do dangerous things.

His teacher reported that the parents were very young but that they seemed caring and concerned for Mark. He was dressed fashionably and appeared to be well looked after. However, scores on the P.S.Q. were unusually high for punitiveness and neglect, and low on accurate monitoring.

Mark had bullied other children since he was in first school. He could recall, without apparent emotion, an incident from the past when he acted aggressively towards Ali:

Mark: When it was my ball, I brought it to school. He goes, 'I'll pop it,' and I said, 'I'll pop *your* brain!' Then he popped it and I gave him one . . . [pauses] . . . he had a broken nose. I broke his nose!
H.C.: You broke his nose?
Mark: He was on the floor before it got broken. I just stamped on it like that.
H.C.: You stamped on his nose? Were you sorry afterwards?
Mark: No . . . He admitted that he started the fight.
H.C.: That's quite a reaction on your part now, wasn't it? To break his nose you must have stamped on it pretty hard.
Mark (coolly): Not pretty hard 'cos on the side it's soft there.

H.C.: How do you think that he felt?
Mark: Nowt. He just ran out and went home.

This pattern of responding to other children with a strong counter-attack persisted throughout the first year of the project. He usually showed no remorse for his overreactions and always seemed convinced that the victim deserved all he got, even when there was no obvious provocation. Here is how Shoukat, a boy nominated by 75 per cent of his classmates as a victim, described his experience of being with Mark:

When I'm doing good work, Mark and Yussef start confusing me, like calling me nasty names and pushing my chair. Or they get a piece of paper and tear it and tell Miss I did it. That's what they did today. I think why they're doing it is just that they are jealous. Like they got hold of my chair and started pushing it. I said 'Stop it!' but they wouldn't so I moved my chair to the other side of the table so they couldn't push it, and then Miss moved them, because they were messing about.

At that time, other children tried confronting Mark with specific examples of aggressive behaviour but he did not then find it easy to listen to honest feedback and reacted angrily to any hint of criticism from others. He would, for example, shout almost hysterically 'Shut up!' or 'You liar!', so that small-group evaluation sessions, which worked well with other children in the class, were not successful when Mark was a member of the group.

Mark's teacher saw that some children teased and annoyed him but also noticed how quickly he went on the defensive when faced with something that he did not like:

He can be so silly. Someone will pull a face and he'll go up and say 'Don't you do that again!' I think it's as if they offend him. He can be so aggressive. Then he'll take it to the extreme.

During the first year of the project no one, it seemed, had been able to challenge Mark. He expressed the view that, although there might be some penalties for aggressive behaviour, on the whole they were a small price to pay: 'I just got to do lines for a few weeks and miss playtime.' His philosophy, as interpreted from his karate lessons, remained 'No pain, no gain.'

In November 1991, Mark was interviewed in his group. This group was a quarrelsome one where, as they readily admitted, the boys and girls did not get on. The other members of the group – Murban, Zabir,

Fatima and Naheed – were able to voice their feelings about Mark who, this time, listened without interrupting. What he heard was mixed:

> 'Mark has changed [from last year]. He used to fight but now he doesn't so much.'
> 'And we let him draw.'
> '. . . because he's better at drawing.'
> 'He's great. I found him bossy but he isn't now.'

However, Fatima, Murban and Naheed also commented on his temper during group work:

> *Fatima:* When we work if he starts teasing he'll say 'I'll box you up' and then he starts quarrelling.
> *Murban:* He starts fighting every day.
> *Naheed:* When we wanted to draw something good he goes 'I'll give you a punch' and draws it no more.
> *Fatima:* He's a brat!

Mark's view of the others was uncomplimentary:

> 'Fatima needs a smaller mouth.'
> 'Murban is right bossy. He jumps about like a gorilla.'

Mark seemed to be a little more able to deal with the interactions within his group and was certainly less physically aggressive towards the others. However, he still showed very little capacity to be supportive towards others and a continuing tendency to use insults towards his peers, some of which appeared to be racist.

By February 1992 Mark had become subdued. He was no longer having so many outbursts but was complaining of being bullied himself. This was confirmed by peer nominations towards the end of the year. Only 38 per cent of his classmates now saw him as a bully but 69 per cent nominated him as a victim. He was having particular problems with Joshua and Delroy because 'they always ask you for money'; he felt that he had to pay up because otherwise 'they beat you up. One of them is cock o't' school [Joshua] and one of them's third [Delroy].' He was not experiencing the class as a cooperative place to be in 'because of all the fighting and arguing'. However, he admitted that 'sometimes I fight and argue' and was beginning to express some awareness that he might play some part in it. He was still justifying past bullying behaviour by saying:

> I never asked money off them [the victims]. I did pick on Richard. He caused trouble so I caused it back.

This time he selected Amin as someone nice to work with and be with in the playground because 'He's funny' and 'He don't always say his words right' but there was more than a hint of ambivalence towards this new friend.

Karate was still an important activity for him but he seemed less confident that it could solve all his problems: 'If I have to use it I will.'

By the end of the second year his teacher had become so concerned about his behaviour in class and his under-achievement in work that she had visited the home to discuss ways in which she and the parents might collaborate to control him. She had noted that he was finding particular difficulty in groups and that he continued to be ambivalent towards his peers, especially towards vulnerable boys like Ralph:

> Even now, if Ralph's in a bad mood Mark will go over and help him, but sometimes he can have put Ralph in a bad mood in the first place.

Margie had visited the home and, in collaboration with Mark's mother, was monitoring his behaviour in class. His mother had agreed to keep a closer watch on him at home and Margie was finding that this was some help 'because she has pushed him'.

Mark remained acutely aware of the dominance hierarchies within the class and was unable to benefit greatly from the potential for power-sharing and collaboration which CGW can offer.

Sean: a bully

(time 1: 68 per cent; time 2: 87 per cent; time 3: 89 per cent; time 4: 100 per cent)

In the first year Sean was nominated 'controversially' in the sense that some children stated that they liked him very much while others disliked him strongly. The headteacher, who had devoted hours of her time in talking through his feelings, commented: 'The biggest bullies are often the ones who are the most insecure – like Sean.' Pat, his teacher in the second year of the project, noted: 'You can't touch him – yet he needs to be touched – but he won't accept it.'

He is tall, physically fit and attractive. He is aware of his power to draw people to him and explained this as being due to: 'Good looks . . .

personality ... I'm clever at sport and just share things and that.' At the beginning of the project, Margie, his teacher, acknowledged his skill in relating to other people but showed some concern:

> He's a very strong personality that usually acts for the good but he has a very strong sense of devilment. And he has a very good general knowledge and lots of ideas... so he's a fun person to have around. But I think people's relations with him are tinged with fear. You've got to be friendly with him, otherwise ... because he's quite tough.

Sean never denied that there had been times when he abused his power in the class:

> *H.C.:* Have you ever bullied anybody?
> *Sean:* No, but I hit someone for doing something little to me ... It was Jamie ... He got on my nerves. Every time you tap him he says 'Stop tickling me!' so I just hit him.

He was open about the fact that he could be envious of children who seemed to be cleverer than him and that he would then be at pains to put them down in some way, usually by 'beating them up'.

In the first year of the project he had forged friendships with two other dominant boys in the class. They played football at breaktimes and after school and they made sure that only good players were in their team. Sean justified excluding 'crap players' on the grounds that 'There's millions of footballs int' yard and they know they just want to annoy me 'cos they don't like me saying no to them.' The impression then was that, while low-status children felt left out, favoured children became highly positive about Sean's personal qualities of loyalty, liveliness and sheer fun:

> 'He always plays football with me and he's always been friends for years.' (Brian, another bully)
> 'Sean makes me laugh.' (Laura, a popular girl)

There was certainly a side to Sean which was caring and supportive. He would spend time helping Ian, a boy who had reading difficulties. However, he could be extremely prejudiced in his attitudes towards Black children and, at the same time, form close mutually acceptable friendships with them. For example, he played with a group of Asian boys but openly expressed his negative feelings towards them:

> None of them like me because they think I hate their sisters and they are thinking 'I hate him' behind my back, and they are always talking about me. They know if I catch them they've had it. (H.C.: What does that mean?) I'll knock them out because I don't like people talking about me.

In the course of the first year Sean developed a strong friendship with Imtiaz who became a member of Sean's close-knit friendship group. Furthermore, he became close to Olivia, a popular African-Caribbean girl and spent a lot of time with her in class. His prejudiced attitudes, readily expressed on issues of gender or race, were not so rigid that they could not be modified in the light of experience. He seemed, despite his bullying and domineering behaviour, to command attention within the peer group and even liking on the part of some children.

However, by the second year of the project, any hopes that his more positive attributes might redeem him were firmly dashed. His behaviour in groups was becoming increasingly overbearing. Pat, his teacher, noted that, although some children said that they liked him, it was her impression that they were only pretending through fear and because 'it is bad if you get the wrong side of him'. She was aware that he was intimidating the others and that they were afraid to tell her. He was especially nasty to Asian girls, with the exception of Abida, 'a sporty girl, not unassertive like the other Asian girls' (in the words of her teacher).

Pat commented on his impatience in CGW towards any child who could not work at his pace. His intolerance of any criticism of his behaviour was confirmed during an interview tape-recorded in November 1991 which attempted to focus on some complaints which members of his group had made about him but which they had been too afraid to voice to his face. The group consisted of Sean, Olivia (the popular, high-achieving African-Caribbean girl with whom he often associated in class), Brian (a White boy, also a bully, with whom he associated) and Alex (a shy mixed-race boy):

> *Sean* (to Olivia): Looks like you've got eczema, dunnit?
> *H.C.:* Sean, it sounds as if some people in this group have found it hard to get on with you.
> *Alex* (in an appeasing tone): Sean's okay . . .
> *Sean* (interrupting loudly): Just tell 'em! I'm not going to beat you up!
> *Alex* (continues timidly): . . . but he can be a bit bossy.
> *Sean* (shouts angrily): Bossy! That's it! That's it! . . . 'cos I'm 'ardest, you see. Just tell 'em! I'm not going to beat you up. (Olivia attempted to speak.)
> *Sean* (interrupts loudly): Close your lips, Olivia! Close your arse! (Laughs

knowingly) Now Alex, he's okay. Sometimes he's a bit too slow for us. He's not actually Christopher Columbus. He's not cleverest in class. I mean Olivia is – and I am! Shut up (to Olivia). Shut up your beep hole! (Laughs) So he's okay but sometimes he's too slow and we have to wait for him.

H.C.: You've said some positive things about Olivia. You've said she's clever . . .

Sean (shouts): I've seen people at spastics club are cleverer than you, Olivia.

H.C.: I think what I'm hearing is that you all find it hard to work together – but especially Sean.

Sean: NO!

H.C.: I wonder if there are any ways in which the group could change to make it better for everyone?

Olivia: Split up. Sit in a corner on our own.

Sean: Cooperate, Miss.

H.C.: You know the word cooperate.

Olivia: He thinks he knows the word cooperate.

Sean: Alex, you're sat there like Michelin man not saying anything.

The interview came to an end abruptly as Sean's shouting made it impossible to continue. He was clearly very threatened by the slightest suggestion that others might not like his behaviour and attitudes.

By the end of the year many children were feeling more confident about voicing their feelings about Sean and he was becoming increasingly isolated in the class. The others were able to share with one another their distaste at the way Sean and 'a little gang' bullied all the rest of the class. As Matt put it:

> Sean just acts cocky, hits you and gets his pencil and goes like that [gestures] to you in your face and no one likes it. And he talks about other people and, like, parts of the body and that, like, gets you mad . . . and no one likes him. All t' bad people do but good people don't.

Pat noticed a dramatic change in the children's attitudes towards him, in part due to the openness which she encourages in CGW:

> When I tried to tell him that some people might be shy of saying things, he just shouted at them 'You're not shy, are you?' He finds it hard to see it . . . He's very impatient. The others have learned to trust 'the establishment' [herself and the headteacher] in the way that they will now tell us if anything happens. We have a book on him that they can go to in confidence and write anything that they feel we ought to know.

Sean was becoming aware of his waning popularity and there were a few chinks in his armour. As Pat said:

> He used to think that he was popular but now he says sometimes, 'I don't know.' Before he was saying, 'I'm really popular' and now he is very insecure.

But it was still hard to challenge him, especially as he did not value the qualities which are enhanced by effective CGW. Although it was clear that he did not work well in groups it seemed to be beyond the power of his peer group to modify his behaviour since any attempt on their part to begin to talk freely and openly was met with outright rejection. He could be friends with a child one day and the next day have no compunction about stealing that child's sweets. Shy children were completely dominated by him; assertive children who tried to stand up to him provoked anger which then usually escalated into a conflict. As Pat put it:

> He doesn't see it as a positive trait to be a listener. He sees it as weak or negative so he can't give them any respect ... In CGW he hates it if anyone else is not quick and he does not like it if they have to discuss something. He is receptive and quick. It is such a shame that he doesn't channel it into different directions. He needs to learn to be less dominant and more sensitive. It's not a case of the other children being more assertive. It's of him being less dominant.

Sean's popularity in the first year of the project had indicated that it was possible for him to win the respect of others through his prowess at sport, his colourful personality and through his social skills when he chose to use them. Unfortunately, the insensitive, domineering side of his character came more to the forefront. Whereas many of his peers had grown through positive interactions in groups, Sean did not take this opportunity and stayed with power-assertive methods of influencing other children.

Alan: a bully-victim

(time 1: 55 per cent (bully)/65 per cent (victim); time 2: 56 per cent (bully)/50 per cent (victim); time 3: 71 per cent (bully)/47 per cent (victim); time 4: 87 per cent (bully)/60 per cent (victim)
Alan is a small boy and throughout the time we knew him he said he

was very unhappy at school because of being bullied. His wish at the beginning of the project was that 'all the bad people left and friendly people came back into school'. At that time he found it hard to think of anything positive to say about his classmates, could not think of a person whom he would like to work with and was unable to name a single person who could be described as a friend. His conversations were dominated by complaints about arguments and fights.

At the same time, he readily admitted that he often bullied other children, for example Ralph, a vulnerable boy who was often targeted as a victim, but considered that they had usually started the fight:

H.C.: What sort of things do you do when you bully Ralph?
Alan: We, he starts it first, like, comes to my table, punches me on the back, then we have a fight and then we get done by the teacher.
H.C.: Do you usually win these fights?
Alan: Yes, 'cos he's only little. Sometimes he cries, sometimes he tells.

Other children confirmed this quarrelsome attitude. A typical comment was: 'Alan thumps me on the back when we're working. He thumps me so I thump him back.'

His teacher noticed how hard he found it to work cooperatively within groups for any length of time. On the occasions when he was rash enough to annoy a stronger boy like Mark, he would get into real trouble:

Mark: Alan drew this love-heart and he gave it to Michelle. He said I drew it so I went up to him and went right hard on his nose.
H.C.: You punched him on the nose!
Mark: It didn't break . . . It only started bleeding.
H.C.: How do you think he felt when you made his nose bleed?
Mark: Sad.
HC: Sad. Did that worry you at all?
Mark: No. I knew what would happen when I did it.
H.C.: You mean you knew you were going to punch him hard?
Mark (corrects this misunderstanding): No. I do that automatically. When anyone gets me mad, I just swing me fist out . . . It was Alan's fault 'cos he drew the love-heart and gave it to Michelle . . .

At that stage, Alan was certainly contributing to his alienation from the rest of the class and did provoke attacks from other children. But a major difficulty for him was that he assumed that other children did not like him and did very little himself to win friends. As his teacher pointed out, he typically anticipated that he was not likely to be chosen in situations where children take partners:

> He will stand up and say 'I don't want to be with anybody!' Whether he knew that nobody would pick him, I don't know. He had a hot temper and nobody wanted to be near him, I suppose.

Because he was quarrelsome, it was easy for others to blame him for any fights that occurred. He was not a pleasant working partner and so, even in small-group work, he did not sustain closeness with other children.

By the second year of the project, Jane, his new teacher, was not optimistic about his potential for cooperation in groups. As she said: 'He spoils things for everyone. He's nasty and picks on people's weaknesses. He is a real problem.' She placed him in a small supportive group of children who had all experienced rejection or victimisation by peers – Nazia, Cath and Raj – and who placed high value on qualities of sharing and helping. At last he began to get positive feedback from his peers:

> 'Alan's good . . . and when we draw pictures, if we can't do a bit, he finishes it for you.' (Cath)
> 'Alan's helpful. He cooperates.' (Nazia)
> 'He helps me.' (Raj)

Alan in turn was beginning to see positive qualities in the others:

> 'Cath helps me with me work when I'm stuck. She shares and lends things.'
> 'Raj is funny and he pulls daft faces.'
> 'Nazia shares things with me.'

The atmosphere within the group was friendly and the others seemed to be able to tolerate Alan's outbursts when they came and to show some degree of understanding. Through Raj, Alan made friends with Shoukat who had also experienced victimisation when he first joined the class. Shoukat was able to offer Alan support when unpleasant events took place:

> Alan, he's like Saleem, like when Saleem's at school. I think he's a bit scared from inside . . . Yeah, he's scared inside, because the other day we were lining up and everyone just started pushing him. I don't know why. And then they pushed him off the chair and he fell on the floor – teacher weren't there –

and they all started kicking him and kicking him. Children from our class
– I don't know why – they get bad tempered. They are a real laugh but they
get bad tempered. And they were doing this to him. When Miss said, 'Who
were the first to hit Alan?', I looked at some of these people . . . If they really
wanted to beat Alan up they wouldn't volunteer [i.e. admit to having done
it], but they did. They volunteered and they said, 'We're really sorry. We
won't do it again.'

Shoukat had not felt able to protest at the time but he did go up to Alan afterwards and offer him genuine friendship.

Alan moved to a new group after Christmas and found a similar level of support and friendship. He was still cross and bad tempered at times but there were many more instances where he was interacting warmly with other members of his group. While he was still a target of bullying in the wider class, at least the small groups offered a kind of haven for him.

By the very end of the year, Jane was able to confirm a change:

He's been getting on much better with all of us – with me and with everybody else in the room . . . People have been willing to work with him and he's been willing. He's had one or two things thrown at him across the room but he has been more steadily applying himself to what was going on in the classroom. We did something at assembly last week which required us all working together and he was very good – so much so that he was given the plum job of operating the tape recorder at the end.

Alan had benefitted from the support of the small groups and the opportunity to interact over a sustained period of time. He was able to experience some positive outcomes from his peers, especially those who could easily empathise with his unpleasant experiences within the class.

Sudha: a victim

(time 1: 63 per cent; time 2: 59 per cent; time 3: 38 per cent; time 4: 37 per cent)
Sudha is a very quiet child and easily overlooked in class. She is unusually small for her age. When her teacher asked children to choose partners, Sudha was seldom chosen. She was often alone and there was a sense of inevitability about this state of affairs since, as Sue, her teacher put it, 'I haven't noticed anyone palling up with her. Her brother was a bit like that last year.' At the beginning of the project 63 per cent of the children in her class nominated her as a victim. The most that she

could expect was, in the words of her teacher, 'to be tolerated not chosen'.

Her P.S.Q. scores were high on punitiveness and neglect. Both her mother and her father had, according to Sudha:

locked me in my room for punishment a lot;
shout at me a lot;
make me cry a lot.

Her mother:

often threatens to punish me;
hits me for every little thing I do;
does not enjoy talking things over with me.

Her father:

doesn't like to hug me;
lets me watch any T.V. programme I want.

On the F.A.S.T. test Sudha put herself in a corner far away from the rest of her family. Her mother and father, a brother and a cousin were all given three power blocks. The constellation was more typical of a bully than of a victim. However, since Sudha is so small, it may be that physically she is unable to bully others.

Sudha could never be sure that anyone would play with her at breaktime and, on the few occasions when she tried to join in games, she was often violently rejected by domineering children. As she said, in her own words:

Jonah [African-Caribbean], Nathan [White] and Nazar [Asian] are three boys that fight. Jonah swears at me and hits me and bosses me around.

She had certain strategies which sometimes kept the worst of the aggression against her at bay. In the playground: 'I share and give them nice things to eat ... I give them some of my snack.' In the class: 'I don't be in fights. I just carry on with my work.' But these strategies only worked sometimes and she was very vulnerable to exploitation. Two White girls, each very friendly with the other and one, Susan, a popular girl in the class, spoke of Sudha with disdain in her presence:

Lara: I don't know much about her. I hardly see her. She's quiet.

Susan: You can't see her she's so small. (Long silence broken by giggles on the part of Lara and Susan.) She lets you use things you want cos she's too shy to say 'no'. (A long painful silence.)

Sudha chose to say nothing about the other two. With children like Susan and Lara, she reverted, understandably, to her withdrawn, silent behaviour.

In CGW situations, however, by the second year of the project Sudha began to find that she could be more involved when the other members of the group were supportive. Where members of her group were kind and friendly, she was able to make a little more contribution, and while she was not a highly popular child, she was able to begin to form relationships within the group. As Sally, her teacher, said in July 1992:

> Sudha is not left out in CGW so she gets involved. She is nice and she really tries, and she is not left out if they're actually working in a group. They'll give her something to do and she'll join in so if they're made to be in a group then she is involved, but if they're allowed to choose partners she won't usually be chosen.

Sudha was cautiously in favour of CGW provided that there were no boys in the group and that there was no fighting. Clearly for a shy, unforthcoming child like Sudha it will take time for her to develop positive relationships with more than a few of her peers. The positive impact of CGW was that her nomination as a victim decreased quite markedly over this time period.

Afsal: a popular boy

(time 1: other; time 2: popular; time 3: popular; time 4: other)
Afsal was new to the class when the project began. His parents were supportive, with a combination of warmth and accurate monitoring. The F.A.S.T. test showed a very close-knit family, possibly somewhat over-protective of Afsal. They both, according to Afsal:

> understand my problems and worries;
> show that they love me;
> enjoy talking things over with me;
> make me feel better when I am upset.

They gave him reasonable freedom but liked to know where he was and with whom he was playing.

Initially, he was extremely quiet and confined his friendships to a small group of Asian boys. As Sally, his teacher, said then:

> Afsal is new. I haven't found out whether he has a friend as yet but he's very quiet and hard-working. He doesn't stand out. He sits and gets on with his work. He is a lovely boy.

Fairly soon he was extending his network of friendships more widely and was liked by most children in the class. He was nominated as popular in each year of the project. He stated his strong liking of CGW and enjoyed the camaraderie of working in groups where you could get to know new people. His peers saw him as an open, friendly boy who readily 'lends you things' and 'is generous.' He was perceived as an asset in groups since he had lots of ideas to contribute himself and, in addition, he was always prepared to help others.

Afsal's CGW group had become a friendship group. They acknowledged one another as friends and openly said that CGW had strengthened this bond. They also spontaneously mentioned friends who were Asian, African-Caribbean, White, and who were boys and girls. His group was unanimous in the view that it is important to work outside friendship groups in order to get to know other children. If a person has talent, they said, he will be in demand: 'We don't care if he's Black or White.'

Olivia: from a controversial to a popular girl

(time 1: controversial; time 2: popular; time 3: popular; time 4: other) Olivia, a popular African-Caribbean girl, was much sought after in the class. She was good at her work and she combined this with a very positive, helpful attitude towards others. Olivia was able to describe her own good qualities without sounding boastful. She believed that she was popular because she 'listened to people' and because she 'liked working with both boys and girls'. She excelled at sports and especially enjoyed playing football. She was friendly with boys and girls from different ethnic backgrounds. At the beginning of the project, peer nominations indicated that, while she was strongly liked by a large number of children she was also strongly disliked by others: she was a controversial member of the class. Many children, when interviewed, mentioned Olivia spontaneously, some praising her for her talents and others criticising her for her forthrightness. At times Olivia's honest opinions could be seen in a less favourable light. Pat said of her in July 1992:

> I think it stems from her parents because they – I mean they are lovely but they haven't got any tact and she's got that off them as well, you know, and I think she does the same with the children . . . Sometimes it comes out. She's not a sensitive person . . . She'll say it aggressively. I think that some of the children – that would fire them up a bit.

She was not afraid to speak her mind but she was also open to people who were not close friends and said, of her early experiences of CGW, 'You don't need to work with your friends all the time but it's nice to work with people you know.'

As the project progressed, she claimed to get on with everyone in her class and found that football games offered a good opportunity for boys and girls to play together. By the second assessment time this self-perception proved to be accurate. Special friends included her cousin Cecile, Claire, Beth, Alex and Geordie. She valued their friendship because:

> 'If I'm ever feeling sad I can go and talk to them.'

> 'Well, there's Gavin. I like working with him because he listens to your ideas. And Nadine does and all. When they listen you can say things.'

Olivia clearly had friends to whom she could turn when things were not going so well for her, but she was also ready to help other children who were not close friends. This capacity developed within her groups where she had a warm but realistic view of peer interactions. For example, everyday conflicts were not viewed by Olivia as events to be feared:

> Sometimes children have little fights with pencils and that but they always make friends after two minutes . . . Like they say things wrong to each other sometimes and then they split up for a day and then they get back together and the next day they work well together.

She also stood up for children who were being bullied and was proactive in telling bullies to stop picking on other children. Olivia would say that if they did not stop she would tell a teacher. She also went out of her way to walk with vulnerable children who were afraid to walk home alone. Then she would even tell their parents. She went on:

> Yes, I know what their problem is. And if I was like in a situation like that they would do the same for me.

She was aware that this did not endear her to bullies but she did not let it bother her. In fact, she was not bullied.

But she also had a strong sense of identity so that when, for example, some boys decided arbitrarily to ban girls from playing football, she did not experience it as a rejection (as Sudha did) but had a plausible explanation for it which maintained her own positive feelings about herself:

> *Olivia:* Sometimes I ask to play with boys' football and sometimes they say, 'We're not having any girls today.' But int' end they let us play because they haven't got enough players.
> *H.C.:* How often does this happen?
> *Olivia:* About once a week..
> *H.C.:* Why do you think they do this? Is it because you're girls?
> *Olivia:* No, it's not because we're girls. If we're in group playing anyway, it's just because sometimes the girls can play football better.
> *H.C.:* And they don't like that?
> *Olivia:* No ... Charles would let all the girls play. It's just Sean and some of the other boys.

Unfortunately, her final group was not a very cohesive one and her experience of it coloured her overall evaluation of CGW as a method. In this group, which included Sean, Olivia was prepared to voice publicly what he was like in the group. Other children were more fearful of doing this but Olivia was not afraid:

> When we're sitting next to him [Sean] and he's doing it, he works it all out and then just sits there doing nothing. Then he sits and does just one thing and it takes him about an hour and then when us lot have done all the work he's only done one picture.

Sean's response to her was rude and overbearing at the time (see the case study of Sean) and she was understandably upset by it, especially as it had become a characteristic form of communication within the group. She may have been aware that, on other occasions, he expressed grudging admiration for her. Although there were practical outcomes in the sense that Pat, her teacher, and the headteacher took the criticisms of Sean by the group very seriously, Olivia was clearly discouraged by the experience and, by July 1992, was somewhat negative about group work, even though she was perceived by the other children as such an asset in their groups. Although she was able to stand up to him and often did, it seemed to have spoiled things for her. She said:

> We've been in the same group with Sean and Brian and theren't no point in talking to them. They just mess about ... They say, 'Lend us your book'

or when you're doing summat they say not to do it and when you've been doing something they say, 'Oh, Miss, she's just been sitting there doing nowt!' ... We've learned that they mess about – and that they smell!

When Olivia was in a more congenial group, her attitude was dramatically different. In a group consisting of Alex [mixed-race], Jay (White) and Sorbia (Asian) she was enthusiastic about CGW.

Douglas: a bully-victim

(time 1: 63 per cent rejected bully/79 per cent victim; time 2: 65 per cent rejected bully/53 per cent victim; time 3: 73 per cent rejected bully/ 69 per cent victim; time 4: 31 per cent rejected bully/81 per cent victim)

In Sally's opinion, Douglas, at the beginning of the project, had not been able to make very many friends in the class. He scored highly on prejudice on the stereotypes test. This prejudiced attitude did not change in the course of the project, and he related very badly to Black and Asian children. The main reason for his rejection by the others was his unpredictable behaviour and his frequent tantrums.

He felt angry about the amount of bullying that he was experiencing and tried to get his own back whenever he could. This in turn escalated quarrels and failed to solve his difficulty in relating positively to the others:

> I don't like people bullying me. They kick me, thump me, smack me in the back, especially Lianne and Andrew... Marie pulls my hair but I get back. I get a rounders bat and whack her round the head... Soon when I'm older I'm going to learn karate so I don't have to be scared. Then I won't have to run away. I'll just fight.

This was confirmed by his teacher who had to take a firm line with his frequent tantrums. Sometimes her firmness worked, sometimes it provoked further outbreaks:

> You can actually say things to him now. He can take what I say to him. This morning when I was trying to sort things out he was in tears. I told him that wouldn't have any effect and that's when he lashed out and kicked Nazir.

Douglas found it hard to accept feedback from others and had difficulty in expressing any empathy for others' feelings. He told how glad he felt when, for example, he had kept Lianne out of his game and recounted many occasions when he had got his revenge on children who were nasty to him. However, despite the apparent warmth and accurate monitoring on the part of his parents, as shown on the P.S.Q. test, Douglas had not been able to tell his parents about the fact that he was experiencing bullying by other children. His arrangement of figures on the F.A.S.T. test was very unusual and suggested a poor relationship within the family.

The other children found him very difficult to have in a group, partly because he was very poor at doing any task, however simple. This reinforced his negative feelings about himself and further escalated his difficulties. Although the children could recognise that he was being bullied, his behaviour did not evoke their sympathies, even in children who were upset by other bullying episodes. For example, his obvious distress after being bullied by Hafeez and Ahmed, was ignored by everyone except his teacher and his response to her was an angry rebuff:

> He was a bit funny in P.E. last week. He sat out at the side and he wouldn't take part. He was crying, moaning and groaning again so I stood them [Hafeez and Ahmed] out in the dining room while the rest went out to assembly and Douglas swore at me, which I wasn't very happy about. I put him on the landing during assembly and afterwards he was lovely all day. The trouble is, one minute he's in that mood, and the next minute he's completely forgotten about it.

By the end of the project Sally reported a slight improvement in his capacity to relate to others within a small group but on the whole he remained a rejected member of the class:

> They prefer not to work with him. He works well alone. He feels that he has nothing to contribute to CGW – he can't draw, write, discuss. He gets very upset about things and has tantrums. He tries but has tantrums...The other kids look at him and they don't really want to be involved with him. Then they see him tantrum and act babyish and it's not something a lot of them want to be associated with.

Douglas continued to be vulnerable to attack by other stronger children. His reaction was to lash out or to have a tantrum, neither of which endeared him to the others.

Seth: a bully-victim

(time 1: 53 per cent bully/53 per cent victim; time 2: 72 per cent bully/39 per cent victim; time 3: 53 per cent bully/29 per cent victim; time 4: 87 per cent bully/0 per cent victim)

His teacher, Tom, nominated him as being 'quite belligerent' at the beginning of the project, though he suggested that he had settled down as the year went on and that he was 'very pleased with him'. In the second year of the project he spent a lot of time in a close-knit group with other African-Caribbean children in the class. Helen Cowie interviewed him in a group with Delroy and Marcia (both African-Caribbean), Amin (Asian) and Jay (White). The group had worked very well collaborating to make a book along the lines of *The Jolly Postman*. They had shared out the work and had all worked very productively together. Each seemed to be able to acknowledge the contribution of the others and to be positive about CGW. They said:

'She's got a sense of humour.' (Seth of Jay)
'He's like patient because when we're speaking English he doesn't understand it.' (Seth of Amin)
'Seth likes to help me but sometimes he can get mad with people.' (Jay)
'Seth likes to get things done quicker.' (Delroy)
'He has patience and, like, listens for ideas, and he can calm his temper.' (Marcia of Seth)

In this kind of group Seth could function very well and the more helpful aspects of his character emerged. However, when he came under the influence of Joshua, who dominated him and told him what to do, his attitude was likely to change. In a group with only Delroy and Joshua Seth was less sure of his opinions and tended to hang back until he had heard what the others, especially Joshua, had to say. In fact, often he would simply echo the exact words of Joshua, as if he were unable to come to an opinion of his own. There were clear advantages in being associated with Joshua since there was protection from being bullied, but the protection seemed to demand that he in turn become involved in bullying himself.

Joshua: a bully

(time 1: 100 per cent; time 2: 85 per cent; time 3: 71 per cent; time 4: 67 per cent)
At the beginning of the project Joshua was perceived as a bully by everyone in the class. Margie and Jane, his teachers, were very aware of his aggressive behaviour towards the others and had even sent a letter home to voice their concern. As Jane put it:

> Well, he always strikes me as a child who has very little contact in chatting to him – I think that this is why he doesn't ever listen to you. I always imagine that he's always out to play... He is well-cared for in the sense of clothes but I feel that he does not have much human contact.

Margie added:

> Yes, at E[feeder infant school] he didn't talk to his mother. I never saw any contact between them... or going round with her or anything. She was with her friends in a little group.

By the end of the first year of CGW Joshua had not changed, it seemed, though his behaviour was more undercover than it had been. What had changed was the willingness of his victims to voice their upset about him to their teachers. Margie thought that what had happened was that he continued to bully but in a more surreptitious way:

> Maybe he just doesn't do it when I'm watching now. I mean, there has been quite a big change, a big improvement from when he first came [to the school]. He used to be just horrid to other people all the time, taking food off them, making them give things out of their packed lunches. There's been a big improvement but there's still a latent tendency.

This was confirmed by Jane:

> Yes, I've had children tell me that Joshua's been hitting so-and-so. Now they will talk about it. A couple of weeks ago when he was bullying someone we talked about it afterwards and they were all against him, whereas at one time I might have felt that there were people on his side.

Margie also pointed out that his experience of life was very limited. This had become obvious to all the others when the class went on an outing and it emerged that he knew virtually nothing about the countryside. For example:

> He spoke to Ralph about 'those bricks – those big bricks over there' as he pointed to outcrop rocks and mountains... and he couldn't take any teasing from me. He really thought I was going to eat his chocolate which he had asked me to look after for him when I said, for a joke, 'How kind!' and he said, 'I'll have it back now' and I said, 'Oh I thought you were giving it to me!' He couldn't cope with it.

He claimed that a person he got on with well was Sean, another bully, because 'he's been friends for years'. He admitted that he sometimes kept other children out of games though he would not say why. He also admitted that he had bullied other children, in particular Ralph, Leonie, Paul, Michael 'and everyone'. He said that when he bullied he would often punch his victims, and he knew that many people were afraid of him. He claimed that he felt 'nowt' about this and that he never felt sorry.

By the second year Joshua was acknowledged to be 'cock of the school'. Margie, his teacher, saw an improvement but still saw in him 'that hard edge that can be quite hurtful if he wants to be so there's an element of fear in it as well'. At the same time, in her view some of the children perceived him positively: 'The other children, they do love to be with him ... boys mostly and not just from his class.' He spent a lot of time with Seth and Delroy, both African-Caribbean, sometimes with Olivia, sometimes with Jason, a mixed-race boy, who was not in their view 'proper Black'. Margie had heard them discussing their ethnicity:

> I've heard them talking about what proportion of their genetic makeup is Black and 'Oh, you're only an eighth Black' and 'You're very much Black' ... It was a statement of fact – look at our different colours, look at our hair, think why we're like we are.

When he was in a group where he was supported by at least some other African-Caribbean children he seemed to be able to work quite cooperatively.

CHAPTER EIGHT: Conclusions and recommendations

Children may have difficulties in social relationships at school

Children spend a large part of their lives in school. Usually, when we look back at our own school days, we will remember vividly certain other children, our friends and enemies, who got bullied and who did the bullying. And at the time, these are very important for the children concerned – usually more salient to them than the academic aspects of school and arguably just as important for general development. Friendships have their own intrinsic value and a child who is unhappy through lacking friends or through being bullied, is not likely to work most effectively.

We started this book by looking at the very real problems which many children experience in their social relationships with classmates. As in any social situation, the two primary dimensions of social relationships are *affiliation* and *power*. It is problems with these two aspects of relationships with which we have been concerned in our review and in our project.

Firstly, affiliation. Most children of middle school age – 8 to 11 years approximately – have several children they can name as friends. In their own words, these are other children – often, classmates – whom they like playing with and whom they can trust. They may have quarrels now and then, but they know how to make up. Unfortunately, some children lack friends. Isolated or neglected children are not nominated by any classmates as one of their best friends. Sometimes, of course, such children may have good friends in another class or outside school. But quite often such children, who may be timid or socially unskilled, or who perhaps just find making friends difficult because of language barriers, really do lack any close friends. We documented, in chapter one, how this may not only cause unhappiness, but also possibly have longer-term consequences.

Other children are rejected – in other words, they not only have few friends, they also are actively disliked by many classmates. Peer rejection seems to be relatively stable and these children are perhaps even more at risk in the long term than the neglected children. Some children are rejected because of their aggressive and disruptive behaviour ('rejected-aggressive' children) and will often also be seen by classmates as being bullies. Not all such 'bullies' lack friends, however: some will be 'controversial', disliked by many children but liked by others who are in their gang or clique. Although some bullying children lack social skills, others are very skilled in their own terms and do not lack friends.

This leads to our other dimension – power – which is generally orthogonal to, or independent of, friendship. There will always be power relationships in human groups. Sometimes one person will be stronger or sometimes more socially skilled, sometimes more knowledgeable about a task, sometimes just more confident. Then, that person is likely to take the lead, to be more dominant or powerful in the group. But power can be abused. Someone can take advantage of their greater strength, skill, knowledge or confidence, to actually harm someone else, or denigrate what they can do.

The systematic or repeated abuse of power is a good definition of bullying. It is clear that some children, if they can get away with it, will bully others – repeatedly insulting them, taking their belongings, hitting and kicking them. Other children are at risk of being the 'victims' of such bullying – some children being more at risk than others. Bullying tends to be more frequent towards children with difficulties (children with special educational needs, for example) and towards children who have less power in some sense – boys to girls (less strong physically) and across ethnic groups. Although we would argue that racial bullying can occur between any two ethnic groups (not just from White to Black or majority to minority group), in our society White children do belong to the more powerful ethnic group and some aspects of racial name-calling are especially experienced by children of ethnic minority groups, as we saw in chapter one.

Friendship also intersects with characteristics such as sex and ethnic group. Children tend to choose friends of their own race and sex. This in itself need not be too worrying. It is likely that similarity (in various guises) will always be one strong feature determining friendship choice and we certainly cannot legislate about who a child's friends should be! These friendship choices will operate most naturally in the playground. However, it would be unfortunate if classroom work did not give further opportunities for interaction. If children rarely interact across sex or race barriers, there is a danger that stereotypical notions will persist.

In this book we have focussed on race (ethnic group) rather than gender, though clearly both are important. Much research – reviewed in chapter two – has shown that children do have stereotypes of other ethnic groups. Moreover, these stereotypes are often negative. A persistent, negative stereotype denotes prejudice. There is no doubt that some children are racially prejudiced. As Aboud's (1988) review shows, the middle-school years may be an especially fruitful time to tackle such prejudice.

The 'contact hypothesis' – that mere contact with the other group will reduce prejudice – has long been shown to be inadequate. But, it is very likely that contact is one part of prejudice reduction; what is also important is what kind of contact takes place. We return to this later in considering what cooperative group work might achieve. But irrespective of the arguments about CGW, it is unlikely that prejudice will be challenged effectively in the classroom if children only work independently or in friendship groups. Nor will such a way of working have much impact on the problems of social isolation, rejection, bullying and victimisation which are found in many classrooms.

And these problems are quite frequent. Clearly, the frequency will vary: some classes, in some schools, may be models of friendly, cooperative and non-exploitative behaviour. But it is certain that in many classes, in many schools, these difficulties are present to an extent that many children are unhappy and many teachers find their task more difficult. Again, we have documented the extent of such problems in chapters one and two. As became clear in our own project, carried out in innercity schools in quite deprived areas, the average class would contain several very difficult children – often rejected by classmates, often perceived as bullies, sometimes racially prejudiced.

Cooperation and what it means

The work on children's social relationships shows that 'cooperation' is a valued characteristic. As was seen in table 1.2, popular children are also described as cooperative; neglected children are seen as lacking in cooperation and rejected children even more so. And, the 'rejected-aggressive' children, often seen as bullies, seem to have particular difficulties with cooperation (chapter one).

Unfortunately, the word 'cooperation', like many others, can have different shades of meaning and is subject to misinterpretation. In our view, cooperation means 'being fair' and 'being trustworthy'. It does not mean 'being friendly' or 'being unselfish'; and it does not mean 'being obedient' or 'being conformist'. Yet, it can be interpreted in these ways. It is important to consider this before going on to look at the impact of 'cooperative group work' in classrooms.

What cooperation is

Cooperation means working together for a common goal. To do this implies a certain degree of fairness and reciprocity in how the work is done. If both (or all) the persons involved 'pull their weight' and contribute effectively, then the task will get done more quickly than if one person was doing it, and tasks impossible for one person can be achieved.

By contrast, if one person is being an 'easy rider', slacking off while another does all the work, this is not cooperative; and even less so, of course, if one person is disruptive. Usually, the person who finds him/herself doing most/all the work will resent this after a while and take action about it – reasoning or arguing with the other, or abandoning the group effort.

Of course, a person might be 'unselfish' or 'altruistic', carrying on regardless. But there is usually little merit in this as a general principle of behaviour. By and large, social existence requires everyone to do their bit and for there to be sanctions against laziness or disruptive behaviour. In fact, work done on 'the evolution of cooperation' (Axelrod and Hamilton, 1981) shows that purely unselfish behaviour is unlikely to be widespread. Axelrod and Hamilton used 'games theory' to model the effects of different behaviour strategies in situations involving potential conflict of interest. What they found was that neither a 'purely unselfish' strategy, nor a 'purely selfish' strategy, was likely to do best. The optimal strategy was one which they labelled 'TIT FOR TAT'. TIT FOR TAT had three important aspects:

(1) you are prepared to trust (work with) your partner to start with;
(2) if your partner lets you down (cheats, does not reciprocate) then you will stop trusting them;
(3) if your partner who has cheated then 'reforms' and is prepared to work with you again, you too will resume working with them.

TIT FOR TAT thus embodies fairness and reciprocity; it presumes trust unless disillusioned and is prepared to forgive – but only when forgiveness is justified.

We think that TIT FOR TAT – in this sense – is a good model of what we can realistically expect from children in the way of cooperation. If everyone behaved this way, everyone would cooperate effectively. We are not expecting anyone to be unselfish in a saintly way and we are exerting sanctions against those who cheat, are lazy, or are disruptive.

What cooperation is not

This example makes it clear that cooperation does not mean trust or unselfishness at any cost – it only means trust when rules of fairness and reciprocity are operating within reasonable levels of tolerance.

Also, cooperation does not mean friendship. It is quite possible to cooperate with someone, without being friends with them. The two words do not have the same meaning. However, cooperation is importantly related to friendship (chapter one). Friends are much more likely to cooperate with each other and trust each other than are non-friends. Cooperation is one likely precondition of friendship. In fact, cooperating together and the trust that develops from that, may well lead to friendship: indeed, this is one rationale for using CGW in the classroom. But while cooperation may lead to friendship, this is not necessary or inevitable, and the two terms should not be confused.

Finally, some teachers and adults may use the word 'cooperative' to imply children who are obedient and conforming – who do what the teacher says without question. This too is a distortion of the true meaning of cooperation, which again negates the aspects of fairness and reciprocity which we see as central to it. Of course, often the requests of the teacher may be fair; but sometimes they might not be and a truly 'cooperative' child would then point this out, whereas an obedient or conforming child would do what the teacher said without question.

Thus, being 'cooperative' is *an active state of mind which does not avoid conflict*. Conflict need not be present, if trust is not misplaced. But if someone else is taking advantage of you or hindering you, the 'cooperative' person will actively protest this. It is this sense of cooperation which we think should underlie the encouragement of cooperative behaviour and the use of cooperative group work in the classroom curriculum.

The potential of cooperative group work in the classroom

Cooperative learning is a global term which encompasses a wide range of teaching strategies. Within this umbrella are different theoretical traditions, some of which overlap. We reviewed these in chapter three. However, there are, we think, three essential features of cooperative group work; these are very relevant to our discussion of 'cooperation', and to our thinking about the potential of CGW for improving social relationships.

(1) CGW brings children together outside friendship groups

We have seen that, very often, children will play with and work with children who are friends, and/or who are of the same ethnic group and gender as themselves. While there is nothing objectionable in this in itself, there are reasons for arguing that at least some of the *classroom* experience in school should provide children with wider opportunities for interaction. In particular, such interaction – under the right conditions – may help reduce prejudice and foster trust (and *sometimes* friendship) across ethnic and gender groups, and help integrate neglected or rejected children at least to the extent of increasing their peer acceptance.

(2) Children in cooperatively working groups must communicate, and share information and task loads in order to achieve a common goal

In CGW, cooperation is called for. It is fundamentally different from individual learning or from whole-class teaching in which each child still functions as an individual. Instead, different children *must* work together if the goal is to be achieved. Cooperation – trust and a fair division of workload – is needed. Being disruptive, or lazy, will make the task difficult – partly because it makes more work for those who *are* working, and partly because these latter will naturally resent the laziness or disruptiveness of others in their group, and will spend time attempting to change their behaviour.

(3) Conflicts will be discussed and attempts made to resolve them

Inevitably, many groups engaging in CGW – especially since they are often broader than friendship groups – will result in conflict. Some children *will* resent working with others or will not trust others or will be disruptive. Such conflict is not a failure of CGW; rather, it is a precondition for any success in tackling such problems, which will stem from the difficulties in peer relationships we discussed earlier. But the conflicts must not be left there. Through debriefing and perhaps through methods of mediation and conflict resolution, the teacher needs to help the children work through these difficulties; the hope is that (as in TIT FOR TAT) children can forgive each other and that trust can be gradually built up, and effective cooperation resumed.

It was with intentions such as these, that we examined the impact of CGW on social relationships in our project. We felt that we knew from other work that there could be clear academic benefits of CGW (e.g. Dunne and Bennett, 1990). We elected to work with classes where there were marked difficulties in *social* relationships – classes in innercity schools, ethnically mixed, where we had already found quite high levels of social rejection, bullying and victimisation, and racial prejudice. We also had some provisional evidence, from our first study (Smith, Cowie and Boulton, 1993) that CGW might have some positive impact on this state of affairs.

The successes of CGW in our project

There were some successes in our attempt – important to point out, against a general background of lack of effects (chapters six and seven). Firstly, some (not all) of the teachers, after initial reservations, became convinced of the usefulness of the method. Margie, for instance, despite initial scepticism and a reluctance to use CGW very extensively (table 6.9), ended up a strong advocate of its potential. Judy, one of the teachers in School C (which withdrew from the project after the first year) wrote to the project team afterwards to say that CGW had changed her teaching apporach and that it had become an integral part of her way of working with children. In the year following the end of the project Jane was very honest about the difficulties involved in implementing CGW methods with an exceptionally challenging class, but she remained committed to its use.

Secondly, many of the children liked CGW. From the fairly openended interviews with them in their working groups, we found in each year, and for both boys and girls, a majority whose comments could be scored as indicating that they liked CGW (rather than being neutral or disliking it). In fact, around two-thirds of the children indicated that they liked CGW – a clear majority. Also, many could give reasons for liking it which showed that, in their own way, they could appreciate the impact CGW could have on their relationships with others. For example, many children commented on the importance of working outside friendship groups because they 'learned to get on with new people' and because it was 'important to learn to work together'. Furthermore, in those groups which succeeded in working harmoniously across race and gender barriers, there were explicit statements about the need to combat the injustice of racial prejudice. Some children valued these opportunities to share their dislike of discrimination and abuse of power. In the groups which did work cooperatively children learned about working 'as a colleague' with peers; in some cases this working partnership developed into real friendship.

Thirdly, although most of our quantitative outcome or change measures gave inconclusive results, there was one important exception. Compared to the N.C. classes, the CGW classes did show a relative improvement in peer perceptions of who was a victim of bullying. This was a consistent finding: significant in year two and showing the same trend, nearly statistically significant, in year one. This – unfortunately – did not always mean that victimisation scores decreased; in some classes, including CGW classes, they got worse. But where this was the case, they got even worse still in N.C. classes matched for school and year group. At least CGW was slowing down one unfortunate trend in these classes.

Also, the decrease in 'victim' scores was not matched by a decrease in 'bully' scores. This suggests that as many children were attempting to bully others as before, but that fewer children were just submitting to it. In other words, while CGW had not significantly affected the behaviour of children seen as bullying others, it had had some impact on the children perceived as the victims – perhaps by giving them more confidence in themselves or raising their self-esteem. Cooperative group work might do this, if potential victims of bullying gained confidence through being drawn into working groups with other children who did not abuse or take advantage of them – thus providing models of non-abusive, non-exploitative interactions. An example of this progress seems to be Sudha (see chapter seven), whose 'victim' score steadily decreased through the two years she was in a CGW class and of whom Sally commented 'Sudha is not left out in CGW so she gets involved ... they'll give her something to do and she'll join in so if they're made to be in a group then she is involved, but if they're allowed to choose partners she won't usually be chosen.' One can see here that in an N.C. class, Sudha might have made less progress.

The failures of CGW in our project

Although there were some successes, our main aim had been to see whether CGW would have a positive impact on difficulties in children's social relationships in school. In talking about 'impact' here, we are of course considering the relative impact of CGW in these classes, taking the N.C. classes as a 'baseline' to compare against. In other words, would CGW have any more positive impact than just following the normal curriculum, which as we have seen did not involve much cooperative group work (table 6.9). By this criterion, and apart from the findings on 'victim' scores, the picture is one of failure (table 6.1).

Firstly, there was no impact on our measures of friendship and sociometric status. Overall liking scores did not increase more in the CGW classes, nor was there any greater change or decrease in the numbers of children who were sociometrically neglected or rejected.

Secondly, there was no impact on 'bully' scores, or on the numbers of classmates perceived as being bullies.

Thirdly, there was no impact on measures of racial or ethnic prejudice. We had two kinds of measure here – those related to classmates and those projective tests based on photos of unknown children. So far as classmates were concerned, and looking at our two major ethnic groups, there were no changes in Whites' liking of Asian classmates or in Asians' liking of White classmates. Looking at the projective tests based on unknown children, there was no change in social preference and no change on the stereotypes test of White children's stereotyping of Asians or of Asian children's stereotyping of Whites. Nor (based on this latter test) was there any reduction in the number of 'prejudiced' children.

At this point, we should reconsider the reliability, validity and sensitivity of these outcome measures. We have no reason to doubt reliability: all these methods have been widely used by other authors and, in the case of peer nominations (for liking, and for bully and victim scores), each individual child's score is based on the aggregate ratings from some twenty or more classmates.

Validity is a more difficult issue and may be called into question for some measures. In particular, in chapter two we discussed evidence that the projective tests for ethnic attitudes – the social preference and stereotypes tests – may have limited validity when compared against measures of actual friendship choices in the classroom or playground. But the peer nomination measures appear to be valid. Classmates generally showed considerable agreement and often the class aggregate perceptions agreed with that of the class teacher.

Finally, sensitivity to change is important if, like us, you are interested in seeing whether an intervention does produce change. Most of our measures would be sensitive to change. Liking scores can go up or down, for example, because there are no constraints on how many photographs of classmates were put in the 'like a lot' pile or the other two piles. Similarly for bully and victim scores, and for scores on the stereotypes test because of the 'nobody' option.

The sociometric categories are less sensitive. This is because, following standard procedures, they are based on the 'three like most' and 'three like least' nominations of classmates. Thus, the child being questioned is constrained to put three classmates in each category (and the great majority did so). There is obviously less scope for change, if – even in a perfectly harmonious classroom – each child 'has' to pick three children liked least! While the status types are good at picking out individual differences between children – an ability we put to good use in chapter seven – they are not good at showing overall change in the group. We were aware of this problem and regarded the peer nomination 'liking' scores as a much more sensitive indicator in this respect (but one which, unfortunately, showed no clear trends in favour of the CGW classes).

Overall, despite some uncertainties about the validity and the sensitivity of certain measures, we feel that our choice of outcome measures were reasonable. In fact, the general picture of across-the-board non-significant results (apart from 'victim' scores) in itself gives some measure of concurrent validity! It is possible that CGW was having an impact on other outcomes which we did not assess, but measures of liking, bullying, liking of classmates across ethnic groups, and stereotyping, seemed to be good reflections of the kinds of problems in social relationships which we were interested in.

Why did the failures occur?

Putting together our qualitative data with these primarily quantitative results, we feel we have a fairly good picture of why, despite some successes, the overall impact of CGW on social relationships must, in this project, be accounted a failure. These reasons can be divided into those to do with the teachers and the application of CGW; and those to do with pupils and the reception of CGW. Having said that, the two obviously interact.

Teachers and the application of CGW

Eight teachers took part in our CGW training – four of them for one year, four over two years (table 4.1).

As was shown in chapters five and six, the teachers generally had mixed feelings about CGW and mixed success in applying it. Although all had some commitment to trying it out and most had already experienced training in CGW methods through the World Studies curriculum package, many of them felt some fear or reluctance about 'letting go' of control or 'sharing power' with their pupils. There was an expressed anxiety, for example, about 'lifting the lid' for fear of what might happen to class discipline. As we have indicated, these fears were often justified since all the classes contained challenging children who were difficult to manage by any standards. At the same time, we know from numerous classroom observation studies that the didactic style of teaching has remained firmly in place in many primary schools. The philosophy and culture of the school are factors which strongly influence the impact which the introduction of a cooperative curriculum will have.

In addition some teachers did not use CGW very much. Margie's use of it was within the range found in N.C. classes and Sally did not use it very much more. Clearly these two teachers, who used CGW through two years, did not feel confident or willing enough to extend their use of CGW through much of the classroom curriculum. Equally clearly, we could not expect to find a differential impact of CGW compared to N.C. if there is no great difference in the amount of CGW actually used in the two conditions!

This of course would not apply to the other CGW teachers, who at least reported using CGW considerably more. However, the quality of CGW also needs to be considered, bearing in mind the three essential aspects discussed earlier. One teacher at least – Judy, in year one – sometimes allowed groups to be self-chosen. We do not know how often this happened, but if it was frequent it would negate the thrust of CGW on social relationships. And as far as all the teachers are concerned, it is not clear how thoroughly the debriefing procedures were followed when conflicts arose. The importance of debriefing in CGW is often overlooked, particularly when there are pressures of time. Sometimes, perhaps naturally enough after a tiring period, the essential debriefing and working through aspects of group work may have been foreshortened or even dropped. This again would mitigate against the social effects of CGW and in some respects might actually make matters worse. In retrospect, we should probably have put more emphasis on debriefing and included training in relevant skills such as mediation and conflict resolution, in our initial and continuing training programme.

Pupils and the reception of CGW

It is quite clear from the diary records (chapter six) that many of our teachers experienced great difficulties with certain children: Margie/Jane, Pat and Sally are prominent examples. Quite independently, we had identified certain children (often, the very same children) as having problematic social relationships, on the basis of peer nominations. Our CGW classes had between two and seven of these very difficult children – an average of four or five in each class of some 20 to 25 children. Such children – some of them detailed in our case studies in chapter seven, for example Mark, Sean, Alan, Alex, Seth, Joshua – could make things very difficult for the class teacher. But, especially, they would be likely to make CGW difficult.

Many of these 'difficult' children were boys and they were generally not well liked by most classmates, and were seen as bullies or sometimes as bully-victims. We saw in chapter seven (table 7.1) how these children often actively disliked CGW and quite openly expressed this. They did not like being placed outside friendship groups or away from their 'cronies', they did not (if boys) like mixing with girls, and they sometimes expressed racial prejudice. More generally, it would seem, they did not want to run the risk of losing power. A properly functioning cooperative group would mean sharing power, sharing responsibility, give and take, even with less powerful or dominant classmates. Many of these 'difficult' children just did not want to do this. The non-cooperativeness of the 'rejected-aggressive' child was very strikingly shown in these situations.

Such children could make it very difficult for a group to work effectively. In chapter seven we saw how Sean (independently nominated by *all* his classmates as a bully at time 4!) could be unpleasant and disruptive with Alex (a shy boy) and Olivia (a popular girl). He could clearly spoil their experience of CGW, which might otherwise have been positive; indeed, Olivia had liked CGW but after being placed with Sean came to have a somewhat negative view of it.

To cope with these difficulties and conflicts would require much time, skill and expertise from the class teacher. Given that our teachers using CGW varied in commitment, and through lack of specific training and pressures of time did not deal with these conflicts thoroughly – perhaps in any event a near impossible task for one person – it is not, in retrospect, so surprising that CGW had such a limited impact on social relationships. We suspect that in 'easier' classrooms – ones where the great majority of children were well-behaved, with only one or two persistently troublesome children – and given good training and support, CGW could still be a very effective curriculum method, both academically and socially. But for classes with many disruptive children, and with limited resources, the outlook seems more problematic.

Conclusions: the future of cooperative group work for improving social relationships

On the basis of our project, we feel that CGW is not a panacea for coping with social relationship difficulties in classrooms. Nevertheless, we still feel that the approach has potential. If we want cooperation to be developed in children with anti-social tendencies who find cooperation difficult, then the goal is still a desirable one even if it is difficult to reach. In fact, most children like cooperative group work. In many classrooms – for example those described by Dunne and Bennett (1990) – it appears to work effectively. We suspect that these classes may sample less socio-economically disadvantaged families than our own classes did, with many fewer *really* disturbed children. Many children present some difficulties to teachers, of course, but as our case studies make clear, some of our children were exceptionally difficult and aggressive, and often came from quite unsupportive home backgrounds.

Many of the U.S. and Israeli studies have pointed to benefits of CGW, also (see chapter three). Again this reinforces our belief in its potential. But many of these studies were short term, in selected classroom situations. We believe our study to have been much more 'ecologically valid' in the sense of what is achievable in more difficult but – for some inner cities – quite realistic conditions.

So, what lessons can be drawn for the future? We think there are three.

(1) If classes contain difficult children, implementing CGW will not be easy

If CGW is to be used in classes with appreciable numbers of difficult children – and by difficult, we mean children who find cooperation difficult, children who will often be disliked by classmates and often seen as bullies – then its successful application will not be easy. There is a possibility, if not a probability, that these difficult children will hinder the working of cooperative groups and effectively spoil the benefits of it for the majority of classmates.

With experience and with the support of teachers and members of the peer group, there is a realistic hope that even difficult pupils can develop the qualities which will help them to solve problems, to complete tasks and to interact effectively with one another. Teachers and their pupils can work together to overcome personal fears and anxieties about the approach. By ensuring that group members understand the importance of participation, supportiveness and turn-taking, groups can help members, for example, to search for the right words to capture an experience or encompass an idea. Empathic awareness of another person's feelings – an essential ingredient of effective cooperation – can also play a key role in exploring the processes of controversy and conflict. Pupils learn by challenging one another as they reformulate points of view and practise the skills of constructive criticism.

(2) In such classes, teachers wishing to implement CGW will need considerable help and training

If the disruption of cooperative groups by difficult pupils is to be prevented, the class teacher will need considerable help and training. This will consist of training not only in CGW methods *per se* (which we feel we did effectively), but also in sustained debriefing and working through the inevitable conflicts and disagreements which will arise when children who find it difficult to cooperate are put in groups required to cooperate. This, after all, is the core process by which CGW might really affect and change social relationships, where such change is needed most. Quite specific training in mediation and conflict resolution skills may be needed in addition to that in CGW tasks.

But if teachers are to do this well, even when specifically trained, they also need time to work with individuals and small groups. In the pressures of the normal school classroom, this time is just not available. In a class of 25 children, 5 of whom are severe problems, the teacher cannot spend a great deal of time working through problems with one child or one group. They will just be 'firefighting' – dealing temporarily with issues as they arise rather than working through them in any depth. Although a few of our CGW teachers had a helper in the class for children with difficulties with the English language or for some weeks a trainee teacher, these forms of help are not broad or long term enough to make much difference as far as children's relationship problems are concerned. Many such problems might be more the province of the educational psychologist; but the latter would not be able to spend a long time in the classroom and could not deal with problems as they arise in CGW groups. If we believe that classroom groups and their conflicts are the natural way to work on cooperation and on relationship problems, we need to find some new ways of both training teachers, and helping or resourcing them better. For example, training in counselling skills could enhance teachers' capacity to deal with interpersonal difficulties in the classroom (Cowie and Pecherek, 1994).

(3) Schools can achieve something, but the wider social context cannot be ignored

The relationship problems of difficult children have a wider dimension than the school. Many of these children come from families where conflict is itself endemic (chapter seven). As with the wider issues of conduct disorder and delinquency, it has become clear that while schools can achieve a great deal, their impact will be limited while severe problems exist in the family, community and wider society. The problems of difficult children cannot be separated from issues such as attachment quality between parents and children, in turn related to prior parenting history, and to socio-economic stress; nor can they be separated from the extent of conflict and racial prejudice which children see and experience outside the school. Prejudiced attitudes are reflected in the community and the wider society, and these attitudes are often further reinforced by social institutions. Children are being brought up in a society where minority groups are discriminated against at every level.

The task facing schools is a daunting one. But while schools cannot achieve everything, they can achieve something. The recent work on the impact which schools can have on rates of bullying, through school policy development as well as curriculum and playground work, is encouraging (Olweus, 1993; Smith and Sharp, 1994). We believe too that in the long run, CGW methods have an important part to play in building relations of trust and cooperation in the school environment, with at least the possibility that these can serve as models for behaviour outside the school. Such action does not absolve us from trying to help families and to improve communities; rather, it should go along with it. In any event, some combined or integrative approach is going to be needed if CGW is to be used effectively in schools with many difficult and disruptive pupils – arguably the situation where it is needed most. Without some form of wider support, teachers will find its application difficult or impossible. Yet if the status quo continues, these children are not being 'helped' until they emerge as special cases for the educational psychologist, or later in the statistics for delinquency and criminal behaviour. The class teacher is in the front line for dealing with these problems at an early stage and we believe CGW could provide an effective approach; but these teachers will need much more support from us to have a hope of doing the job properly.

BIBLIOGRAPHY

Aboud, F. (1988) *Children and Prejudice* (Oxford: Basil Blackwell).
Ahlberg, J. and Ahlberg, A. (1986) *The Jolly Postman* (London: Heinemann).
Aronson, E. (1978) *The Jigsaw Classroom* (Beverley Hills: Sage).
Arora, C. M. J. and Thompson, D. A. (1987) 'Defining bullying for a secondary school', *Education and Child Psychology*, **4**, 110-20.
Asher, S. R. and Allen, V. L. (1969) 'Racial preference and social comparison processes', *Journal of Social Issues*, **25**, 157-66.
Asher, S. R., Hymel, S. and Renshaw, P. D. (1984) 'Loneliness in children', *Child Development*, **55**, 1456-64.
Asher, S. R. and Parker, J. G. (1989) 'Significance of peer relationship problems in childhood' in B. H. Schneider, G. Attili, J. Nadel and R. P. Weissberg (eds.) *Social Competence in Developmental Perspective* (Dordrecht: Kluwer).
Asher, S. R., Parkhurst, J. T., Hymel, S. and Williams, G. A. (1990) 'Peer rejection and loneliness in childhood' in S. R. Asher and J. D. Coie (eds.) *Peer Rejection in Childhood* (New York: Cambridge University Press).
Asher, S. R. and Williams, G. A. (1987) 'New approaches to identifying rejected children at school'. Paper presented at the American Educational Research Association, Washington DC.
Ashley, M. (1992) 'The validity of sociometric status', *Educational Research*, **34**, 149-54.
Axelrod, R. and Hamilton, W. D. (1981) 'The evolution of cooperation', *Science*, **211**, 1390-96.
Balaam, J. and Merrick, B. (1988) *Exploring Poetry 5-8* (London: National Association for the Teaching of English).
Barnes, D. (1976) *From Communication to Curriculum* (Harmondsworth: Penguin).
Barnes, D., Britton, J. and Rosen, H. (1969) *Language, the Learner and the School* (Harmondsworth: Penguin).
Bennett, M., Dewberry, C. and Yeeles, C. (1991) 'A reassessment of the role of ethnicity in children's social perception', *Journal of Child Psychology and Psychiatry*, **32**, 969-82.
Bennett, N. (1985) 'Interaction and achievement in classroom groups' in N. Bennett and C. Desforges (eds.), *Recent Advances in Classroom Research*, British Journal of Educational Psychology, Monograph Series no. 2 (Edinburgh: Scottish Academic Press).
Bennett, N. (1991) 'Cooperative learning in classrooms: processes and outcomes', *Journal of Child Psychology and Psychiatry*, **32**, 581-94.
Bennett, N. and Dunne, E. (1992) *Managing Classroom Groups* (Hemel Hempstead: Simon and Schuster).

Berndt, T. J. (1984) 'Sociometric, social-cognitive, and behavioral measures for the study of friendship and popularity' in T. Field, J. L. Roopnarine and M. Segal (eds.) *Friendships in Normal and Handicapped Children* (Norwood, N. J.: Ablex).
Besag, V. E. (1989) *Bullies and Victims in Schools* (Milton Keynes: Open University Press).
Bjorkqvist, K., Lagerspetz, K. M. J. and Kaukainen, A. (1992) 'Do girls manipulate and boys fight? Developmental trends in regard to direct and indirect aggression', *Aggressive Behavior*, 18, 117-27.
Blaney, N. T., Stephen, S., Rosenfield, D., Aronson, E. and Sikes, J. (1977) 'Interdependence in the classroom: a field study', *Journal of Educational Psychology*, 69, 121-28.
Boulton, M. J. (unpublished) 'Playground behaviour and peer interaction patterns of bullies, victims and not involved children'.
Boulton, M. J. and Smith, P. K. (1992) 'Ethnic preferences and perceptions among Asian and White British middle school children', *Social Development*, 1, 55-66.
Boulton, M. J. and Smith, P. K. (1993) 'Ethnic, gender partner and activity preferences in mixed race schools in the U.K.: playground observations' in C. H. Hart (ed.) *Children on Playgrounds: Research Perspectives and Applications* (New York: State University of New York Press).
Boulton, M. J. and Smith, P. K. (1994) 'Bully/victim problems among middle school children: Stability, self-perceived competence, and peer acceptance', *British Journal of Developmental Psychology*.
Boulton, M. J. and Smith, P. K. (unpublished) 'Sociometric status, rough-and-tumble play and aggression: Participation and social skill'.
Boulton, M. J. and Underwood, K. (1992) 'Bully/victim problems among middle school children', *British Journal of Educational Psychology*, 62, 73-87.
Bowers, L., Smith, P. K. and Binney, V. (1992) 'Cohesion and power in the families of children involved in bully/victim problems at school', *Journal of Family Therapy*, 14, 371-87.
Bowers, L., Smith, P. K. and Binney, V. (1994) 'Family relationships as perceived by children involved in bully/victim problems at school', *Journal of Personal and Social Relationships*, 11, 215-32.
Brandes, D. and Phillips, H. (1979) *Gamester's Handbook* (London: Hutchinson).
Brown, A. and Palinscar, A. (1989) 'Guided cooperative learning and individual knowledge acquisition' in L. Resnick (ed.) *Knowing, Learning and Instruction* (Hillsdale, N.J.: Lawrence Erlbaum Associates).
Bruner, J. S. (1986) *Actual Minds, Possible Worlds* (Boston: Harvard University Press).
Bukowski, W. M. and Hoza, B. (1989) 'Popularity and friendship: Issues in theory, measurement, and outcome' in T. J. Berndt and G. W. Ladd (eds.) *Peer Relationships in Child Development* (New York: Wiley).
Bullock Report (1975) *A Language for Life* (London: H.M.S.O.).
Cairns, R. B., Cairns, B. D., Neckerman, H. J., Gest, S. D. and Gariepy, J. (1988) 'Social networks and aggressive behavior: Peer support or peer rejection', *Developmental Psychology*, 24, 815-23.
Carrington, B. and Short, G. (1993) 'Probing children's prejudice – a consideration of the ethical and methodological issues raised by research and curriculum development', *Educational Studies*, 19, 163-79.
Cassidy, J. and Asher, S. R. (1992) 'Loneliness and peer relations in young children', *Child Development*, 63, 350-65.
Charlesworth, W. R. and LaFreniere, P. (1983) 'Dominance, friendship, and resource utilization in preschool children's groups', *Ethology and Sociobiology*, 4, 175-86.

Cillessen, A. H. N., van IJzendoorn, H. W., van Lieshout, C. F. M. and Hartup, W. W. (1992) 'Hetereogeneity among peer-rejected boys: subtypes and stabilities', *Child Development*, **63**, 893-905.

Clark, K. B. and Clark, M. P. (1939) 'The development of the consciousness of self and the emergence of racial identity in negro preschool children', *Journal of Social Psychology*, **10**, 591-99.

Coates, D. L. (1985) 'Relationships between self concept measures and social networks characteristics for black adolescents', *Journal of Early Adolescence*, **5**, 319-38.

Cohn, T. (1988) 'Sambo – a study in name calling' in Kelly, E. and Cohn, T. *Racism in Schools: New Research Evidence* (Stoke-on-Trent: Trentham Books).

Coie, J. D., Christopolous, C., Terry, R., Dodge, K. A. and Lochman, J. E. (1989) 'Types of aggressive relationships, peer rejection, and developmental consequences' in B. H. Schneider, G. Attili, J. Nadel, and R. P. Weissberg (eds.) *Social Competence in Developmental Perspective* (Dordrecht: Kluwer).

Coie, J. D. and Dodge, K. A. (1988) 'Multiple sources of data on social behavior and social status in the school: A cross-age comparison', *Child Development*, **59**, 815-29.

Coie, J. D., Dodge, K. A. and Coppotelli, H. (1982) 'Dimensions and types of social status: A cross-age perspective', *Developmental Psychology*, **18**, 557-70.

Coie, J. D. and Kupersmidt, J. B. (1983) 'A behavioral analysis of emerging social status in boys' groups', *Child Development*, **54**, 1400-16.

Commission for Racial Equality (1988) *Learning in Terror: A Survey of Racial Harassment in Schools and Colleges* (London: C.R.E.).

Cowie, H. (1994) 'Involving children in decision-making' in P. Blatchford and S. Sharp (eds.) *Understanding and Managing School Breaktime Behaviour* (London: Routledge).

Cowie, H. and Pecherek, A. (1994) *Counselling: Approaches and Issues in Education* (London: David Fulton).

Cowie, H. and Rudduck, J. (1988a) *Cooperative Group Work: An Overview* (London: B.P. Educational Services).

Cowie, H. and Rudduck, J. (1988b) *School and Classroom Studies* (London: B.P. Educational Services).

Cowie, H. and Rudduck, J. (1990) *Cooperative Group Work: Transitions and Traditions* (London: B.P. Educational Services).

Cowie, H and Sharp, S. (1992) 'Pupils themselves tackle the problem of bullying', *Pastoral Care in Education*, **10**, 31-37.

Crick, N. R. (1991) 'Subgroups of neglected and rejected children'. Paper presented at meeting of the Society for Research in Child Development, Seattle, W.A.

Davey, A. G. (1983) *Learning to be Prejudiced: Growing up in Multi-Ethnic Britain* (London: Edward Arnold).

Davey, A. G. and Mullin, P. N. (1980) 'Ethnic identification and preference of British primary school children', *Journal of Child Psychology and Psychiatry*, **21**, 241-51.

Davies, B. (1982) *Life in the Classroom and Playground: The Accounts of Primary School Children* (London: Routledge and Kegan Paul).

Denscombe, M. (1983) 'Ethnic group and friendship choice in the primary school', *Educational Research*, **25**, 184-90.

DeVries, D. and Slavin, R. (1978) 'Teams – Games – Tournaments: a review of ten classroom experiments', *Journal of Research and Development in Education*, **12**, 28-38.

DFE (1992) *Choice and Diversity: A New Framework for Schools* (London: H.M.S.O.).

Dodge, K. A. (1983) 'Behavioral antecedents of peer social status', *Child Development*, **54**, 1386-99.

Dodge, K. A. and Coie, J. D. (1987) 'Social-information-processing factors in reactive and proactive aggression in children's peer groups', *Journal of Personality and Social Psychology*, **53**, 1146-58.

Dunne, E. and Bennett, N. (1990) *Talking and Learning in Groups* (London: Macmillan).

Eggleston, J. (1985) *The Educational and Vocational Experiences of 15–18-Year-Old Young People of Minority Ethnic Groups* (Keele: Department of Education, University of Keele).

Eitan, T., Amir, Y. and Rich, Y. (1992) 'Social and academic treatments in mixed-ethnic classes and change in student self-concept', *British Journal of Educational Psychology*, **62**, 364-74.

Epstein, J. L. (1983) 'Selection of friends in differently organized schools and classrooms' in J. L. Epstein and N. Kareweit (eds.) *Friends in School: Patterns of Selection and Influence in Secondary Schools* (New York: Academic Press).

Epstein, J. L. (1989) 'The selection of friends: Changes across the grades and in different school environments' in T. J. Berndt and G. W. Ladd (eds.) *Peer Relationships in Child Development* (New York: Wiley).

Farrington, D. P. (1994) 'Understanding and preventing bullying' in M. Tonry (ed.) *Crime and Justice: A Review of Research*, **17**, 381-458 (Chicago: University of Chicago Press).

Fine, G. A. (1980) 'The natural history of preadolescent male friendship groups' in H. C. Foot, A. J. Chapman and J. R. Smith (eds.) *Friendship and Social Relations in Children* (New York: Wiley).

Finkelstein, N. W. and Haskins, R. (1983) 'Kindergarten children prefer same-color peers', *Child Development*, **54**, 502-08.

Fisher, S. and Hicks, D. (1987) *World Studies* (Edinburgh: Oliver and Boyd).

Furman, W. and Buhrmester, D. (1985) 'Children's perceptions of the personal relationships in their social networks', *Developmental Psychology*, **21**, 1016-24.

Furman, W. and Childs, M. K. (1981) 'A temporal perspective on children's friendships'. Paper presented at the biennial meeting of the Society for Research in Child Development, Boston.

Galton, M. and Patrick, H. (eds) (1990) *Curriculum Provision in Small Primary Schools* (London: Routledge).

Galton, M., Simon, B. and Croll, P. (1980) *Inside the Primary Classroom* (London: Routledge and Kegan Paul).

Galton, M. and Williamson, J. (1992) *Group Work in the Primary Classroom* (London: Routledge).

Gillborn, D. (1990) *'Race', Ethnicity and Education* (London: Unwin Hyman).

Gilmartin, B. G. (1987) 'Peer group antecedents of severe love-shyness in males', *Journal of Personality*, **55**, 467-89.

Gregor, A. J. and McPherson, D. A. (1966) 'Racial preference and ego identity among white and Bantu children in the Republic of South Africa', *Genetic Psychology Monographs*, **73**, 217-54.

Hammersley, M. (1992) A response to Barry Troyna's 'Children, "Race" and Racism: the limits of research and policy', *British Journal of Educational Studies*, **40**, 174-7.

Harter, S. (1985) *Manual for the Self-Perception Profile for Children* (University of Denver).

Hartup, W. W. (1989) 'Behavioral manifestations of children's friendships' in T. J. Berndt and G. W. Ladd (eds.) *Peer Relationships in Child Development* (New York: Wiley).

Hayvren, M. and Hymel, S. (1984) 'Ethical issues in sociometric testing: impact of sociometric measures on interaction behavior' *Developmental Psychology*, **20**, 844-9.

Hertz-Lazarowitz, R. (1992) 'Understanding interactive behaviors: Looking at six mirrors of the classroom' in R. Hertz-Lazarowitz and N. Miller (eds) *Interaction in Cooperative Groups: Theoretical Anatomy of Group Learning* (Cambridge: Cambridge University Press).

Hertz-Lazarowitz, R. and Miller, N. (eds) (1992) *Interaction in Cooperative Groups: Theoretical Anatomy of Group Learning* (Cambridge: Cambridge University Press).

Hirano, K. (1992) 'Bullying and victimisation in Japanese classrooms'. Paper presented at the 5th European Conference on Developmental Psychology, Seville, Spain.

H.M.I. (1983) *9-13 Middle Schools: An Illustrative Study* (London: H.M.S.O.).

Hopson, B. and Scally, M. (1981) *Lifeskills Teaching* (London: McGraw Hill).

Howes, C. and Wu, F. (1990) 'Peer interactions and friendships in an ethnically diverse school setting', *Child Development*, **61**, 537-41.

Hymel, S., Franke, S. and Freigang, R. (1985) 'Peer relationships and their disfunction: Considering the child's perspective', *Journal of Social and Clinical Psychology*, **3**, 405-15.

Jahoda, G., Thompson, S. S. and Bhatt, S. (1972) 'Ethnic identity and preference among Asian immigrant children in Glasgow', *European Journal of Social Psychology*, **2**, 19-32.

Jelinek, M. M. and Brittan, E. M. (1975) 'Multi-racial education: 1. Inter-ethnic friendship patterns', *Educational Research*, **18**, 44-53.

Johnson, D. W. and Johnson, R. T. (1982) *Joining Together: Group Theory and Group Skills* (Englewood Cliffs, N.J.: Prentice Hall).

Johnson, D. W. and Johnson, R. T. (1987) *Learning Together and Alone* (Englewood Cliffs, N.J.: Prentice Hall).

Johnson, D. W., Johnson, R. T., Johnson, J. and Anderson, D. (1976) 'Effects of cooperative versus individualized instruction on student prosocial behavior, attitude towards learning, and achievement', *Journal of Educational Psychology*, **68**, 446-52.

Johnson, D. W., Johnson, R. T. and Scott, L. (1978) 'The effects of cooperative versus individualized instruction on student attitudes and achievement', *Journal of Social Psychology*, **104**, 207-16.

Kagan, S. (1986) *Beyond Language: Social and Cultural Factors in Schooling Language Minority Students* (California: Evaluation, Dissemination and Assessment Centre, California State University).

Kelly, E. (1988) 'Pupils, racial groups and behaviour in schools' in Kelly, E. and Cohn, T. *Racism in Schools: New Research Evidence* (Stoke-on-Trent: Trentham Books).

Kelly, E. and Cohn, T. (1988) *Racism in Schools: New Research Evidence* (Stoke-on-Trent: Trentham Books).

Kerry, T. and Eggleston, J. (1988) *Topic Work in the Primary School* (London: Routledge).

Kreidler, W. (1984) *Creative Conflict Resolution* (Glenview, Illinois: Scott, Foresman and Co).

Kutnick, P. (1988) *Relationships in the Primary School Classroom* (London: Paul Chapman).

Ladd, G. W. (1983) 'Social networks of popular, average, and rejected children in school settings', *Merrill-Palmer Quarterly*, **29**, 283-308.

LaFontaine, J. (1991) *Bullying: The Child's View* (London: Calouste Gulbenkian Foundation).

Lagerspetz, K. M. J., Bjorkqvist, K., Berts, M. and King, E. (1982) 'Group aggression among school children in three schools' *Scandinavian Journal of Psychology*, **23**, 45-52.

Lane, D. (1989) 'Violent histories: Bullying and criminality' in D. P. Tattum and D. A. Lane (eds.), *Bullying in Schools* (Stoke-on-Trent: Trentham Books).

Lewis, D. O., Lovely, R., Yeager, C. and Femina, D. D. (1989) 'Towards a theory of the genesis of violence: A follow-up study of delinquents', *Journal of the American Academy of Child and Adolescent Psychiatry*, **28**, 431-6.

Lewis, J. and Cowie, H. (1993) 'Kooperative Gruppenarbeit: Versprechungen und Begrenzungen – Eine Untersuchung der Werte der Lehren' in G. Huber (ed.) *Neue Perspektiven der Kooperation* (Tubingen: Schneider Verlag Hohengehren).

Malik, G. (unpublished) *Bullying – an Investigation of Race and Gender Aspects* (University of Sheffield: MSc thesis).

Mannarino, A. P. (1976) 'Friendship patterns and altruistic behavior in preadolescent males', *Developmental Psychology*, **12**, 555-6.

Masheder, M. (1986) *Let's Cooperate* (London: Peace Education Project).

Milner, D. (1973) 'Racial identification and preference in 'black' British children', *European Journal of Social Psychology*, **3**, 281-96.

Milner, D. (1975) *Children and Race* (London: Cox and Wyman).

Mooney, A., Creeser, R. and Blatchford (1991) 'Children's views on teasing and fighting in junior school', *Educational Research*, **33**, 103-12.

Moran, S., Smith, P. K., Thompson, D. and Whitney, I. (1993) 'Ethnic differences in experiences of bullying: Asian and white children', *British Journal of Educational Psychology*, **63**, 431-40.

Mortimore, P., Sammons, P., Stoll, L. D. and Ecob, R. (1988) *School Matters: The Junior Years* (Wells: Open Books).

Newcomb, A. F., Brady, J. E. and Hartup, W. W. (1979) 'Friendship and incentive condition as determinants of children's task-oriented social behavior', *Child Development*, **50**, 878-81.

Newcomb, A. F. and Bukowski, W. M. (1983) 'Social impact and social preference as determinants of children's peer group status', *Developmental Psychology*, **19**, 856-67.

Olweus, D. (1978) *Aggression in the Schools: Bullies and Whipping Boys* (Washington DC: Hemisphere).

Olweus, D. (1979) 'Stability of aggressive reaction patterns in males: a review', *Psychological Bulletin*, **86**, 852-75.

Olweus, D. (1984) 'Aggressors and their victims: Bullying at school' in N. Frude and H. Gault (eds.) *Disruptive Behaviour in Schools* (Chichester: Wiley).

Olweus, D. (1987) 'Bully/victim problems among schoolchildren in Scandinavia' in J. P. Myklebust and R. Ommundsen (eds.) *Psykologprofesjonen mot ar 2000* (Oslo: Universitetsforlaget).

Olweus, D. (1989) 'Prevalence and incidence in the study of anti-social behavior: Definitions and measurement' in M. Klein (ed.) *Cross-National Research in Self-Reported Crime and Delinquency* (Dordrecht: Kluwer).

Olweus, D. (1991) 'Bully/victim problems among school children: Basic facts and effects of a school based intervention program' in D. Pepler and K. Rubin (eds.) *The Development and Treatment of Childhood Aggression* (Hillsdale, N.J.: Erlbaum).

Olweus, D. (1993) 'Bullies on the playground: The role of victimization' in C. Hart (ed.) *Children on Playgrounds: Research Perspectives and Applications* (New York: State University of New York Press).

O'Moore, A. M. and Hillery, B. (1989) 'Bullying in Dublin schools', *Irish Journal of Psychology*, **10**, 426-41.

Orlick, T. (1978) *The Cooperative Sports and Games Book* (New York: Pantheon Books).

Orlick, T. (1982) *The Second Cooperative Sports and Games Book* (new York: Pantheon Books).

Parker, J. G. and Asher, S. R. (1987) 'Peer relations and later personal adjustment: Are low-accepted children at risk?', *Psychological Bulletin*, **102**, 357-89.

Parker, J. G. and Asher, S. R. (1988) *Peer Group Acceptance and the Quality of Children's Best Friendships*. Paper presented at the N.A.T.O. Advanced Study Institute, Savoy, France.

Parker, J. G. and Gottman, J. M. (1989) 'Social and emotional development in a relational context: Friendship interaction from early childhood to adolescence' in T. J. Berndt and G. W. Ladd (eds.) *Peer Relationships in Child Development* (New York: Wiley).

Perry, D. G., Kusel, S. J. and Perry, L. C. (1988) 'Victims of peer aggression', *Developmental Psychology*, **24**, 807-14.

Pike, G. and Selby, D. (1988) *Global Teacher, Global Learner* (London: Hodder and Stoughton).

Plowden Report (1967) *Children and their Primary Schools* (London: H.M.S.O.).

Radke, M., Sutherland, J. and Rosenberg, P. (1950) 'Racial attitudes of children', *Sociometry*, **13**, 154-71.

Rampton Report (1981) *West Indian Children in our Schools* (London: H.M.S.O.).

Renninger, C. A. and Williams, J. E. (1966) 'Black-white colour-connotations and race awareness in pre-school children', *Perceptual and Motor Skills*, **22**, 771-85.

Roland, E. (1987) Lectures held at the Council of Europe conference 'Bullying in schools', Stavanger, Norway. Cited in E. Roland and E. Munthe (eds.) *Bullying an International Perspective* (London: David Fulton).

Roland, E. (1989) 'Bullying: The Scandinavian research tradition' in D. P. Tattum and D. A. Lane (eds.) *Bullying in Schools* (Stoke-on-Trent: Trentham Books).

Rubin, K. H., Hymel, S., LeMare, L. and Rowden, L. (1989) 'Children experiencing social difficulties: Sociometric neglect reconsidered', *Canadian Journal of Behavioral Science*, **21**, 95-111.

Ruiz, R. O. (1992) *Violence in Schools: Problems of Bullying and Victimization in Spain*. Paper presented at the 5th European Conference on Developmental Psychology, Seville, Spain.

Russell, H. (1986) *Play and Friendships in a Multi-Cultural Playground* (Melbourne: Australian Children's Folklore Publications, Institute of Early Childhood Development).

Salmon, P. and Claire, H. (1984) *Classroom Collaboration* (London: Routledge and Kegan Paul).

Schofield, J. W. and Francis, W. D. (1982) 'An observational study of peer interactions in racially mixed "accelerated" classrooms', *Journal of Educational Psychology*, **74**, 722-32.

Schofield, J. W. and Sagar, H. A. (1977) 'Peer interaction patterns in an integrated middle school', *Sociometry*, **40**, 130-8.

Sharan, S. (1980) 'Cooperative learning in small groups: recent methods and effects in achievement, attitudes and ethnic relations', *Review of Educational Research*, **50**, 241-71.

Sharan, S. (1985) 'Cooperative learning and the multi-ethnic classroom' in R. Slavin (ed.) *Learning to Cooperate: Cooperating to Learn* (New York: Plenum).

Sharan, S. (1990) 'Cooperative learning and behaviour in the multi-ethnic classroom' in H. Foot, M. Morgan and R. Shute (eds.) *Children Helping Children* (London: Wiley).

Sharan, S. and Sharan, Y. (1976) *Small Group Teaching* (Englewood Cliffs, N.J.: Educational Technology Publications).

Slavin, R. (1983) *Cooperative Learning* (New York: Longman).
Slavin, R. (1987) 'Developmental and motivational perspectives on cooperative learning', *Child Development*, **58**, 1161-7.
Smith, P. K., Bowers, L., Binney, V. and Cowie, H. (1993) 'Relationships of children involved in bully/victim problems at school' in S. Duck (ed.) *Learning about Relationships: Understanding Relationship Processes*, **2**, pp.186-212 (Newbury Park: Sage).
Smith, P. K., Boulton, M. and Cowie, H. (1993) 'The impact of cooperative group work on ethnic relations in middle school', *School Psychology International*, **14**, 21-42.
Smith, P. K. and Sharp, S. (eds) (1994) *School Bullying: Insights and Perspectives* (London: Routledge).
Smoller, J. and Youniss, J. (1982) 'Social development through friendship' in K. H. Rubin and H. S. Ross (eds.) *Peer Relationships and Social Skills in Childhood* (New York: Springer-Verlag).
Stephenson, P. and Smith, D. (1989) 'Bullying in the junior school' in D. P. Tattum and D. A. Lane (eds.) *Bullying in Schools* (Stoke-on-Trent: Trentham Books).
Stevenson, H. W. and Stewart, E. C. (1958) 'A developmental study of racial awareness in young children', *Child Development*, **29**, 399-409.
Swann Report. (1985) *Education for All* (London: H.M.S.O.).
Tigwell, T. (1990) *The National Curriculum and the World Beyond* (Sheffield: South Yorkshire World Development Education Centre).
Tizard, B., Blatchford, P., Burke, J., Farquhar, C. and Plewis, I. (1988) *Young Children at School in the Inner City* (Hove: Lawrence Erlbaum).
Troyna, B. and Hatcher, R. (1992) *Racism in Children's Lives* (London: Routledge).
Vaughan, G. M. (1964) 'The development of ethnic attitudes in New Zealand school children', *Genetic Psychology Monographs*, **70**, 135-75.
Vygotsky, L. S. (1978) *Mind in Society* (Boston: Harvard University Press).
Webb, N. (1985) 'Student interaction and learning in small groups: A research summary' in R. Slavin, S. Sharan, R. Hertz-Lazarowitz, E. Webb and R. Schmuck (eds.) *Learning to Cooperate, Cooperating to Learn* (New York: Plenum).
Whitney, I. and Smith, P. K. (1993) 'A survey of the nature and extent of bullying in junior/middle and secondary schools', *Educational Research*, **35**, 3-25.
Wilson, A. (1987) *Mixed Race Children: A Study of Identity* (London: Allen & Unwin).
Wright, C. (1992) *Race Relations in the Primary School* (London: David Fulton).

Index

Name Index

Aboud, F. 31, 34, 36, 66, 190
Ahlberg, A. 92
Ahlberg, J. 92
Allen, V. L. 28
Amir, Y. 62
Anderson, D. 10
Aronson, E. 54, 61
Arora, C. M. J. 15
Asher, S. R. 8, 10–14, 28
Ashley, M. 77
Axelrod, R. 191

Balaam, J. 51, 53
Barnes, D. 49, 51, 64
Bennett, M. 30–31
Bennett, N. 50–51, 57–58, 63, 84, 96–98, 194, 200
Berndt, T. J. 3
Berts, M. 22
Besag, V. E. 41
Bhatt, S. 28
Binney, V. 164
Bjorkqvist, K. 21–22
Blaney, N. T. 61
Blatchford, P. 35
Boulton, M. J. 12–13, 16–26, 28–29, 31–36, 39, 67–68, 74, 76, 194
Bowers, L. 164
Brady, J. E. 9
Brandes, D. 46
Brittan, E. M. 29
Britton, J. 49
Brown, A. 62–63
Bruner, J. S. 44
Buhrmester, D. 3
Bukowski, W. M. 3, 7
Bullock Report 43

Burke, J. 35

Cairns, B. D. 23
Cairns, R. B. 23
Carrington, B. 76
Cassidy, J. 11
Charlesworth, W. R. 9
Childs, M. K. 10
Christopolous, C. 5, 7
Cillessen, A. H. N. 7
Claire, H. 64–65
Clark, K. B. 28
Clark, M. P. 28
Coates, D. L. 9
Cohn, T. 35, 37
Coie, J. D. 4–7, 9, 117
Commission for Racial Equality 47–48
Coppotelli, H. 4, 9
Cowie, H. 44, 48–49, 52, 59, 64–65, 67, 74, 76, 80, 164, 194, 201
Creeser, R. 35
Crick, N. R. 7–8
Croll, P. 58–59

Davey, A. G. 28–31, 118
Davies, B. 12
Denscombe, M. 76–77
DeVries, D. 53–54
Dewberry, C. 30–31
DFE 59
Dodge, K. A. 4–7, 9
Dunne, E. 50–51, 57–58, 98, 194, 200

Economic and Social Research Council 67, 70
Eggleston, J. 47–48, 57

Eitan, T. 62
Epstein, J. L. 9–10

Farquhar, C. 35
Farrington, D. P. 14
Fine, G. A. 9
Finkelstein, N. W. 29, 32, 39–40
Fisher, S. 46
Francis, W. D. 33
Franke, S. 11
Freigang, R. 11
Furman, W. 3, 10

Galton, M. 49–50, 57–59, 63
Gariepy, J. 23
Gest, S. D. 23
Gillborn, D. 41
Gilmartin, B. G. 26
Gottman, J. M. 8
Gregor, A. J. 28

Hamilton, W. D. 191
Hammersley, M. 78
Harter, S. 25
Hartup, W. W. 7, 9
Haskins, R. 29, 32, 39–40
Hatcher, R. 38, 40, 77
Hayvren, M. 76
Hertz-Lazarowitz, R. 59–61, 63–64
Hicks, D. 46
Hillery, B. 17, 20
Hirano, K. 17
H.M.I. 57
Hopson, B. 46
Howes, C. 29
Hoza, B. 3
Hymel, S. 8, 11, 76

Jahoda, G. 28
Jelinek, M. M. 29
Johnson, D. W. 10, 14, 59–60
Johnson, J. 10
Johnson, R. T. 10, 59–60

Kagan, S. 59–61
Kaukainen, A. 21
Kelly, E. 35, 39
Kerry, T. 57
King, E. 22
Kreidler, W. 99–100
Kupersmidt, J. B. 6

Kusel, S. J. 20, 22, 24
Kutnick, P. 46

Ladd, G. W. 12
LaFontaine, J. 15
LaFreniere, P. 9
Lagerspetz, K. M. J. 21–22, 25
Lane, D. 26
LeMare, L. 8
Lewis, D. O. 26
Lewis, J. 59
Lochman, J. E. 6–7

Malik, G. 35
Mannarino, A. P. 3
Masheder, M. 47
McPherson, D. A. 28
Merrick, B. 51, 53
Miller, N. 59
Milner, D. 28, 30
Mooney, A. 35, 37
Moran, S. 37
Mortimore, P. 57
Mullin, P. N. 28

Neckerman, H. J. 23
Newcomb, A. F. 7, 9

Olweus, D. 15–19, 21–27, 37, 202
O'Moore, A. M. 17, 20
Orlick, T. 47, 55

Palinscar, A. 62–63
Parker, J. G. 8, 11, 13–14
Parkhurst, J. T. 11–12
Patrick, H. 58–59
Pecherek, A. 201
Perry, D. G. 20, 22, 24
Perry, L. C. 20, 22, 24
Phillips, H. 46
Piaget, J. 44–45
Pike, G. 46
Plewis, I. 35
Plowden Report 43

Radke, M. 30
Rampton Report 47–48
Renninger, C. A. 29
Renshaw, P. D. 11
Rich, Y. 62
Roland, E. 15, 23–24

Rosen, H. 49
Rosenberg, P. 30
Rowden, L. 8
Rubin, K. H. 8
Rudduck, J. 44, 48–49, 59, 64–65, 80
Ruiz, R. O. 18
Russell, H. 35

Sagar, H. A. 32
Salmon, P. 64–65
Scally, M. 46
Schofield, J. W. 32–33
Scott, L. 10
Selby, D. 46
Sharan, S. 42, 54, 59, 62
Sharan, Y. 54
Sharp, S. 52, 202
Short, G. 76
Simon, B. 58
Slavin, R. 53–54, 59–61
Smith, D. 19, 22–23
Smith, P. K. 12–13, 16–22, 24–25, 28–29, 31–37, 39, 67–68, 74, 76, 164, 194, 202
Smoller, J. 10
Stephenson, P. 19, 22–23
Stevenson, H. W. 28–29
Stewart, E. C. 28–29
Sutherland, J. 30
Swann Report 37, 47–48

Terry, R. 5, 7
Thompson, D. A. 15, 37
Thompson, S. S. 28
Tigwell, T. 52
Tizard, B. 35, 57
Troyna, B. 38, 40, 77

Underwood, K. 17, 20–22, 24–26

van IJzendoorn, H. W. 7
van Lieshout, C. F. M. 7
Vaughan, G. M. 28
Vygotsky, L. S. 44–46

Webb, N. 63–64
Whitney, I. 18, 20–22, 35, 37
Williams, G. A. 10–11
Williams, J. E. 29
Williamson, J. 49–50, 57, 63

Wilson, A. 29, 118
Wright, C. 40–41
Wu, F. 29

Yeeles, C. 30–31
Youniss, J. 10

Subject Index

Academic performance 59, 75, 127, 130
aggression 5–8, 24, 156–157

bullying 14–27, 66, 70, 115, 117–118, 120, 124–125, 127, 134–153, 154, 188–190, 194–196, 202
 age differences in 20–22
 and race 35–38
 correlates and consequences of 25–27
 definition of 14–16
 prevalence of 16–21
 sex differences in 19–21
 stability of 24–25

Case studies of children 154–187
 who dislike CGW 159–160, 161–163
 who liked CGW 154–159
Class profiles 133–152
conflicts 95–100, 156, 192–193, 200–201
Cooperation 9–14, 45, 47, 58, 63, 154, 190–193, 200, 202
cooperative games 55, 95
Cooperative group work 43–65, 66–75, 79–114, 192–202
 application of by teachers 197–198
 cycle of change in 80–82
 effect on social relationships 115–153
 failures of in project 195–197
 in-service training in project 73, 79–114
 negative aspects of 89
 positive aspects of 88
 potential of in classroom 42, 192–194, 199–202
 range of activities 86–87
 reception of by pupils 198–199
 successes of in project 194–195
 three models of 50–51, 95–99

Cooperative learning 46, 57, 61–62, 64–65
  evaluation of 59–65
  in the U.K. 48–53
  in the U.S.A. and Israel 53–54
counselling skills 201

Debriefing *see* Group processing
Diary records 67, 74, 131–133, 198
Difficult children 131–132, 136, 141, 143–146, 148–149, 151–153, 198–200, 202
Discussion method 51, 83

Ethical issues 76
Ethnicity 28–42, 189–190, 196

F.A.S.T. test 164–166, 178, 184
Forming and maintaining the group 54–57
Free riders 102
Friendship 1–3, 8–14, 22–24, 61–62, 66, 155–156, 158–159, 188–190, 192–193
  and race 28–34, 38–40

Group investigation method 54, 60
Group processing/debriefing 56–57, 83, 89, 95, 193, 198
Group projects method 52, 83

Jigsaw method 51, 54, 61, 97

Liking 74, 116, 120–122, 124, 134–152, 194–196
  by race 120–121, 124, 134–152
  of CGW 75, 131–132, 180, 194–195
Loneliness 11, 23

Neglected children 4–5, 7–8, 9, 12–13, 22, 66, 75, 153, 188–189

Parenting Style Questionnaire (PSQ) 164, 166–7, 178, 184
Peer acceptance 3–5, 9–14, 22–24
Play-fighting *see* Rough-and-tumble play
Prejudice 30–34, 66, 74, 118–119, 127, 134–153, 190, 194, 196, 202

Problem-solving method 52, 83

Qualitative data 68–70, 75–78, 115, 154–160, 164–187, 194
Quantitative assessments 68–70, 74–78, 115–133, 161–187, 195

Race
  and bullying 35–38
  and friendship/peer acceptance 38–40
Rejected children 4–8, 9, 12, 22–23, 66, 75, 153, 161–162, 188–190, 194
  rejected-aggressive 7, 131, 189, 190, 199
  rejected-withdrawn 7
Role-play method 53
Rough-and-tumble play 13, 100

Schools in the project 70–73
self-esteem 25–26, 61–62, 66, 166
Separation Anxiety Test 164
Simulation method 52
Social context of schooling 201–202
Social preference 74, 118, 120, 124, 128
Sociometric status 4–8, 11–12, 67, 74–78, 115–117, 127, 161–163, 196–197
  and ethnic relations 67–69
Stereotyping 30–34, 74, 76, 118, 120, 124, 127, 129, 134–153, 190, 196–197
Student-team learning method (STAD) 53, 60–61

Teacher-pupil relationships 40–41
Teams games tournament method 53–54, 60
TIT-FOR-TAT 191, 193
Trust-building exercises 55, 83

Victimisation 14–27, 70, 115, 117–118, 120, 124, 126–127, 130 134–153, 154, 162–187, 188–190, 194–197
  stability of 24–25
  correlates and consequences of 25–27

Zone of proximal development (ZPD) 45, 60, 63, 82